How Buildings Work

How Buildings Work

THE NATURAL ORDER
OF ARCHITECTURE
Second Edition

EDWARD ALLEN

Drawings by David Swoboda and Edward Allen

NEW YORK • OXFORD

OXFORD UNIVERSITY PRESS

1995

OXFORD UNIVERSITY PRESS

Oxford   New York
Athens   Auckland   Bangkok   Bombay
Calcutta   Cape Town   Dar es Salaam   Delhi   Florence
Hong Kong   Istanbul   Karachi   Kuala Lumpur   Madras
Madrid   Melbourne   Mexico City   Nairobi   Paris
Singapore   Taipei   Tokyo   Toronto

and associated companies in
Berlin   Ibadan

Library of Congress Cataloging-in-Publication Data
Allen, Edward, 1938–
How buildings work : the natural order of architecture
Edward Allen;drawings by David Swoboda and Edward Allen.—2nd ed.
p.   cm.
Includes bibliographical references and index.
ISBN 0–19–509100–0
1. Buildings—Environmental engineering.   I. Title.
TH6021.A44   1995   721—dc20   94–38032

9 8 7 6 5 4 3 2 1

Printed in the United States of America
on acid-free paper

With thanks to the people
who helped make it happen

JOYCE BERRY

NOEL CARR

ALBERT G. H. DIETZ

ELLEN B. FUCHS

N. J. HABRAKEN

FRANK JONES

DONLYN LYNDON

DOUGLAS MAHONE

JAMES RAIMES

J. N. TARN

and especially
MARY M. ALLEN

Preface
to the First Edition

I often wished for a single volume, broad in scope, that would summarize in simple, graphic fashion what a building does and how it does it, much as an introductory book on physiology summarizes the structure and function of the human body. Such a book would be useful to almost anyone involved with buildings, including architects, engineers, students of those professions, critics and historians of architecture, building owners, building occupants, armchair architects, and sidewalk superintendents. When no one appeared ready to write such a book, I saw that there was no alternative but to produce my own. The first version, prepared in a couple of weeks' time in 1974 as a classroom handout, was a sketchy forty pages in length. Two years later, when my turn came for a sabbatical leave from M.I.T., I was ready to attempt an augmented edition. The present volume, four years in preparation, is derived from my own experiences as an architect and builder, from library research in England and the United States, and from a lifetime of interaction with other architects and builders, engineers, building scientists, skilled tradespeople, and students of architecture.

These four years of work have served to reinforce in my mind a theory that I have held from the beginning: There is a natural order to architecture, an order not bound by time, place, or style; more enduring than the Doric or Ionic orders of the ancient Greeks and more orderly than the cleanest modern style. It is the order of physical function, of the ways in which buildings work. When understood as a whole, it has an elegance and utility that cannot otherwise be appreciated or exploited. I hope this book will help its readers acquire such an understanding.

There are many ways in which a book such as this could be organized. I have started from what seems to me to be the beginning, a comparison of the outdoor environmental conditions of the earth with the conditions required by human beings for a healthy, fulfilling existence. From this comparison I list the ways in which we expect buildings to reconcile the differences between the two. I then devote the main chapters of the book to answering in detail the involved and sometimes difficult question of how buildings can fulfill these expectations.

South Natick, Mass.   E. A.
June 1979

Preface to the Second Edition

Over the last fifteen years the practice of building has undergone significant evolution in several areas, most notably mechanical, electrical, and communications systems. Our understanding of building function has also evolved during this period, thanks to research by many individuals and organizations. This new edition, in the tradition of its predecessor, sticks to the basics, but includes hundreds of changes both small and large that reflect the current state of the art and science of building. I have retained the basic organization and the look and feel of the original version, all of which seem to have worn well. The premise and mission of the book remain unchanged.

South Natick, Mass.   E. A.
September 1994

Contents

What Buildings Do

1
The Outdoor Environment

The Earth and the Sun

Earth is unique among the planets of our solar system in offering all the basic necessities of life. But human life is far from easy on most parts of the globe. A planet-sized atmospheric engine, fueled by radiation from the sun and cooled by the radiation of heat back into the emptiness of space, moves air, moisture, and thermal energy across its surface in restless patterns that create an outdoor environment of varied and often extreme conditions.

The sun is the single most important factor in the lives of people and their buildings. The oxygen we breathe, the food we eat, and the fuels we burn are created by the action of sunlight on green plants. The water we drink is purified in an atmospheric distillation process powered by heat from the sun. Sunlight warms our bodies and buildings directly or through sun-warmed air, sometimes enhancing our comfort and other times making us uncomfortable. Sunlight illuminates the outdoors, disinfects the surfaces it touches, creates vitamin D in our skin, and has an uplifting effect on our dispositions. Sunlight also disintegrates the materials with which we build and burns our skin. The sun is both the giver of life and its destroyer.

Sunlight includes electromagnetic radiation of varying wavelengths. Less than 1 percent of the sun's rays that reach sea level on earth are too short in wavelength to be visible. These ultraviolet rays range between about 160 and 400 nanometers (nm) in wavelength. The visible solar wavelengths, ranging between 400 and 780 nm, contain about half the energy of sunlight. The other half of the energy lies in the infrared part of the spectrum, the invisible wavelengths between 780 and 1500 nm. (A nanometer is one-billionth of a meter).

1.1

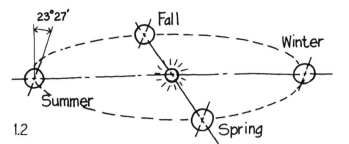

1.2

The earth loops around the sun in a slightly elliptical orbit with a mean radius of 92.9 million miles (149.5 million kilometers), rotating about its own axis once each day and completing an orbit every 365¼ days. The half of the globe oriented away from the sun at any moment is in darkness, and the other half is sunlit (1.1). The eccentricity of the earth's orbit is about 3 percent, a difference that causes a variation of about 7 percent in the intensity of solar radiation on the earth over a six-month period. This variation is not the creator of the earth's seasons, for the earth is closest to the sun in winter, so the orbital eccentricity helps slightly to moderate the seasons. The seasons are created, instead, by the inclination of 23°27′ between the axis of the earth's rotation and a perpendicular to the plane of its orbit (1.2).

At the position in the earth's orbit where the North Pole is tilted closest to the sun, the sun's rays in the Northern Hemisphere pass through the atmosphere and strike the earth's surface at a steep angle (1.3). The atmosphere absorbs and scatters a minimum of sunlight before the radiation reaches the ground, where it is received in maximum concentration per unit area. The sun's rays are at their hottest at this orbital position, which is known as the *summer solstice*, occurring about June 21 of each year. The total solar heat gathered by the Northern Hemisphere on June 21 is further increased by another important factor: The sun is seen for a longer period of time on this day than on any other day of the year. The sun rises to the north of east before six o'clock in the morning and sets to the north of west after six o'clock in the evening. How long before and after six o'clock sunrise and sunset occur is wholly dependent on latitude. On the equator, the day from sunrise to sunset is always twelve hours long regardless of the time of year. Moving northward to the Tropic of Cancer, June 21 is only slightly longer than twelve hours, and the sun at noon appears directly overhead at an altitude of exactly 90°. (From this we can deduce that the Tropic of Cancer is at 23°27′ north latitude.) As we move farther and farther to the north, we find June 21 to have longer and longer hours of sunlight, with the sun rising and setting farther and farther toward the north, until at the Arctic Circle the sun never sets at all but merely skims the horizon at midnight, giving twenty-four hours of sunlight. Simultaneously, however, the noontime sun's altitude decreases as one moves northward, from 90° at the Tropic of Cancer, to 70° at the latitude of New York City, to 47° at the Arctic Circle, and to 23°27′ at the North Pole, thus decreasing the heating effect on the earth's surface and ensuring that in general, the farther north one goes, the cooler the climate will be.

Not surprisingly, the summer solstice occurs during the warm season of the year. On the average, however, the hottest weather of

Summer

Spring/Fall

Winter

1.3

the year comes four to six weeks later than the summer solstice, in late July and early August. This delay occurs because the land and water have been absorbing and holding considerable solar heat since late June. By late in the summer, however, the earth is reemitting this stored energy, thus moderating the effect of the lower solar flux in that season.

In the opposite orbital position, which occurs about December 21, the *winter solstice*, the North Pole is tilted directly away from the sun. In the Northern Hemisphere, the sun's rays arrive at a low angle, taking a long, flat passage through the atmosphere, and their heating effect on the ground is correspondingly weak. This day has the fewest hours of sunlight of any day of the year, with the sun rising late and to the south of east, climbing to a low noontime, and setting early and to the south of west. Above the Arctic Circle, the sun never rises at all but merely gives a faint glow in the southern sky at midday. The land and seas are still giving off stored heat from the previous warmer weather, however, so that the coldest part of the winter does not come until late January or early February.

On March 21 and September 21, known respectively as the *vernal equinox* and the *autumnal equinox*, the North and South Poles are equidistant from the sun. Everywhere on earth, the sun rises exactly in the east and sets exactly in the west twelve hours later, except at the extreme poles, where the sun travels just along the horizon for twenty-four hours.

It is useful to keep in mind that the seasonal variations in length of day and the maximum daily sun altitude are least pronounced in the tropics and most exaggerated in the polar regions. In the tropics, the length of day is always close to twelve hours but, except on the equator itself, is slightly longer in summer and slightly shorter in winter. The sun always rises in the vicinity of due east, a bit to the north in summer and a bit to the south in winter, and sets in the vicinity of due west, traveling very nearly directly overhead at noon. The sun always intercepts the horizon in the mornings and evenings at a steep angle, producing very brief sunrises and sunsets (1.4).

As one moves northward in latitude, seasonal variations increase gradually. Summer days here are longer than they are in the tropics, and winter days are shorter. Noontime sun altitudes are lower, giving a lower solar flux per unit of ground area. The directions of sunrise and sunset show a more marked seasonal swing, and sunrises and sunsets are more prolonged (1.5). In the Northern Hemisphere the limiting case is the North Pole, where day and night each are six months long: The sun rises on March 21, climbs to a low "noon" on June 21, and sets on September 21 (1.6). On a year-long basis, every point on the globe is exposed to direct sunlight exactly half the time. At the poles, the half comes in one continuous period. At the

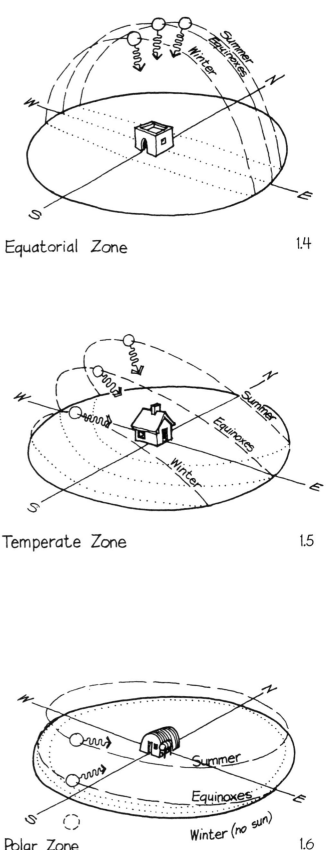

Equatorial Zone   1.4

Temperate Zone   1.5

Polar Zone   1.6

equator, each day of the year is evenly divided between sunlight and darkness. At intermediate latitudes, longer days in summer compensate for shorter ones in winter.

In the Southern Hemisphere, the sun resides in the northern half of the sky, and the seasons are reversed from those in the Northern Hemisphere, with longer days and higher solar fluxes occurring while the days are short and the sunlight is weak in the Northern Hemisphere. The progression of seasonal effects from the equator to the South Pole is the same as for the Northern Hemisphere.

Effects of Solar Radiation on the Earth

A number of factors affect the amount of solar radiation that reaches a given surface. As we have already seen, these include the length of day, the angle of incidence of sunlight on the ground at each time of day, and the amount of atmosphere traversed by the radiation at each time of day. Atmospheric interference is the most difficult factor of all to evaluate. Solar intensity just outside the earth's atmosphere is about 130 watts per square foot (1400 watts/m^2). At an altitude of about fifteen miles, a stratum of ozone and nascent oxygen absorbs most of the ultraviolet portion of the solar waves. In the lower reaches of the atmosphere, carbon dioxide, water vapor, clouds, dust, and pollutants work in various ways to reflect, scatter, absorb, and reradiate different parts of the spectrum. The shorter wavelengths of sunlight are the most affected, and they produce the blue appearance of the daytime sky. A considerable portion of the sunlight's energy is stripped away by the "clear" atmosphere—nearly half, on the average, worldwide. Most of this energy is then reradiated from the atmosphere into space, but a significant amount is reradiated to earth as diffuse sky radiation, thus slightly increasing the total amount of solar energy available at the earth's surface. Clouds, which cover roughly half the earth's surface at any given time, cut out much of the sun's direct radiation but still pass a considerable quantity in diffuse form. Taking all these factors into account, a square foot of land at 45° latitude, in a location with a 50 percent incidence of cloud cover, receives about 75 kilowatt-hours of direct solar radiation each year, plus roughly another 20 kilowatt-hours of diffuse sky radiation, for a total of nearly 100 kilowatt-hours annually. A square meter of land receives about ten times these quantities.

Little heat is imparted directly to the atmosphere by the sun. Instead, the ground and its objects are warmed by solar radiation, and they in turn pass some of their heat to the air. The rate at which a patch of ground is warmed depends first on how much solar energy arrives at the surface. Assuming equal atmospheric conditions, a patch of ground nearer the equator receives more solar flux than does one farther from the equator because of the higher angle of incidence. The slope of the ground also has an important effect on solar intensity, for the same reason. A second factor affecting the rate at which ground is warmed is the portion of solar radiation that the ground reflects; this is typically about 20 percent, leaving 80 percent to be absorbed. Of this 80 percent, a portion may go to warm the soil and thus is stored temporarily. Some is expended in evaporating moisture from the soil. Some is radiated at long infrared wavelengths from the soil back to the sky and to cooler terrestrial objects that the patch of ground can "see": teetops, fences, buildings, and so forth. The remainder of the 80 percent warms the air above the patch of ground.

So far we have been considering what happens during the daytime. At night, the flow of radiation is reversed, with the dark side of the earth releasing energy into space by means of infrared radiation at wavelengths ranging from 4000 to 80,000 nm, considerably longer than the sun's infrared rays. On cloudy, humid nights, the water vapor in the atmosphere, which is particularly absorptive of this longwave infrared radiation, serves to block much of the outflow of energy, but on clear, dry nights, a very powerful cooling effect is exerted by rapid radiation from the warm earth to the cold blackness of the sky. Dew frequently condenses from the air onto the radiationally cooled ground surfaces and the roof surfaces of automobiles and buildings. The cold ground surface cools the adjacent air. A stagnant layer of cold air may form near the ground in a stable atmospheric configuration known as an *inversion*. Ground fog may form from moisture condensation in this cold layer, and frost may occur along the ground even when thermometers at eye level are reading temperatures well above freezing. A nighttime wind tends to mix earth-cooled air with warmer air, making dew, frost, and ground fog less likely to form. Over bodies of water, the large heat capacity of the water and its convective mixing generally result in a less pronounced nocturnal cooling of the air than over land.

Weather

If atmospheric conditions are equal, nighttime heat loss by radiation occurs at an equal rate in all parts of the world. But daytime heat gain, as we have seen, is not equal in all locations. On any day of the year, the tropics and the hemisphere that is experiencing its warm season receive much more solar radiation than do the polar regions and the colder hemisphere. Averaged over the course of the year, the tropics and latitudes up to about 40° receive more total heat than they lose by radiation. Latitudes above 40° have a negative annual

1.7

balance of radiation. Thus the necessary conditions are created for the operation of an atmospheric engine: It takes on heat in the tropics, and it gives off heat in the polar regions. Its working fluid is the air, especially the moisture contained by the air. Air is heated over the warm earth of the tropics, expands, rises, and flows away both northward and southward from the equator at high altitudes, cooling as it goes, to descend and flow toward the equator again from more northerly and southerly latitudes. Meanwhile, the earth's eastward rotation deflects these currents westward along the earth's surface to form the trade winds. Farther toward the poles, similar but weaker cells of air convection are set in motion, resulting in a generally eastward flow of air (1.7).

The heat of the sun continuously evaporates water from the seas and land into the air. The warm, moist air thus produced eventually rises, either because of convection or because the air is blown by winds up the slopes of rising landmasses. As it rises, the air expands because of decreasing atmospheric pressure. As it expands, it undergoes adiabatic cooling until the temperature at which moisture begins to condense is reached. The condensing moisture then evolves latent heat into the air, offsetting some of the cooling effect of expansion. But a slower rate of cooling continues as the air continues to rise; moisture continues to condense; and clouds of water droplets and ice crystals are formed. Considerable quantities of water are often involved; a single large cumulus cloud is estimated to weigh a hundred thousand tons (10^8 kg).

The exact mechanism by which a cloud releases its moisture is not well understood, but it generally involves both further cooling and the presence in the cloud of microscopic particles of dust around which the tiny cloud droplets can aggregate to form raindrops or ice crystals. Precipitation tends to be heavier over mountain ranges because of the rapid cooling of the rising winds and is usually sparse to the leeward side of mountains, where the descending winds have already been wrung dry of excess water (1.8). Rainwater and snow melt are gathered by the earth's surface into streams and rivers and eventually flow to the seas, evaporating moisture into the air along the way to start the cycle again.

In the temperate latitudes, large masses of warm, moist air from more tropical climates advance northward to meet masses of cooler, drier air from the polar regions. The warm front, characterized by low barometric pressure, and the higher-pressure cold front collide and swirl about each other, increasing the local wind velocities and releasing precipitation where the warm air is suddenly cooled by contact with the cold air (1.9). Weather patterns in the temperate latitudes are predominantly the result of such frontal systems and are less stable and predictable than tropical weather, which is dominated by the general sun-induced circulation of the atmosphere.

8

1.8

Wind serves an important function in the earth's weather, distributing both water and heat more equitably about the globe. Wind flow at high altitudes is generally rapid and fairly smooth. In the vicinity of the earth's surface, however, the wind is subjected to interference from hills, mountains, trees, buildings, and various convective flows of air. The average wind speed is progressively reduced by these obstacles nearer the ground, and the wind flow becomes more turbulent, fluctuating rapidly in both velocity and direction.

Vast quantities of energy are converted from sunlight to wind, and from sunlight to falling precipitation, by the atmospheric engine. Despite being only about 3 percent efficient in transforming radiation into motion, the engine operates at a level that would be measured in trillions of horsepower (multiples of 10^{12} watts). But this vast flow of energy is difficult to tap for direct human use: As wind, it is diffuse and is difficult to harness at the high altitudes and polar latitudes where it is strongest. As water, only a minute percentage of all precipitation falls in mountain valleys that may be dammed for power generation; the rest falls on the oceans or on watersheds that are not suitable for hydroelectric installations.

1.9

Both water and land are capable of absorbing and storing heat, but water, with its higher specific heat, is considerably more efficient as a storage medium. As a result, large bodies of water tend to moderate the temperatures in their vicinities as compared with the temperatures farther inland. This effect is particularly noticeable where prevailing winds pass over water before reaching the land. The West Coast of the United States, under the influence of the prevailing west winds off the Pacific Ocean, has a much milder climate, cooler in summer and warmer in winter, than does the East Coast, where the prevailing winds come off the continental landmass. Water can also transport heat for great distances, as in the case of the warm Atlantic Gulf Stream, which gathers heat in the tropics and carries it northward to soften (and moisten) the weather in western Europe. London, warmed by winds off the Gulf Stream, has little subfreezing weather in winter, whereas Minneapolis, landlocked in the central United States at a somewhat more southerly latitude than London, has considerable snow and protracted periods of bitter cold. Thus latitude alone is not a good index of precisely what climate can be expected in any given area of the world.

At an individual building site, even more climatic variables may come into play. The apparent movement of the sun across the site is rigidly fixed according to the geographic latitude, but the effect of the sun's radiation varies according to the orientation and steepness of the ground slope, the infrared absorbance of the ground surface, the presence or absence of shading vegetation, and reflected and reradiated solar heat from surrounding buildings and geological features. The air temperature on the site is further affected by the altitude of the site above sea level, its proximity to bodies of water, the direction of prevailing winds, the presence of shading vegetation, and so on. Fountains, waterfalls, and trees on the site may diffuse enough moisture into the air to raise the local humidity and depress the local air temperature. Local wind patterns are largely dependent on local obstructions to the passage of wind such as forests, trees, buildings, and hills. Plowed ground or dark pavement are warmed by the sun to a higher temperature than are surrounding areas, thereby increasing the radiational heating of nearby surfaces and causing small updrafts of warm air. Topography may have an important role in local convective airflow: A valley may be more protected from wind than a hilltop, but on still, cool nights, rivers of cold air flow down the valley to collect in pools in low areas while warmer air rises toward the hilltop. Cities, too, affect local weather. The energy released by vehicles and buildings is gradually dissipated in the form of heat to the outdoors, often warming the air by 5 to 10 degrees Fahrenheit (3°C–6°C) above that of the surrounding countryside. Large cities often create considerable convective updrafts that can have significant climatic effects on a regional scale.

Other Solar Phenomena

Besides its thermal effects—those of warming the earth and creating wind and precipitation—the sun also has important nonthermal effects. It provides visible light; it furnishes energy for photosynthesis in plants; and it radiates ultraviolet light.

The role of sunlight in lighting buildings will be discussed later in detail, but we should note here that direct sunlight is often far too bright for comfortable seeing. Much more useful during the daytime is the visible light scattered by the atmosphere, the even, restful illumination of a shaded area. If we need light at night, or under dense cloud cover, we must use alternative sources of illumination.

It would be difficult to overemphasize the value to humankind of the photosynthetic reaction in plants. We could not live without it. The human organism cannot create nutrients from sunlight. Plants, however, produce sugars, starches, and proteins from water, carbon dioxide, nitrogen, and soil nutrients through solar-fueled processes. They take carbon dioxide from the air during photosynthesis and give back oxygen as a waste product. (Animals consume oxygen in their metabolic processes and give off carbon dioxide, thus forming the other major link in a self-sustaining environmental chain.) Simultaneously, people and other animals eat plants that they are capable of digesting, and/or the flesh of other animals that ultimately are nourished by plants. Animal excrement contains nitrogen, phosphorus, potassium, carbon, and other substances that become available to plants through soil and water, and thus food production is perpetuated through other self-sustaining chains (1.10). Even dead plants and animals have a role to play. Their corpses are broken down by other animals and by microorganisms into basic chemical compounds that become once more part of the soil, available to nourish plants and begin life again.

Photosynthesis also produces useful nonfood products such as wood for construction, fibers for the manufacture of fabrics and paper, and decorative plants, flowers, ornamental trees and shrubs, and climbing vines. Photosynthesis is responsible for our entire supply of fossil fuels—coal, oil, and gas—which were formed millions of years ago by the effects of geological heat and pressure on large masses of decaying vegetable matter. Except for geothermal energy, nuclear energy, and tides, all our energy sources are solar in origin: not only direct sunlight but also wind energy, water energy, plant energy, and, of course, fossil fuels.

Ultraviolet radiation from the sun is important for its role in photosynthesis, but it has other roles as well. Ultraviolet kills many harmful microorganisms, an effect that is important in purifying the atmosphere and in ridding sunlit surfaces of disease-carrying bacteria. Vitamin D, essential to human nutrition, is formed by the

O_2

CO_2

Sugars
Starches
Amino acids
Vitamins
Minerals
Cellulose

N, P, K, C

1.10

action of ultraviolet light on the skin. On the negative side, ultraviolet rays are responsible for the rapid and soon fatal burning of human skin exposed too long to sunlight and for the high incidence of skin cancer among people who are constantly in the sun. Ultraviolet rays also fade dyes in fabrics, decompose many plastics, and contribute to the deterioration of paints, roofing, wood, and other organic building materials. It is because of these bad effects that there is such concern about preserving the high-altitude ozone layer that intercepts most ultraviolet radiation before it can reach the earth.

Other Aspects of the Outdoor Environment

The earth's geology has a great deal to do with the ways in which we build. Many of our building materials, of course, are mineral in origin: earth, stone, concrete, brick, glass, gypsum, asbestos, steel, aluminum, copper, and dozens of others. In many cases the simplest of these can be obtained directly from the building site or from sources in the neighborhood. The subsoil, subsurface water levels, topsoil, and rocks of a site affect the sorts of excavations, foundations, and landscaping that are likely to be undertaken. The contours of the site—its hills, valleys, and slopes—help determine how water will drain during storms, where erosion of soil may occur, where roadways and paths may run without being excessively steep, what areas will be more or less sheltered from wind, what areas will be exposed most favorably to sunlight, where various sorts of plants will grow best, and where and how the buildings will be built. These are exceedingly complex factors, rich in both positive and negative implications for a designer.

Certain biological factors of the building site are important, too. Microorganisms are universally present in such forms as the bacteria, molds, and fungi that break down dead vegetable and animal matter into soil nutrients. Higher plants such as grasses, weeds, flowers, shrubs, and trees play important roles in trapping precipitation, preventing soil erosion, providing shade, deflecting wind, and other functions already mentioned. Insects can affect building design: Biting insects and food-contaminating insects must be excluded from interior spaces. Building-destroying insects such as termites need to be discouraged from attacking the structure. Native reptiles, birds, and mammals also may figure importantly in the planning process. We may want bird songs to filter into the breakfast room, but not the birds themselves. Mice, rats, raccoons, foxes, deer, squirrels, lizards, and the neighbor's dog, to name a few, can be nuisance animals in one's building. But a cow, sheep, or horse may be welcome in a barn, and one's own dog, cat, or hamster in a house.

1.11

Nearby buildings often affect what we are likely to build. They may shade certain areas of the site, divert the wind in unforeseen ways, upset natural drainage patterns, or cause areas of the site to lack visual or acoustical privacy (1.11). Buildings or remains of buildings erected on the site by previous builders may have to be dealt with, along with their associated driveways, parking areas, walks, gardens, wells, septic systems, and underground utilities. Bad land-use practices of previous or abutting owners may have caused problems of weeds or soil erosion.

Environmental factors caused by people include air that is polluted with smoke, gases, dust, or chemical particles; noise from traffic, industrial processes, a nearby discotheque, or a rowdy family next door; and surface or ground water that is fouled with sewage or chemicals. Sadly, too, a designer must commonly come to terms with the fact that the outdoor environment includes unknown persons who would deface, destroy, or intrude on the building being designed, often before its construction is complete and almost always to the detriment of the building and its occupants.

This, then, for better and for worse, is the outdoor environment, portions of which we may select and modify for human occupancy. It has a warming sun that rises and sets, a procession of seasons, a more-or-less predictable pattern of weather, a unique geology, a varied colony of flora and fauna, and a history of human use and misuse extending through the present and into the future. We must ask ourselves who will occupy and use this environment, what their needs are, and how their needs differ from what this environment can furnish.

Further Reading

David I. Blumenstock. *The Ocean of Air*. New Brunswick, N.J., Rutgers University Press, 1959.

T. F. Gaskell and Martin Morris. *World Climate: The Weather, the Environment and Man*. London, Thames and Hudson, 1979.

2
The Human Environment

The Human Body

The quality of a human environment can be measured only in terms of its effect on the people who experience it. But people, both physically and emotionally, are creatures not easily understood, and evaluations of quality are seldom simple. Even a simple question such as "Is this place warm enough?" does not have a simple answer in quantitative terms, for the same person, under varying circumstances of season of the year, amount of clothing, radiant temperature, relative humidity, and air movement, will find the place exactly "warm enough" at a range of air temperatures extending over many degrees, a surprising spread for an animal whose internal temperature cannot vary by more than a couple of degrees either way without distress. To understand how to evaluate environmental quality, then, we must begin by looking within the body itself to find out how it works.

The human body is, in its most fundamental mechanical behavior, a heat engine. The fuel for the engine is derived from food, in the form of proteins, carbohydrates, and fats. The digestive process breaks these down by means of various chemicals, bacteria, and enzymes into substances that the body can use. These useful substances are then pumped into the bloodstream, for transportation to the living cells throughout the body where they will be used. Waste products and harmful substances are filtered out in the digestive process and stored for periodic excretion. Urine consists primarily of nitrogenous wastes dissolved in water. Feces, though mainly water, contain the indigestible fibers, minerals, and particles that could not be used in the metabolic process.

We need a regular supply of water to facilitate the chemical processes in the body, to move the products of these processes about the

2.1

body, and to help cool the body. We need air too, because in the
critical set of chemical reactions that combust the food-derived fuels
to keep the human heat engine operating, oxygen is a necessary
reactant. When we breathe air into our lungs, we absorb a portion of
its oxygen into our bloodstream. We mix carbon dioxide and water,
waste products of the combustion, with the air in our lungs before
we breathe it out again. Less than a fifth of the air's oxygen is
replaced by carbon dioxide in each lungful, but a continuous supply
of outside air must be available to the body to avoid oxygen depletion
and carbon dioxide narcosis through repeated breathing of the same
air (2.1).

2.2

2.3

The normal internal operating temperature of the human engine is just under 99° Fahrenheit (37°C), a temperature that must be maintained within narrow tolerances in order to avoid metabolic malfunction. But our bodies are only about one-fifth efficient in converting food energy to mechanical work. They must give off four times as much heat as they use in order to maintain a stable internal temperature. An adult working at a desk produces excess heat at about the same rate as does a 100-watt lightbulb. The same person walking generates two to three times as much heat and, when exercising strenuously, six to ten times (2.2). These necessary rates of cooling are achieved through an admirable collection of physiological mechanisms.

The body is continuously cooled by the heating of respired air, the vaporization of water from the lungs and breathing passages, the convection and radiation of heat from the surface of the skin, and the diffusion of small amounts of water vapor through the skin (2.3). The surface temperature of our skin, and hence its rate of heat loss, is controlled by the dilatation or constriction of the small blood vessels of the skin. As the vessels dilate, the flow of warm blood near the surface of the body increases, and the skin temperature rises, giving off heat more quickly to the surrounding environment. The increased volume of blood, which is a good thermal conductor, also partially displaces fatty tissues, which are poor thermal conductors, near the surface of the body, and direct heat loss from the underlying body tissues to the surrounding environment is thus increased. This very sensitive vasomotor system can regulate the body's rate of heat loss under a fairly wide range of conditions.

When the rate of cooling by respiration, skin diffusion, skin radiation, and skin convection is not enough to meet our body's demands, we sweat. Water is exuded from the pores of the skin, to be evaporated into the atmosphere, with the latent heat of vaporization furnished primarily by the body. Large quantities of heat can be lost in this way, and perspiration is sufficient under most conditions to provide the additional cooling required. But how well this works depends on the degree of moisture in the air. If the surrounding air is very dry, perspiration will evaporate very quickly, and considerable cooling is possible even when the air temperature is higher than our body temperature. When the humidity is high, evaporation is slow, and so the rate of perspiration increases as the body attempts to compensate. The situation can be helped to some extent by increasing the rate of air movement past the body: The moving air is more effective not only in evaporating perspiration but also in speeding convective heat loss from the skin, provided that the air temperature is lower than skin temperature (2.4). If the body is in a situation in

16

which none of these strategies is sufficient, however, the deep-body temperature will rise until metabolic function is impaired, bringing heat stroke and death.

Under conditions in which heat is being removed too quickly from the body, heat loss tends to be especially rapid from the back of the neck, the head, the back, and the extremities. Clothing and furniture that are designed to obstruct the flow of heat from these areas are particularly effective in aiding thermal comfort under cold conditions (2.5). Because the body is capable, through the blood-stream, of transferring heat from one of its parts to another, symptoms of excessive heat loss are sometimes difficult to interpret. Warm footwear may not be of much help for cold feet if rapid cooling is occurring in some other part of the body. Outdoorspeople have a saying, "If your feet are cold, put your hat on." This seemingly odd strategy works in a surprisingly high proportion of cases, because the head, with a high ratio of heat transfer surface to internal volume, is capable of radiating and convecting very large amounts of heat to a cold environment, much as a relatively small automobile radiator can cool a very large engine. The body responds by lowering the temperature of the feet and hands, in order to keep vital internal organs at an optimum temperature. If rapid heat loss continues, "goose pimpling" occurs, in which the hairs of the skin are erected to trap still air as an insulating layer next to the skin. One's instinct generally leads one, quite correctly, to cut down the exposed surface area of the body by folding the arms, hunching the shoulders, and bringing the legs tightly together, or to exercise, in order to raise the level of metabolic heat production to match the rate at which heat is being lost (2.6). If these measures are insufficient, shivering—an involuntary form of heat-generating muscular exercise—commences, and if even this cannot restore equilibrium, the deep-body temperature will begin to fall, a condition known as *hypothermia*. Hypothermia can be reversed in its early stages by the direct conduction of heat into the body by means of hot food and drink and a hot bath or sauna, but in its later stages a deepening coma is followed by death.

The human body is not comfortable when it is placed under thermal stress. Excessive sweating is uncomfortable and annoying. So is goose pimpling or shivering. Prolonged overheating or over-cooling of the body results in increased fatigue and weakens resistance to disease. A suitable human thermal environment, then, is fundamentally one in which the body is able to give off its excess heat at the required rate without having to resort to its more drastic thermal control mechanisms.

Besides food, water, fresh air, and optimum thermal conditions,

2.4

2.5

2.6

2.7

2.8

the human environment has other requirements. The most vital is adequate sanitation (2.7). The human body is a biological organism, susceptible to attack by a very large assortment of bacteria, viruses, and fungi. The skin, respiratory system, and digestive tract are particularly fertile environments for these microorganisms. The basic sanitary requirements for a human environment include the provision of food and drinking water that are free of harmful microorganisms, the prompt removal and processing of excreta and food wastes to render them free of disease-causing organisms, adequate ventilation to carry away air-borne bacteria and excessive moisture, adequate sunlight to dry and sterilize the environment, the exclusion of disease-carrying rodents and insects from buildings, and facilities for washing foodstuffs, dishes, skin, hair, and clothing. Inadequate sanitation is costly in human terms: Poor ventilation encourages tuberculosis and other respiratory diseases. Contaminated food and water spread hepatitis and typhoid. Pest-borne diseases include typhus, yellow fever, malaria, sleeping sickness, encephalitis, plague, and various infestations of parasites. These are but a few examples.

Human eyes and ears, the most important sensory organs of the body, have their own sets of environmental requirements. The eye can be damaged if it looks even momentarily at the sun or if it looks too long at a sunlit landscape of snow or light-colored sand. Seeing becomes difficult or painful if the eye must look at a very bright object against a very dark background, and vice versa. Seeing is difficult and less accurate at very low levels of illumination. The eye is able to adjust in order to see objects fairly well at moderately low levels of illumination, but the adjustment mechanism, which probably evolved in order to give humans the ability to see during the twilight period of the day, is very slow, acting over a period of minutes.

The ear is somewhat similar in its characteristics: It can be damaged by sounds of excessive loudness, especially if they occur over a protracted period of time. Hearing is difficult at very low sound intensities or if a strong background of noise obscures the sounds that one wishes to hear. But there is one very important difference between our eyes and our ears: By closing our eyelids, we can shut off nearly all visual stimuli, but we cannot stop our ears so easily (2.8). We can find visual relief in any but the very brightest environments, but for relief from a disturbingly noisy environment, we have to move to a quieter location.

The human body needs space in which to move—to work, to play, or merely to maintain its muscle tone, skeletal movement, and heart and lung function through exercise. Even when at rest, the body needs to be able to shift about in order to unburden and relax

18

its various components in turn. In its motions, the soft body requires protection from injury. It needs smooth surfaces underfoot to prevent ankle damage or tripping. The body needs help in ascending or descending between surfaces at different levels without an excessive danger of falling, and something to prevent it from accidentally falling over edges of surfaces. Hard or sharp objects must be kept out of the volumes of space normally traversed by the body in its movements. Fire and very hot objects must be kept away from the delicate human skin. The body must be kept safe from falling objects and explosions and from poisons, corrosive chemicals, harmful radiation, and electric shocks, any of which can cause it severe injury or sudden death.

The Environmental Necessities of Human Civilization

To this point we have considered the human body primarily as a machine that will not run properly except under a certain set of conditions. But of course, a person is much more than just a physical mechanism, and much of human nature emerges through social activities, those contacts with others through which people create, grow, and enjoy life.

At the most basic individual level, each person requires a place to sleep, facilities with which to carry out the basics of personal hygiene, a source of water, sources of food, and facilities to prepare the food for eating. But most people live as part of a family and in somewhat less Spartan surroundings, a place called *home*. Family life requires places for reproduction and for the rearing of children. Preparing and eating food become more elaborate processes in the family, a source of enjoyment as well as bodily nutrition and a setting for social interaction at several levels. Home becomes a place for certain kinds of work carried out by various members of the family: pursuing hobbies, studying, writing letters, cleaning and repairing things, managing financial affairs. Home is also a place for play and for entertaining friends. Home is where you hang your hat—along with your coat, your shoes, your wardrobe, your dishes, your books, and all the rest of your belongings. It is meant to be a safe, secure, familiar place, filled with the things of one's life, closed and private at times, open and outgoing at other times, at the option of its occupants (2.9).

Outside the home, we require a variety of other sorts of places. We need workplaces—workshops, warehouses, markets, offices, studios, barns, laboratories—where the goods of civilization are designed, produced, and distributed. Each has to furnish the basic

2.9

19

2.10

necessities of life, plus the special requirements of the processes that take place there. We need gathering places of various sorts, places of worship, places to exercise, places to play, places in which to be entertained, places in which to view interesting and beautiful things, and places in which to carry out the functions of government and education. Large numbers of people need to be accommodated at once, and all their needs satisfied simultaneously (2.10).

Human society implies human mobility. We need to move around to enjoy the various amenities of a city or a countryside. A network for human movement must be provided, starting with the doors of rooms; the hallways, stairs, and elevators that connect them; the entrances that merge the building and the outdoors; and continuing with footpaths, streets, roads, and long-distance mechanisms for moving both people and goods (2.11). This requires clear

2.11

rights-of-way, pavements, vehicles, stations of transfer—and understandable information on how to get where one is going.

The requirements of a high-quality human environment are numerous and often exacting. They include physiological and social requirements, as well as psychological ones that are much more difficult to define. Taken together, they describe an environment that exists nowhere in the natural world. The outdoor environment is too variable, too frequently extreme, too often destructive and unstable, to be hospitable to human life and civilization. In the course of its development, humankind has had to learn not merely to seek sheltered areas of the natural landscape but also to create artificially sheltered areas of more constant and comfortable qualities than Nature is capable of providing on its own.

Further Reading

B. Givoni. *Man, Climate, and Architecture*. New York, Elsevier, 1969, pp. 19–95.

3
The Concept of Shelter

Shelter at its most basic is not a human invention; it is something we seek instinctively, as do all animals, in a world that is seldom attuned exactly to our physiological and social needs. On a hot summer day, we picnic under a tree or near a shady waterfall or cascade. On bitter winter days, we gravitate instinctively toward the lee side of any landscape feature that will deflect the wind, especially if a patch of warming sunlight is available there. The experienced outdoor traveler, when selecting a spot on which to roll out a sleeping bag for the night in any season of the year, avoids the low spots and valleys, which channel nighttime flows of cold air and moisture, and, animal-like, beds down on the higher ground, perhaps on an eastward slope, to be wakened by the morning sun.

In an agrarian society, the search for shelter begins with a judicious use of the natural landscape. People choose building sites for their sheltering qualities—orientation, topographic features, trees and vegetation, and sources of water. In northern climates, higher ground that slopes toward the south is reserved for growing the most essential crops. Farmers know from personal experience that the earliest frosts of autumn and the latest frosts of spring occur only in the low spots of the landscape and that plants in south-sloping fields receive life-giving sunlight of an intensity higher than that of flat or north-sloping fields (3.1). Rural towns are sited, where possible, next to rivers or springs on leeward, generally southerly slopes.

Artificial shelter starts with such gentle manipulations of the landscape as planting a shade tree or a row of shrubbery for a windbreak. A simple, freestanding east–west wall of piled-up rocks, through its vertical profile and its thermal capacity, can create a small zone of shaded coolness immediately to its north in hot weather and a sun-

3.1

warmed, less windy zone to its south in cold weather (3.2). The wall retains some of the sun's heat and releases it gradually after sundown, extending the sheltered zone's period of habitability. A paving of stones or a platform of wood provides a drier footing for the inhabitant, and a lean-to roof keeps off rain and snow (3.3). East and west walls increase the wind-deflecting capabilities of the shelter and interfere little with the entry of winter sunshine. At night, a fire at the mouth of this simple shelter warms its occupants by both direct and wall-reflected radiation, and a small portion of its heat is stored in the stones to moderate the temperature of the sheltered space even after the fire has died (3.4). One can easily imagine further steps in the improvement of such a rudimentary shelter: the use of fabric or skins to close off the open side after dark or on cloudy days, the moving of the fire to an interior hearth, and so on (3.5). Perhaps many primitive building forms evolved in much this same way, to join later in the stream of development that led ultimately to modern building techniques.

Modern buildings are much more complicated than this primitive example, of course. Each genuine new improvement in shelter wrought by our ancestors was at first a novelty, but soon afterward it became standard practice and then the acceptable minimum as later improvements superseded it. A shelter that represented the height of comfort and convenience to one generation might be considered substandard a generation or two later. We have grown to expect more and more of our buildings, to the point that buildings now are expected to perform functions that are not strictly "sheltering" at all, such as providing water, removing wastes, and furnishing energy for

3.2

3.3

3.5

3.4

23

3.6

use in mechanical tools. Our buildings are becoming, in fact, comprehensive life-support mechanisms (3.6).

Many of the functions we now expect of our buildings were formerly the functions of other devices. Clothing and shelter are to a considerable extent interchangeable in function, but with the passage of time, people have tended to ask less of their clothing and proportionally more of their shelter. Some functions formerly expected of pieces of furniture, such as the provision of enclosed storage for various household articles, are steadily being subsumed by building components such as closets and cupboards. Sinks, bathtubs, cookstoves, and dishwashers are less portable nowadays and more common as fixed parts of a house. Offices were once lit by portable lamps that had to be refilled periodically with oil. Today office illumination is usually provided by fixtures that are a part of the building, and the building conducts the energizing electricity directly to the fixtures (3.7).

Our concept of what a building is, therefore, is more than what would be found in a dictionary definition of shelter. A building is functionally what we expect it to be. The list that follows attempts to include all the functional expectations we are likely to have for a building at this point in history, arranged roughly in descending order according to the relative importance of each to the support of life:

1. We expect a building to provide most of the immediate necessities for human metabolism:

   A. Clean air for breathing.
   B. Clean water for drinking, food preparation, cleaning, and flushing of wastes.

3.7

C. In some types of building, facilities for the preparation and consumption of food.

D. Removal and recycling of wastes, including excrement, wash water, food wastes, and rubbish.

2. We expect a building to create the necessary conditions for human thermal comfort:

A. Control of the mean radiant temperature.

B. Control of the air temperature.

C. Control of the thermal characteristics of surfaces contacted directly by the human body.

D. Control of the air's humidity and the flow of water vapor.

E. Control of the air's circulation.

F. Control of the entry of precipitation or other water into inhabited space.

3. We expect a building to create the necessary conditions for sensory comfort, efficiency, and privacy:

A. Optimal seeing conditions.

B. Visual privacy.

C. Optimal hearing conditions.

D. Acoustical privacy.

4. We expect a building to control the entry and exit of living creatures of every kind, from viruses to elephants, including human beings.

5. We expect a building to distribute concentrated energy to convenient points for use in powering various tools and appliances.

6. We expect a building to provide certain channels of connection and communication with the world outside: windows, telephones, mailboxes, computer networks, video cables, and so on.

7. We expect a building to facilitate bodily comfort, safety, and productive activity through the provision of useful surfaces: floors, walls, stairs, shelves, countertops, benches, and the like.

8. We expect a building to provide stable support for the weights of all the people, belongings, and architectural devices in the building and to provide sufficient structural resistance to the physical forces of snow, wind, and earthquake.

9. We expect a building to protect its own structure, surfaces, internal mechanical and electrical systems, and other archi-

tectural devices from wetting by precipitation or other water.

10. We expect a building to adjust to its own normal movements without damage to itself or its contents.
11. We expect a building to furnish reasonable protection to its occupants, its contents, and itself against damage by fire.
12. We expect a building to be built without excessive expense or difficulty.
13. We expect a building to be capable of being operated, maintained, and changed in a useful, economical manner.

This list begins with expectations that arise more or less naturally from human needs amid a hostile outdoor environment. From item 8 to the end of the list, however, the expectations are of a different sort. They arise largely from needs created by the building itself and relate only in a secondary way to human needs. A structural beam, for example, is not related in a primary way to the solution of any human need. It is a secondary device supporting a surface (a floor or roof) that is of primary importance to the users of a building. Movement and fire are problems that arise only because the building exists, but unless the building solves these problems of its own, they constitute a danger to its occupants.

The following chapters explain the ways in which buildings meet these functional expectations. They proceed in the same general order as this list, with several exceptions: All building functions having to do with movement of air are discussed together in the chapter entitled "Controlling Air Movement," and the chapter entitled "Keeping Water Out" incorporates the material on all the water-resisting functions of buildings. Various aspects of the function of controlling the entry and exit of living creatures are discussed in several of the chapters; the function is far too diverse to fit logically into a single chapter. It is noted throughout the book that although we have complex functional expectations of our buildings and complex ways of meeting some of these expectations, most building functions can be met by any well-informed designer, even in very large buildings, with architectural devices as straightforward and direct as the instinctively sought, simple shelters of the natural landscape.

How Buildings Work

4
Building Function

In order to understand how a building works, we can dissect it and study its various elemental functions. But few building functions take place in isolation. Almost every component of a building serves more than one function, with some components commonly serving ten or more simultaneously, and these functions are heavily interdependent. For example, if we decide to build the partitions in a school building of gypsum wallboard over steel studs, instead of brick, we will affect the thermal properties of the building, its acoustics, the quality and quantity of light in the classrooms, how the wiring and piping are installed, the usefulness of the wall surfaces, the deadweight that the structure of the building must support, the fire resistance of the building, which trades will construct it, and how it will be maintained. Some functions of the school building will be improved by the change, and some will be impaired. The accompanying diagram shows how the functions we expect of buildings are linked with one another (4.1). A designer cannot expect to change the way in which one function is served without affecting others. A building has its own ecology, a delicate internal balance of connected mechanisms that function not in isolation but as a richly interconnected whole. Thus our dissection runs the risk of overlooking or obscuring natural linkages among the various building functions and of giving too simplistic a view of how a building works. We will attempt to minimize these risks in the final chapter, in which the combination of elemental functions in buildings' common components are discussed, but in the intervening pages we constantly ought to be asking questions about the connectedness of things: What are *all* the functional repercussions of a very massive building? Of a light-colored or a dark-colored building? Of a sunny building?

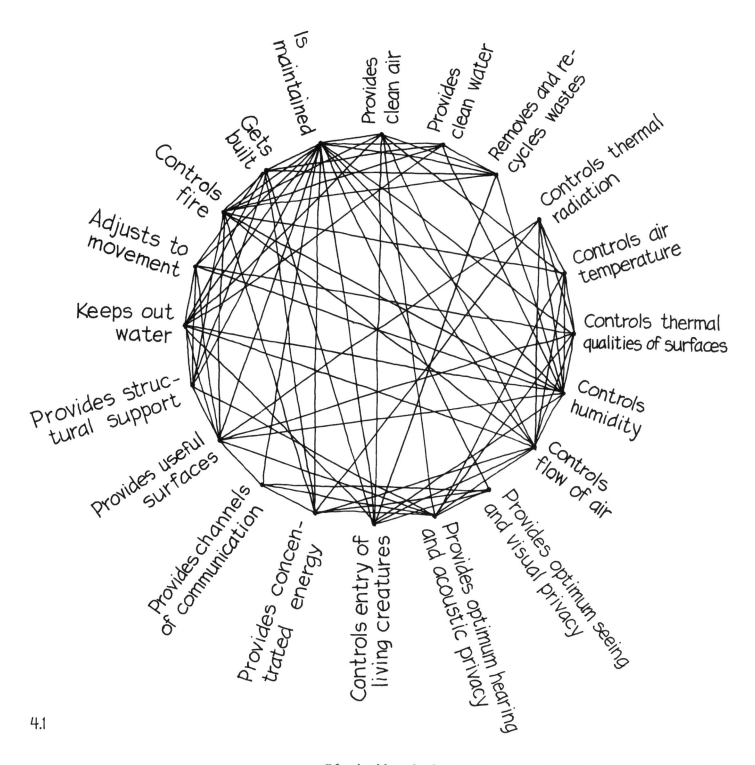

Is maintained

Provides clean air

Provides clean water

Removes and re-cycles wastes

Controls thermal radiation

Controls air temperature

Controls thermal qualities of surfaces

Controls humidity

Controls flow of air

Provides optimum seeing and visual privacy

Provides optimum hearing and acoustic privacy

Controls entry of living creatures

Provides concen-trated energy

Provides channels of communication

Provides useful surfaces

Provides struc-tural support

Keeps out water

Adjusts to movement

Controls fire

Gets built

4.1

Of a building built entirely of wood? Of a building in a windy location? What are *all* the ways in which we may warm a building, cool a building, or illuminate a building? These questions come naturally to mind in response to themes that recur again and again under various functional headings, and the answers, as they accumulate, begin to reveal the larger functional patterns underlying every building.

5
Providing Water

Buildings and settlements must always have access to an adequate source of clean water. In primitive circumstances people take water from ponds or streams and either drink it on the spot or carry it short distances in containers before using it. But most surface waters in "civilized" areas are unsafe to drink because of biological or chemical pollution, so specially protected sources of water must be developed. Piped, pressurized distribution safeguards the purity of the water to the point of use and provides convenient service even in buildings remote from sources of water.

To obtain the purest possible water on a large scale, we attempt wherever possible to harness the atmospheric distillation process by collecting and impounding rainwater as it falls. For municipal water systems, we may take over whole mountain valleys as catchment areas and dam them to form storage reservoirs. We closely regulate the human use of the catchment areas and reservoirs in order to avoid water contamination. Large aqueduct pipes carry the water from the reservoirs to the municipality, with gravity usually furnishing the motive power. Communities without access to sparsely inhabited mountains are forced either to draw water of a lesser purity from rivers or to tap subterranean water flows with wells. Well water or water from mountain reservoirs usually requires little or no treatment to make it suitable for human consumption. River water and some other waters require treatment for any or all of a number of contaminants. Sand filters and settling basins remove particulate matter. Chemical precipitation is used to remove such contaminants as iron and lead compounds. Special filters may be necessary to remove hydrogen sulfide, radon, or other dissolved gases. Finally,

5.1

5.2

Main

Shutoff

Meter

if necessary, chlorine gas is dissolved in the water in controlled amounts to kill microorganisms.

Municipal water systems are usually pressurized by water elevated above the level of the buildings, in reservoirs or water towers. Water is distributed around the town through a grid of pipes under the streets. Fire hydrants are connected directly to these pipes or, occasionally, to their own separate underground supply network (5.1).

Plumbing contractors or municipal crews make the connection between understreet water mains and individual buildings (5.2). They install an underground shutoff valve in the service pipe of each building, most often at the curb or sidewalk, so that the local water authority can shut off water service in cases of emergency or nonpayment of bills. The flow of water is usually metered inside the building, and charges are assessed periodically based on the amount of water used, often at a level covering the expenses of both water supply and sewage disposal services.

In rural areas and in many small communities, each building must develop its own supply of water. A few fortunate sites possess reliable springs from which water can be pumped, but most buildings must either catch rainfall or utilize a well. Rain water systems are still the most satisfactory watersource in many areas of the world. Although a special catchment area may be constructed on an unbuilt portion of the site, it is generally more economical to use the roof of the building to collect water. By means of gutters and downspouts, the water is brought to a cistern for storage, from which it can be withdrawn by pump or by hand (5.3). Depending on the weather, the size of the catchment area, and the volume of water storage provided, such a system may or may not be able to furnish sufficient quantities of water for use throughout the year. Cleanliness of the water is a continuing problem, especially where leaves and bird droppings fall on the catchment area, encouraging the growth of colonies of algae and bacteria in the cistern.

A well usually provides a supply of water that is more reliable, both qualitatively and quantitatively, than a rainwater system. A well is a hole that is dug, driven, or drilled in the ground to reach a porous, subsurface, water-bearing stratum. Water is sometimes found within just a few feet of the surface. Such water has probably seeped into the ground in the immediate neighborhood of the well and is therefore subject to contamination by nearby sewage disposal systems, including a building's own, or by barnyards, outhouses, or garbage dumps in the vicinity. Although deep wells require expensive equipment to drill, they usually encounter strata that are fed by surface water originating tens or hundreds of miles away. The filtering action of the long horizontal passage through the stratum results in water that is often totally free of bacteria, although it may be laden with dissolved minerals. Most such minerals do not affect the potability or usefulness of the water. Certain calcium salts, however, can cause the internal scaling and eventual obstruction of water pipes and form an insoluble scum when combined with ordinary household soap. Water rich in calcium ions is known as *hard water*. Hard water is usually pleasant in taste and deposits little scale in pipes as long as it is cold. When hard water is heated, however, its chemical activity is greatly increased, and both the water heater and the hot-water pipes quickly become encrusted with rock-hard internal deposits. Therefore a *water softener*, a simple ion-exchange column, is installed on the pipe feeding the water heater in buildings served with hard water, to replace the troublesome calcium ions with soluble sodium ions. Chemically softened water does not scale pipes, and its cleansing properties are similar to those of mineral-free rainwater.

An *artesian well* is one that taps a stratum pressurized by a flow of water from a higher elevation. Such a stratum is often encountered, but the pressure is seldom high enough to force the water all the way out the top of the well (5.4). A pump, therefore, must be installed. If the water level in the well is within about twenty-five feet (7 m) of the surface, a pump at ground level can create a sufficient vacuum in a pipe to allow the atmospheric pressure to force the water to the surface (5.5). If the water lies deeper, a pressure stronger than atmospheric is required, and so a pump must be lowered permanently into the bottom of the well to force the water up the pipe. The most common such pump is the submersible pump, which contains a sealed electric motor capable of functioning for years without maintenance at the bottom of a well. Electric wires are run down the well from the surface of the ground to the pump, often for hundreds of feet (5.6).

Pump

Overflow

Cistern

5.3

25'
(7.5m)
max.

Ground-level
hand pump
5.5

Impellers

Motor

Submersible pump
5.6

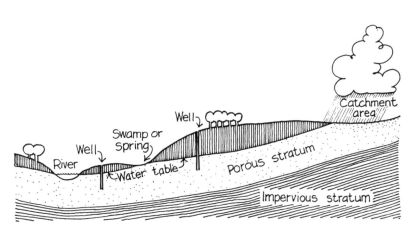

Catchment area

Well

Swamp or
Spring

Well

River

Water table

Porous stratum

Impervious stratum

5.4

33

Water to building

Air

Water

Pressure
switch
controls
pump

Water from pump

5.7

Air
chamber

Shutoff
valve

cold

hot

Excess
pressure
relief
valve

Shutoff

Water
heater

Pressure
tank

Electricity
to heater

Drain

Main shutoff
and drain

From
pump

5.8

Most individual water systems provide pressure within the building by means of a small storage tank into which the water is pumped against a volume of compressed air in the top of the tank (5.7). The pump is engaged automatically when the pressure falls to a predetermined minimum level, to force water into the tank until a predetermined maximum pressure is reached. Water driven by air pressure is always available from the bottom of the tank, whether or not the pump is operating.

If filtration or chlorination is required, appropriate devices are coupled in series with the pressure tank. If no treatment is needed, cold water is simply fed from the tank (or from the main water service pipe from the street) through a network of supply pipes to the various outlets and fixtures in the building (5.8). A parallel network is often installed to carry water that has been heated in a tank to make it more suitable for washing. The size of each pipe is determined by the rate at which it must transport water under conditions of maximum reasonable demand. Thus we find that the pipes in a supply network, treelike, tend to be smaller as we trace them farther and farther away from the water source, toward the points of use. Supply piping is generally made of copper or hard plastics, which offer smooth, low-friction interior surfaces and a high resistance to corrosion and scaling. Zinc-coated steel pipe, once very popular and lower in cost than copper, is very prone to scaling.

At each fixture, a valve is placed in each supply line so either hot or cold water may be shut off when servicing the fixtures without interrupting the flow to other parts of the building. A dead-end, upright branch of pipe is left as an *air chamber*, to absorb the shock created by the almost instantaneous deceleration to zero of the water velocity in the pipe when a faucet is shut off. If such a chamber is

34

not provided, a banging noise known as *water hammer* is heard as faucets are shut off, and momentarily high pressures are created in the pipes, causing the possibility of damage to the system.

In hot-water networks for large buildings, a return pipe to the water heater is provided near each fixture. Water circulates up the supply pipe and back down the return pipe to the heater to be rewarmed, with the circulation force furnished by either convection or a small pump (5.9). Thus hot water is always available at each tap within one or two seconds, despite the cooling that takes place in the pipe. Another way of circumventing the problem of cooling in the pipe is not to have a central water heater but to provide smaller heaters at or near each point of use.

Chilled water for drinking was commonly provided at one time by a central chiller and return piping analogous to the hot-water system just described. In recent times, however, it has become more economical and satisfactory to chill water in small coolers at each point of use.

All water supply pipes should be thermally insulated. In the case of hot or chilled water, energy is saved and water is conserved if the water does not have to be run for a long time before it emerges from the tap at the desired temperature. Cold and chilled water pipes require insulation jacketed by a vapor retarder, to prevent condensate from forming on the pipes in humid weather.

In tall buildings, the municipal water pressure is often insufficient to force water to the fixtures on the upper floors. Here, pumps must be installed in the building to transport the water to the upper reaches of the building. In some cases, these pumps feed the fixtures directly. In other cases, the pumps lift the water to one or more tanks at higher levels, from which it is fed by gravity to pipe networks in the floor below (5.10).

Lavatories, sinks, and bathtubs are designed to catch and hold water for washing and to drain it away after use. For cleanliness and durability, they must be made of hard, smooth materials such as porcelain or stainless steel, which can withstand repeated scrubbing over a period of many years.

Toilets (more precisely called *water closets*) and urinals are designed to flush away body wastes. They are made of porcelain to ensure that they will not accumulate bacteria-harboring scratches as they are being cleaned. Where supply piping is kept economically small, as in houses, it is incapable of directly providing the quick, copious rush of water necessary to operate the siphon trap of the fixture, so water is slowly accumulated for each flush in a tank at the back of the fixture. In public buildings, flushing is so frequent that slow-filling tanks are unequal to the demand, and thus larger water supply pipes must be installed, with special valves to regulate the strength and duration of each flush.

35

Normal Flow   Reverse Flow

Principle of the Vacuum Breaker

5.11

5.12

Most plumbing fixtures are designed in such a way that the level of the open water held by the fixture—the wash water in a bathroom sink, for example, or the water in the bowl of a water closet—cannot possibly reach the level of the opening that supplies fresh water to the fixture. A bathroom sink has an overflow port that drains off excess water before it can reach the end of the faucet. The bowl of a tank-type water closet may clog and fill up to its rim, but the actual inlet from the building's supply network is safely above the rim, above the water level of the tank. Thus if the water pressure in the supply pipes should fail for one reason or another, there would be no chance that contaminated water could be drawn into the pipes as the fresh water drained back away from the fixture. But some fixtures cannot be designed in this way. A water closet or urinal in a public building has a supply pipe connected directly to its rim. The end of a hose connected to an outdoor faucet can be left in a swimming pool or a garbage can filled with water. These *cross connections* between supply pipes and contaminated water, though harmless enough as long as the fresh water is flowing, cause a surprising number of cases of water system contamination through back siphonage when a system is shut off and drained or when the water pressure accidentally fails. It is now legally required in most areas that at each fixture where such a cross connection is possible, a *vacuum breaker* must be installed in the supply line (5.11). Whenever the water pressure fails, the vacuum breaker allows air to enter the line and destroy the siphoning action, thus preventing contaminated water from being sucked into the system. The familiar chrome-plated flush valve on every public toilet fixture contains a vacuum breaker, and appropriate vacuum breakers are manufactured for outdoor faucets and other fixtures as well.

Water supply piping occupies space. Small wood-frame buildings often have enough space inside floors and walls to accommodate it. But the walls of buildings with large numbers of fixtures cannot hold all the pipes, and so special *pipe chases*, both vertical and horizontal, must be provided as a part of the building's basic design. Such chases are sometimes built with access doors to allow occasional change and maintanance of the pipes without disrupting the fabric of the building (5.12). In cold climates, neither chases nor walls containing water piping should be located at the outside perimeter of a building, because the pipes may freeze and subsequently burst.

Further Reading

Benjamin Stein and John Reynolds. *Mechanical and Electrical Equipment for Buildings* (8th ed.). New York, Wiley, 1992, pp. 477–589.

6
Recycling Wastes

Nature works in closed cycles. What is waste to one organism is food to another, in an endless, intricately interwoven web that ultimately wastes nothing at all except small amounts of renewable energy from the sun. An army of insects and microorganisms feed on the excrement and the corpses of higher animals, reducing these wastes to soil nutrients that can be utilized by plants. Dead vegetable matter of all types is similarly attacked, broken down, and used again. In the soil, in the water, and in the air, processes continually take place to ensure that none of Nature's valuable substances is ever left in an unproductive state.

In many agrarian societies, farm families are active participants in these cycles. With the aid of water, air, earthworms, and a host of bacteria, they convert animal and vegetable wastes to rich soil. In the soil, with the aid of sunlight and rainfall, plants grow to feed the family and its animals and to furnish fuel for cooking and heating. The animals provide both food and clothing. The ashes from the spent fuel and the excrement of the animals go back into the soil too, replenishing its nutrient content. The land's fertility decreases little over the family's lifetime, if at all. Even some small, primitive towns are capable of sustaining this sort of relationship to the land. Food scraps and human excrement are carefully gathered and transported by "night soil" collectors to the outskirts of town, where farmers add them to the soil to help produce food (6.1). If adequate composting practices are employed, the wastes will be free of harmful organisms by the time they reach the soil, and diseases will not be communicated through the cycle. Both the health of the community and the richness of its agriculture are maintained.

Unfortunately, it is difficult to ensure that adequate composting

6.1

37

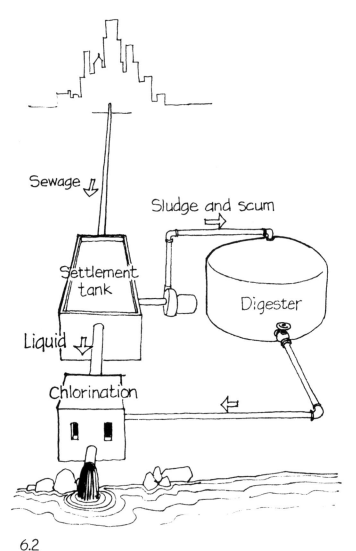

Sewage

Sludge and scum

Settlement tank

Digester

Liquid

Chlorination

6.2

practices are always employed, and careless handling of night soil has caused disastrous epidemics and plagues throughout history. Most modern cities do not use these practices because most are not fed in any large degree by the farms in the immediate vicinity, meaning that wastes would have to be transported considerable distances for agrarian recycling. We have become, furthermore, a society of people who cannot tolerate for more than a few moments the presence of our own excrement, not for reasons of health, but for aesthetic reasons. As a result of all these factors, we have broken the chain of recycling. We directly expend half our urban water consumption in flushing garbage and excrement from our buildings and then mix this half with the half we have used for washing and other purposes. Our buildings are thereby rendered marvelously convenient and free of disease and odor, but new problems arise. The water that the municipality just brought to the town, sparkling clean and bacteria free, at such trouble and expense, is now thoroughly contaminated with odor and disease.

Some towns (as did nearly all not so long ago) simply discharge their sewage, bacteria and all, into a nearby river, lake, or ocean. But most towns nowadays allow the solid material in sewage, the *sludge*, to settle out in a sewage treatment plant. The remaining liquid is chlorinated to kill bacteria and then dumped into the local waterway. The sludge is pumped into a tank where it is allowed to ferment anaerobically for several weeks. This fermentation kills most of the disease-causing bacteria in the sludge and precipitates out most of the minerals it contains. Then this "digested" sludge is also chlorinated and pumped into a waterway (6.2).

Through this process, soil nutrients—brought into the city as fruits, vegetables, grains, milk products, and meats and flushed out of the city as sewage—are now dumped not back onto the soil but into the waterways. Unlike the soil, which needs the nutrients and is capable of finishing their reconversion into food, the waterways are not capable of completing the cycle. Instead, the increased nutrient content of the water accelerates the growth of waterweeds and algae. Soon the water is choked with plant growth, to the extent that sunlight can no longer penetrate the water for more than a few inches. Masses of plants die and decay, and the decay process consumes much of the oxygen dissolved in the water. Fish suffocate in the oxygen-poor environment, and the waterway itself begins to die. Over a few decades it fills with dead plants and eventually becomes a swamp and then a meadow. By that time, of course, no one remembers that people once swam, boated, and fished there. In the meantime, the food-producing farmland is gradually drained of its nutrients. Farm productivity falls, and such plants as are grown there may lack essential human nutrients. Artificial fertilizers must then be manufactured and applied to replace the wasted natural fertilizers that are destroying lakes and rivers instead of replenishing the soil.

Our society also produces nonsewage wastes, which create different sorts of problems. Paper, plastics, glass, and metals enter our buildings, bearing information and containing goods of various sorts. These substances are quickly discarded, along with ashes and cinders, dust and dirt, broken or worn mechanisms, kitchen garbage, old clothing, industrial by-products, and radioactive and chemical wastes from laboratories and industries (6.3). The quantities of these solid wastes produced in the United States average out to hundreds of pounds per person per year. Nearly all the material represent either links in biological recycling chains (such as food scraps or paper) or finite quantities of nonrenewable resources (such as metals and plastics). Many of the waste substances contain useful energy, but the separation and recycling of this mingled refuse is a huge, almost impossible task. Most cities simply burn the mass and bury the ashes or bury the mass without burning it. Whereas the buried organic materials decompose, glass, metals, and plastics simply sit in the soil, wasted.

6.3

As a part of its own curious mechanical metabolism, a building must give off wastes and take in fresh materials to replace them. It is worthwhile to examine both how this is currently done and how buildings might contribute to a more sound system of waste recycling.

Waste pipes from sinks, lavatories, tubs, showers, water closets, urinals, and floor drains all come together in a network that is drained by gravity (6.4). In order to maintain gravity flow, large pipes are necessary; all the pipes must run consistently downhill; and normal atmospheric air pressure must be maintained in all sections of the network at all times. Furthermore, since the waste piping is handling suspended solid wastes of various kinds, it is prone to clogging, and so access to the pipes must be provided at frequent intervals to allow for cleaning.

A fixture such as a lavatory, sink, or tub empties into the waste piping network through a *trap*, a U-shaped piece of pipe that retains enough water to prevent the odors and gases of decomposition from the waste piping from passing back into the fixture and into the building. The water seal in the trap can be broken, however, if waste water from the fixture siphons through the trap or if gas pressure or air pressure builds up in the piping. For this reason, a *vent pipe* is attached to the waste piping a short distance downstream from each trap. The vent allows air to enter the waste pipe to break any potential siphoning action, and it releases to the atmosphere any decomposition gases such as methane or hydrogen sulfide. Thus a complete network of waste piping for a building includes two treelike

6.4

6.5   Water closet

6.6   Septic Tank

configurations, one that collects the sewage and leads it down and another, upside down, that allows air to enter the first tree at the tips of its branches. The piping in each tree grows steadily larger from fixture to outlet, to serve the greater number of fixtures at each stage.

The contemporary water closet is simply a large trap that is forced to siphon rapidly during the flushing process and is then refilled with fresh water to maintain the seal against the entry of sewer gases (6.5). Like any other trap, it must be vented nearby, to prevent accidental siphoning between flushes.

We have already sketched the means by which a municipality gathers and treats sewage from its buildings. Each rural building must treat and dispose of its own sewage. This was formerly accomplished through the use of a *cesspool*, a porous underground container of stone or brick that allows the sewage to seep into the surrounding soil. The cesspool is unsatisfactory, however, in that it does nothing to remove disease-causing organisms from the sewage, and it clogs the surrounding soil with solids in a relatively short period of time, after which it is likely to overflow onto the surface of the ground and cause sewage to back up into fixtures inside the building. Its much more satisfactory successor is the nonporous *septic tank* (6.6). The septic tank is configured in such a way that it holds sewage for a period of days, allowing it to decompose anaerobically and to separate into a clear, relatively harmless liquid effluent and a small amount of mineral matter, which settles to the bottom. The effluent runs out of the tank and into a *leaching field*, a system of porous pipes or porous tanks, from which it is allowed to seep into the soil (6.7). The sludge from the bottom of the tank must be pumped out every several years, to be hauled away and processed into harmlessness at a remote plant. If the septic tank is too small, however, or if the soil in the leaching field is not sufficiently porous or if the system is installed too near a well, a body of water, or a steep slope, even a septic system may malfunction and contaminate the water or soil. For this reason, most municipalities and states have stringent regulations requiring soil testing and the utilization of approved techniques of design and construction in the installation of septic systems. It is not uncommon for a potential building site to prove incapable of accommodating a septic system and therefore to be incapable of supporting a building.

In an effort to improve small sewage disposal systems, new devices are being introduced into the market each year. Some aim to improve the digestion of sewage in the tank, through such expedients as aerating the sewage to encourage the more thorough digestive action of aerobic organisms. Others attempt to improve the leaching process by distributing the effluent more evenly throughout the field or by allowing access to the leaching surfaces for inspection and cleaning.

Garbage and trash are most commonly collected by hand within buildings, to be transported to containers where they are left for periodic removal by municipal or private trucks. Some buildings have incinerator systems, in which wastes are jettisoned down a chute, to be consumed by a gas- or oil-fueled fire at the bottom. Only the ashes need then be carried away, but the air pollution generated by incomplete combustion in faulty incinerators has caused their use to be strictly regulated in many areas. Garbage grinders macerate and flush food scraps into the sewage system, but the sewage disposal installation, whether municipal or private, must be sufficiently large to handle this additional burden of water and solid material.

In some buildings, the laborious manual transport of solid wastes has been largely eliminated through the installation of systems of very large vacuum pipes that suck all the wastes to a central location for incineration or for compression into bales for easier trucking.

Some cities utilize the heat of combustion of their rubbish to fuel electric power plants or central heating installations. Others have systems for the automatic reclamation of valuable constituents of rubbish, through either mechanized sorting or pyrolysis. In an increasing number of cities, householders and building owners sort out the various components of their trash before having it collected, thus avoiding the need for complicated central sorting plants. This means, however, that each house or building needs separate, clearly labeled storage containers for garbage, clean paper, steel, aluminum, glass, and various types of plastics. The solid waste disposal system of the building can no longer be a garbage can or two in a leftover corner but, rather, must be carefully planned and constructed for its purpose.

As water becomes a more precious resource, we may see more buildings with systems for separating discarded wash water from toilet wastes. After a minimum of filtration within the building, wash water can serve such secondary uses as the flushing of toilets or the watering of lawns and gardens. Much of the heat from warm waste water can be recovered through a heat exchanger to preheat fresh water before it enters the water heater or to contribute to the comfort heating of the building.

Most new water closets are designed to use less than half as much water per flush as do older water closets. Many areas of the United States permit only this type of toilet in new installations. There are even more water-efficient options available, however: A toilet with a mechanical seal rather than a water trap uses only about 5 percent of

Septic Tank

Leaching Field   6.7

the ordinary amount, and a toilet using recirculating chemicals is even more efficient than this. Several types generate no sewage at all. One such type has a small aerobic digestor built into the fixture and generally loses enough water by evaporation through a vent pipe to the outside air to maintain a constant level of liquid inside. A second type incinerates the excrement with a gas flame after each use, leaving only a bit of clean ash. A third type is a much-improved version of the traditional outhouse, ventilated in such a way that it can be maintained odor free inside the house and configured internally so it continuously reduces both excrement and kitchen garbage to a small volume of disease-free garden compost. Such a device may offer one small-scale way of mending a part of the break in the nutrient chain.

Anaerobic digestion of excrement and kitchen wastes produces methane gas, potentially valuable as a fuel, as a natural by-product. Such insignificant quantities of methane are developed from domestic sewage that it is not worthwhile to build a gas-generating apparatus for home use, but for livestock farmers and operators of large sewage treatment plants, the possibilities are much greater. Many municipal treatment plants are at present heated, illuminated, and powered by methane gas from their digesters, and some farmers are experimenting with their own methane generation systems. Some cities are even able to extract useful quantities of methane from their old garbage dumps by drilling wells to tap underground pockets of decomposition gases.

Many municipal sewage treatment plants are improving the efficacy of their treatment processes, using aerobic digestion and various sorts of chemical treatment and filtration to produce, in some cases, an effluent that is suitable for drinking. In some cities, clean effluent is pumped into the ground to replenish the depleted water-bearing strata. In a few others, the digested sludge is dried, bagged, and sold for fertilizer. Some municipal plants spray their processed sewage directly on forests or croplands, simultaneously irrigating and fertilizing them. Many such possibilities exist for making more responsible and productive use of the wastes we generate, and many more experiments are under way, but we have only begun to deal with the waste-recycling problems that we, our buildings, and our cities have created.

Further Reading

Benjamin Stein and John Reynolds. *Mechanical and Electrical Equipment for Buildings* (8th ed.). New York, Wiley, 1992, pp. 590–646.

7
Providing for Thermal Comfort

Despite the ingenious physiological mechanisms the human body employs, it can seldom achieve thermal equilibrium without the external help of clothing and buildings. Clothing and buildings are similar in that both use passive devices to control natural flows of heat, air, and moisture vapor for the increased comfort of the wearer or occupant (7.1). They differ in two important respects: First, buildings enclose a volume many times as large as that contained by clothing, in order to house not only the bodies of the occupants but also all the space occupied and traversed in the course of their activities. Second, buildings are usually equipped to take an *active* as well as a *passive* role in creating thermal comfort, through the controlled release of energy to create a more favorable indoor climate.

We often characterize the active thermal comfort control systems in buildings as "heating" systems or "cooling" systems. Except in rare cases, however, a "heating" system does not create an overall net flow of heat into the human body but merely adjusts the thermal characteristics of the indoor environment to reduce the rate of heat loss from the body to a comfortable level. Though for the sake of convenience, we will continue to talk of heating and cooling systems in buildings, as a matter of strict accuracy it should be remembered that *both* heating and cooling systems are designed to control the rate at which the body is cooled. A "heating" system allows the body to cool less rapidly in cold weather, whereas a "cooling" or "air-conditioning" system helps the body cool more rapidly when the weather is hot.

The accompanying chart (7.2) shows the alternative means normally available for the voluntary regulation of human thermal comfort. It is divided horizontally into two major sections, one contain-

7.1

43

		Physical Activity	Clothing	Radiation	Air Temperature	Humidity	Air Movement	Surface Contact
Means for cooling the body more rapidly	Passive	• Extend body to maximize surface area	• Open or remove layers of clothing • Saturate clothing with water	• Shade body from warm object • Expose body to cooler object	• Keep sun from heating occupied space • Use thermal mass to cool air • Evaporate H_2O to cool air	• Dehumidify air by condensing water onto cool building surfaces	• Allow wind or convection currents to move past body	• Put body against cool, dense surface • Keep body off warm or insulating surfaces
	Active	• Reduce level of muscular activity	• Liquid-cooled space suit	• Mechanically cool building surfaces	• Mechanically refrigerate air	• Mechanical dehumidification	• Use fan to move air	• Take a cool bath or swim • Ingest cool food or drink • Mechanically cool floors and/or seats
Means for cooling the body less rapidly	Passive	• Contract body to minimize surface area	• Close or put on layers of clothing • Dry out wet clothing	• Expose body to warm object • Reflect back body heat with metallic surface	• Allow sun to heat occupied space • Use thermal mass to release stored heat into air	• Allow sun to evaporate water into air	• Shelter body from wind	• Put body against warm or insulating surfaces
	Active	• Raise level of muscular activity • Snuggle with a friend	• Electric blanket • Electric stockings	• Mechanically warm building surfaces • Build fire	• Heat the air	• Boil water into air	• Reduce fan speed	• Hot bath • Hot water bottle or hot brick • Heat floors and/or seats • Ingest hot food or drink

7.2   Voluntary Means for Regulating Thermal Comfort

7.3

ing means for cooling the body *more* rapidly and the other for cooling the body *less* rapidly. Each major section of the chart is again divided into two horizontal subsections, one for passive means and one for active means, those requiring the artificial release of energy. The first two vertical columns indicate the roles of physical activity and clothing. The remaining columns list means of regulating thermal comfort that may be employed in or around buildings, most often by the buildings themselves. These means will be explained more fully in the following four chapters, but note that five separate factors—thermal radiation, air temperature, humidity, air movement, and the thermal properties of surfaces contacted by the body—are involved in creating thermal comfort (7.3).

In a building, these five factors are heavily interdependent. When a floor surface is warmed by the sun, it warms the air above itself, radiates heat to the human body, and conducts heat to the human

44

foot that contacts it (7.4). The warmed air rises above the surrounding air, creating a convective circulation, and the air's relative humidity is reduced as its temperature is raised. Thus a single occurrence—the warming of a floor by a shaft of sunlight—can affect all the factors bearing on thermal comfort. Similarly, an ordinary warm-air heating system heats the air, reduces its relative humidity, blows it past the occupants of a room, and warms the surfaces of the room as they are swept by the warm air. It is impossible to change any one factor without affecting the others, at least to a small extent.

Besides this interdependence, there is also a good deal of interchangeability among these means of thermal comfort regulation. As can be seen by using the chart, two sorts of interchangeability are possible: One is between the *columns* in the chart. We can be quite comfortable in a room in which the air temperature is relatively low, for example, if there is a crackling fire radiating generous amounts of heat from the fireplace to the skin (7.5). Summer air temperatures in the high eighties (30°C–32°C) will seem ideal if the humidity is low, a moderate breeze is blowing, only light clothing is worn, and one is shielded from direct sunlight (7.6). There are limits to this sort of

7.4

7.5

7.6

45

7.7

7.8

interchangeability, but within a rather wide latitude, one parameter may be adjusted to compensate for another without causing discomfort. A second sort of interchangeability is between horizontal *rows* in the chart, between active and passive means of varying the same parameter of thermal comfort. A breeze passing through a room can substitute for an electric fan (7.7). A thick rug over a concrete floor may eliminate the need to warm the floor with circulating hot water (7.8). When passive means can be used in place of active ones, fuel consumption in the building is reduced, and long-term cost savings are likely, depending on the relative costs of installing and maintaining the passive and active devices.

People vary a good deal with respect to such important thermal factors as metabolic rate, tendency to perspire, amount of insulating fat beneath the skin, ratio of skin surface area to body volume, and amount of clothing worn. The same person in the same clothing has different thermal requirements at different times of day, as when exercising more vigorously, digesting a heavy meal, or sleeping. As a result of all these variables, each person in a room is likely to have a slightly different opinion about what set of thermal conditions feels most comfortable. In general, the best that can be done is to seek those conditions that satisfy the greatest number of people and to allow the rest to adjust their clothing to compensate. In some circumstances in which people remain in one place for an extended period, as on an airplane, in a theater, or in an office or workshop, it is possible to give each person control over at least one thermal factor, by such means as individual air vents, small operable windows, or small electric heaters. In other circumstances, especially in dwellings, one has freedom to move a little farther from the fire or to sit in a sunny window while others sit in the shade farther back in the room. If the designer of a building takes care to provide such opportunities for individual adjustment, there can be many of them.

Further Reading

Victor Olgyay. *Design with Climate*. Princeton, N.J., Princeton University Press, 1973, pp. 14–23.

8
Thermal Properties of Building Components

Each material used in building construction has its own unique set of physical properties relating to the flow of heat. An important part of a designer's job is to select and combine building materials in such a way as to result in a building whose enclosure performs as much of the building's climate-control function as possible, leaving as little work as possible to be done by energy-consuming heating and cooling systems and producing the maximum possible comfort for the building's occupants.

We must distinguish clearly among the three basic mechanisms of heat transfer. *Radiation* is a transfer of heat by means of the straight-line passage of electromagnetic waves through space or air from a warmer object to a cooler one (8.1). The skin is warmed by radiation when one stands in the sun or near a fire and is cooled by radiation when one stands near a cold wall or under a clear night sky. *Conduction* is a flow of heat through solid material (8.2). Heat is conducted to or from the skin when the skin is pressed against a warmer or cooler object, such as a hot potato or an ice cube. *Convection* is a transfer of heat by means of a moving stream of air or water (8.3). The skin is warmed or cooled convectively by exposure to warm or cool air. A common kitchen stove employs all three mechanisms of heat transfer: The broiler warms food primarily by radiation, the oven primarily by convection, and the burners primarily by conduction through the metal of the pan.

Radiation

All objects give off heat in the form of infrared electromagnetic radiation, and all receive radiation from surrounding objects. Infra-

Radiation   8.1

Conduction   8.2

Convection   8.3

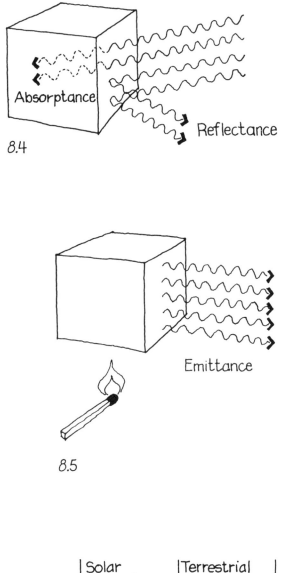

8.4

8.5

	Solar Radiation		Terrestrial Radiation	
	Absorp. Emitt.	Reflect.	Absorp. Emitt.	Reflect.
Bright aluminum	0.05	0.95	0.05	0.95
Galvanized steel	0.25	0.75	0.25	0.75
White paint	0.20	0.80	0.90	0.10
Fresh whitewash	0.12	0.88	0.90	0.10
Lt. green paint	0.40	0.60	0.90	0.10
Dk. green paint	0.70	0.30	0.90	0.10
Black paint	0.85	0.15	0.90	0.10
Concrete	0.60	0.40	0.90	0.10

8.6

red rays are an invisible part of the light spectrum and behave exactly like light. Any two objects that can "see" each other through a medium that is transparent to light, such as air or a vacuum, exchange radiant energy. When line-of-sight contact between the two objects is broken, as by the insertion of an opaque object between them, the exchange stops instantly. The net rate of exchange between the objects is proportional to the difference between the fourth powers of their absolute temperatures. Thus two objects at the same temperature have no net exchange of heat. If one object is a few degrees warmer, there will be a relatively small flow of heat from the warmer object to the cooler one. As the difference in temperature grows, however, the radiant flow grows at an increasingly rapid rate.

The radiative properties of building materials—the ways in which they affect thermal radiation that impinges on them—are of extreme importance to designers. *Reflectance* is the proportion of incoming radiation that bounces off the material, leaving the temperature of the material unchanged. *Absorptance* is the proportion that enters the material and thereby raises its temperature (8.4). The sum of reflectance and absorptance for a given material is always one. *Emittance* is a measure of the material's ability to radiate heat outward to other objects; at any given wavelength it is numerically equal to absorptance (8.5).

The range of infrared wavelengths is quite large, and we find that buildings must commonly deal with thermal radiation in two distinctly different parts of the spectrum. Solar radiation, emitted by a source at a temperature of many thousands of degrees, is of relatively short wavelength. Thermal radiation from most terrestrial sources— sun-warmed earth or floors, warm building surfaces, human skin— is emitted at much lower temperatures and therefore at much longer wavelengths. Most common building materials react quite differently to these two ranges of wavelengths, and these differences account for several interesting thermal phenomena. From the accompanying chart (8.6), we note, for example, that a building painted white reflects about 80 percent of the sun's direct thermal radiation. However, it reflects only about 10 percent of the thermal radiation from surrounding sun-heated lawns and pavement, almost the same as if it were painted black. If the building had a bright metallic exterior, it would be much better protected against the terrestrial reradiation of solar heat. It would also radiate less heat to the outdoors in winter than if it were painted white. This low emittance of polished metals at long wavelengths is of particular use in building construction, because it allows the use of bright metal foils as thermal insulators, provided that they are installed adjacent to an airspace. A material can emit radiation only through a gas that is transparent to infrared wavelengths or through a vacuum. If it is sandwiched snugly between other layers of construction, it cannot emit radiation but can only conduct heat directly. Since metal foils are excellent conductors of heat, it follows that they are valuable as insulation only when they have an adjacent airspace on one side or the other, or preferably both.

Conduction

The resistance of a material to the conduction of heat is a measure of its insulating value. The rate at which a building gains or loses heat through any portion of its enclosure under stable conditions of indoor and outdoor temperature is directly proportional to the difference in air temperature between the inside and the outside and is inversely proportional to the overall *thermal resistance* of that portion of its enclosure. In general, we try to build walls, roofs, and floors so that they have maximum possible thermal resistance, for bodily comfort and for conservation of energy. Solid materials have varying resistances (8.7). Metals have very low resistance (which is the same as saying that they are good conductors of heat, or poor thermal insulators), whereas masonry materials have moderately low resistance, and wood has a moderately high resistance. The best resistor of heat flow that is commonly available for use in buildings, however, is air, provided that it can be kept from moving. If the air layer within the hollow wall of an ordinary wood-frame house is prevented from circulating, by being trapped in a loose tangle of glass or mineral fibers, it will have a very high thermal resistance. The fibers, spun from a dense material, are themselves rather poor resistors to heat flow. Their function is simply to create so much resistance to the circulation of the air they have trapped that the air is held nearly still and acts as a good insulator. If the same air is allowed to circulate freely within the wall, it will set up a pattern of convective flow that fairly effectively transfers heat from the warmer surface to the cooler one (8.8).

Because glass has a notoriously low resistance to the flow of heat, systems of double and triple glazing have been developed, in which air is trapped in thin layers between sheets of glass. The visual qualities of the glass do not noticeably change, but the thermal resistance greatly increases, though not to a value approaching that of a well-insulated wall. In an effort to increase the resistance of double glazing, manufacturers have tried progressively increasing the thickness of the air layer between the panes. What they have discovered is that thermal resistance increases slightly as the layer is thickened to an inch or so and then fails to increase further as the dimension is further increased. What happens is that when the airspace is very thin, friction between the glass surfaces and the air

8.7
Thermal Resistances, R

	$\dfrac{\text{ft}^2\text{hr}\,°\text{F}}{\text{BTU}}$	$\dfrac{\text{m}^2\,°\text{C}}{\text{W}}$
1" (25 mm) aluminum	0.0007	0.00012
1" (25 mm) pine	1.25	0.23
4" (100 mm) brick	0.80	0.14
8" (200 mm) concrete	0.88	0.16
3½" (90 mm) glass fiber batt	10.9	1.96
6" (150 mm) glass fiber batt	18.8	3.38
1" (25 mm) polystyrene foam	4.2	0.76
1" (25 mm) polyurethane foam	5.9	1.06
Single glass	0.9	0.16
Double glass	1.8	0.32
Triple glass	2.8	0.50
Well-insulated wall	15.0 – 19.0	2.7 – 3.4

8.8

8.9

Winter heat flow
8.10

Summer heat flow
8.11

prevents much of the convective flow that would readily transfer heat from one pane to the other, but the very thinness of the air layer prevents it from having a very high resistance. When the airspace is very thick, it could in theory provide a great deal of resistance, except that the air is given enough room to circulate with relative ease. A maximum overall resistance can therefore be achieved with an air layer of intermediate thickness (8.9). Resistance can be increased somewhat by substituting a gas of lower thermal capacity for the air between the panes or by introducing tangled glass fibers into the airspace. Glass fibers affect the optical quality of the window, however, and so cannot be used where a view is desired. They also reduce the amount of light transmitted, forcing the designer to select an optimum compromise between thermal resistance and light transmission.

The resistance of an open airspace is also affected by the emittances of the surfaces on either side. Much of the heat that travels across an airspace is radiated directly from one surface to the other, independently of the convective transfer of the air itself, if the emittances of the surfaces are high at long wavelengths, as they are for most building materials. Thus a layer of bright, nonoxidizing metal foil, usually aluminum, within or on either side of the airspace, can eliminate most of the radiative transfer. In double glazing, thin metallic coatings can be deposited on the surfaces of the glass facing the airspace, to reduce the emittance of the glass. These *low emissivity (low-e) coatings* thereby reduce the conductivity of the entire assembly.

The insulating effectiveness of an airspace—or of any air-containing building material—is also dependent on the position of the assembly and the direction in which the heat flows. In a wall or window, as we have noted, heat flow is horizontal and is abetted by a vertical convective circulation of moderate effectiveness. In a roof, heat flows upward in cold weather, and warm air within the roof assembly rises immediately to the cold upper surface to give up its heat, a relatively (and unfortunately) efficient process (8.10). In hot weather, however the heat flow through the roof is reversed. Air warmed by the hot upper surface tends to remain stratified against that surface rather than circulate toward the cooler surface below, and the heat transfer through the roof is relatively sluggish (8.11). Thus if identical airspaces are provided in the floor, wall, and roof assemblies of a building, convective heat transfer in the winter will be most rapid in the roof, least rapid in the floor, and of intermediate rapidity in the walls. Radiative heat transfer, however, is independent of direction. A reflective foil surface therefore eliminates about half the total outward heat flow through roofs and walls and about two-thirds of the downward flow through floors. Reflective foil is increasingly used as an effective way of reducing the downward transmission of heat from a sun-warmed roof into a building in summer.

Air serves a small but significant insulating role on the exterior and interior surfaces of buildings. Every surface holds a thin insulating *surface film* of air by means of friction between the air and the surface. The rougher the surface is, the thicker the film and the higher its insulating value will be (8.12). Fur is an example of a very rough surface that traps a considerable layer of air; its insulating properties are widely appreciated. Surface films are seriously affected by air movement, however, and exterior films are largely destroyed by high winds, thus accounting for part of the fuel-saving qualities of wind-sheltered building locations. (The other part of the savings comes from the reduced infiltration of cold outside air through cracks in the building.) Convective heat transfer across a surface is roughly proportional to the cube root of the air velocity past the surface. Expected heat losses from buildings are always computed on the basis of maximum prevailing wind velocities in the area.

Walls and roofs of buildings do not usually have uniform thermal resistances across their surfaces, owing to the presence of framing members or structural ties that transmit heat more rapidly through some parts of the assemblies. This is not too severe a problem in wood construction, because wood is itself a fairly good insulator, but metal and masonry construction are often filled with such *thermal bridges*, which can greatly increase the heat loss through an otherwise well-insulated assembly (8.13). In existing walls or ceilings, the presence of thermal bridges can often be detected by *pattern staining*, in which cooler areas of the interior surface collect a thicker layer of dust because of the higher electrostatic charge that they carry in dry air. In cold weather, condensate or frost can form on the portions of interior surfaces cooled by thermal bridges.

Thermal Capacity

Thermal capacity, the ability to store heat, is an important property of building materials. In general, thermal capacity is roughly proportional to mass. Large quantities of dense materials hold large quantities of heat. Fluffy materials and small pieces of material hold small quantities of heat. Thermal capacity is measured as the amount of heat required to raise the temperature of a unit volume or unit weight of material by one degree. Water has a higher thermal capacity than does any other material at ordinary air temperatures (except for certain substances that freeze and thaw at ordinary temperatures), but earth, brick, stone, plaster, metals, and concrete also

8.12
Thermal Resistances, R, of Surface Air Films

	ft²hr°F / BTU	m²°C / W
Interior wall surface	0.68	0.12
Exterior surface, summer wind	0.25	0.05
Exterior surface, winter wind	0.17	0.03

Wood studs   Metal studs

8.13

8.14
Thermal Capacities

	Per unit mass		Per unit volume	
	$\dfrac{BTU}{lb\,°F}$	$\dfrac{kJ}{kg\,°C}$	$\dfrac{BTU}{ft^3\,°F}$	$\dfrac{kJ}{m^3\,°C}$
Water	1.0	4.19	62	4160
Steel	0.12	0.50	59	3960
Stone	0.21	0.88	36	2415
Concrete	0.21	0.88	31	2080
Brick	0.20	0.84	25	1680
Clay soil	0.20	0.84	20	1350
Wood	0.45	1.89	14	940
Mineral wool	0.20	0.84	0.4	27

are materials of high thermal capacity (8.14). Fabrics and thermal insulating materials have low capacities.

In order to appreciate the effect of thermal capacity on building performance, let us first consider the hypothetical case of three identical, very well insulated test chambers, each connected to its own warm-air heating system. Into the first chamber we place a thousand bricks, each standing on end with plenty of airspace between it and the surrounding bricks. In the second chamber, we stack tightly a thousand of the same bricks into a solid cube. In the third chamber we place a thousand blocks of dry wood, each equal in size to a brick, standing on end in a loose array identical to that of the bricks in the first chamber. We now leave the three chambers open to the laboratory air for several days to make sure that the air and contents of each have equilibrated at an identical temperature. Then we adjust the thermostats in the three chambers to identical settings thirty degrees above the laboratory room temperature, close the chambers, and switch on the three heating systems. For each chamber, a recorder plots a graph of total fuel consumption versus time.

After correcting the three graphs for incidental heat losses from the chambers to the air of the laboratory, a striking pattern emerges (8.15). Initially the rate of fuel consumption to heat the three chambers is approximately equal as the air temperatures are raised the first few degrees. Then the fuel consumption of the third chamber, the one containing the wood blocks, begins to fall off as the thermostat calls for less and less heat. The thermostat ceases to call for heat altogether after a relatively short period of time, meaning that both the air and the wood blocks have reached the temperature of the thermostat setting. Meanwhile, the first chamber, with its loose bricks, continues to require heat and consumes both more fuel and more time than does the third chamber before its temperature stabilizes at the higher level. While this is going on, however, the second chamber, with its tight stack of bricks, is burning fuel more slowly than the first chamber, and it continues to consume fuel long after both the other chambers are at equilibrium. After a very long time, it, too, reaches equilibrium after consuming exactly the same amount of fuel as did the chamber containing the same volume of bricks in a loose array. What has happened is that the wood blocks, which have a relatively low thermal capacity, do not require very much heat to warm them up. The bricks, with their higher thermal capacity, require more heat to warm them to the same temperature, and the amount is the same whether the bricks are arrayed loosely or in a compact volume. The loosely arrayed bricks, however, have many times as much surface area exposed to the air as do the bricks in a cube and are thus able to absorb heat from the air relatively quickly. In the brick cube, the heat penetrating from the surface must warm each layer of bricks in turn, and the bricks in the very core of the cube will not be warmed to the air temperature of the chamber until all the surrounding layers have been warmed. This process is a very slow one.

As an application of this experiment, imagine three identical, well-insulated buildings in a cold climate. The first has thin interior partitions of brick. The second contains the same volume of brickwork, but it all is concentrated in a massive, unused fireplace standing free in the middle of the building. The third has wooden parti-

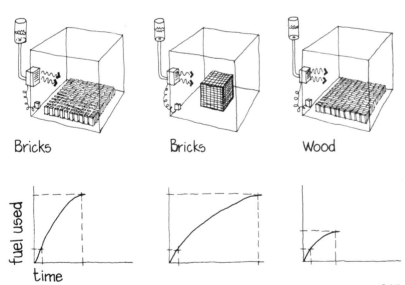

Bricks   Bricks   Wood

fuel used

time

8.15

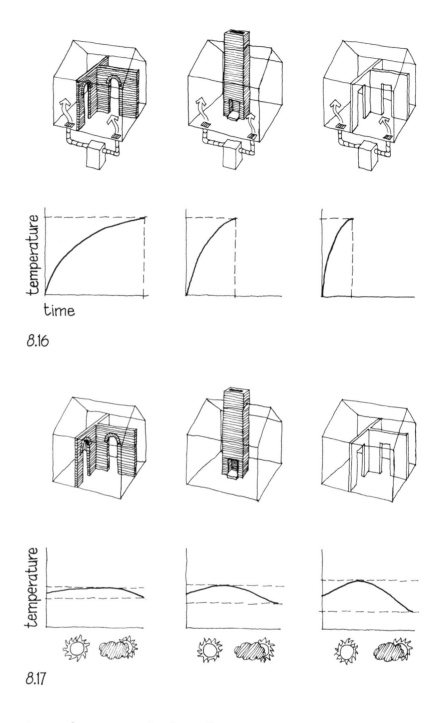

8.16

8.17

tions and contains no bricks at all (8.16). If furnaces are turned on in the three buildings, the third building will heat up very quickly; the first will heat very slowly; and the second will reach the desired air temperature after an intermediate period of time but will continue for a very long time to require additional inputs of heat to warm its masonry mass. If heat is introduced into the three buildings at sporadic but identical intervals as, for example, by sunlight streaming in the windows whenever the sky happens to be clear, the building with

54

wooden partitions will experience wide fluctuations in its air temperature, and the other two will tend to dampen the fluctuations considerably (8.17).

When a massive fireplace has a fire built in it, some of the sudden and intense heat of the flames is radiated and convected directly into the interior of the building, but a great deal goes to warm the masonry of the fireplace and chimney. This heat is released slowly when the fire is low or after it is extinguished, some up the chimney to the outdoors and some through the walls of the chimney and fireplace and through the fireplace opening to the interior of the building. By this means, the fireplace itself serves to even out and prolong the flow of heat from a fire. Some fuel-burning stoves are constructed massively of stone or ceramic, for similar reasons. Masses of masonry or water can be similarly used to accumulate heat from solar collectors for release at night or on cloudy days or to accumulate heat from electric resistance elements during off-peak hours when electric rates are lower, for use in heating the house during the rest of the day.

When an exterior wall is constructed of a thick layer of a high-capacity material such as adobe, stone, brick, or concrete and is subjected to a stable differential in temperature between the outdoors and the indoors, the wall is warmed only slowly by the heat penetrating from the warmer side, as heat is absorbed in turn by each internal layer of the wall. Eventually a stable condition is reached in which the colder side of the wall is at a temperature approaching the cold-side air temperature; the warmer side approaches the warm-side air temperature; and a straight-line gradient of temperature exists through the thickness of the wall. Until this stable condition prevails, the wall transmits heat from the one side to the other at a rate lower than what would be predicted solely from the thermal resistance of the wall. Once a stable condition is achieved, however, heat is transferred at the predicted rate. Because materials of high thermal capacity are characterized by low thermal resistances, this rate is quite rapid compared with a well-insulated wall.

When the air temperature on one side of the wall fluctuates, the wall acts to diminish and delay the fluctuations of air temperature on the other side (8.18). A very useful example of this is the heavy mud or stone architecture that is common throughout the warm desert climates of the world. During the day, the outdoor air is hot, and heat migrates slowly through the wall or roof toward the interior of the building. Before much of the heat can penetrate the thick construction to reach the interior, however, the sun sets. Radiational cooling of the ground results in a considerable cooling of the outdoor air, to temperatures below that of the warm exterior of the building, and convective cooling of the exterior building surfaces

8.18

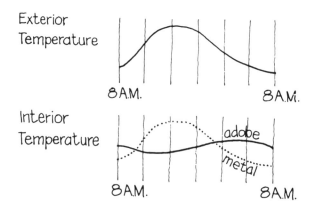

Exterior
Temperature

8 A.M.   8 A.M.

Interior
Temperature

adobe

metal

8 A.M.   8 A.M.

8.19

commences. Direct radiational cooling of exterior surfaces, particularly the roof, also takes place. Much of the heat that was accumulated during the day in the walls and roof now flows slowly back toward the cool exterior surfaces, rather than continuing its migration toward the interior. The net effect is that the building interior is cooler than its surroundings during the day and warmer at night, which is precisely the pattern the occupants require to remain comfortable. The thermally optimal thicknesses of walls and roofs have been arrived at by centuries of trial and error. In many geographical areas, the effect of thermal mass is enhanced by the whitewashing of exterior surfaces. Whitewash reflects most solar infrared radiation but is a fairly efficient emitter of longwave infrared from heated building surfaces to the night sky. Building ventilation is usually minimized during the heat of the day or the cold of the night, by shuttering the small windows tightly.

Contemporary utilitarian buildings in many warm desert areas are constructed with low-capacity roofs of thin corrugated sheets of metal or cement-asbestos. Such building offer a vivid comparison with the buildings of the preceding example (8.19). The lightweight roofs heat almost instantaneously in the sun. Much of this heat is conducted and reradiated to the interior of the building, quickly raising its temperature to unbearable levels. At night, such roofs lose their heat quickly to the sky and chill the interior space and its occupants by means of both convection and radiation. When such a mistaken choice of materials has been made, its thermal effects can be ameliorated by adding a thick layer of insulation and/or high-capacity material below the roof, preferably with a generous, ventilated airspace just below the roofing to allow the escape of solar heat to the outside air.

Materials of high thermal resistance can often be combined with materials of high thermal capacity to help achieve a desired pattern of thermal behavior in a building enclosure. Heavy, warm-climate buildings can be made to function even more effectively by the addition of a layer of insulation outside the masonry enclosure. The insulation reduces the amplitude of the temperature fluctuations to which the masonry is exposed, and the indoor environment is thereby rendered extremely stable (8.20). The same amount of insulation applied inside the masonry enclosure is considerably less effective. In this configuration the mass of the structure is still fully exposed to solar heat gain and to swings in outdoor air temperature, and the insulation on the interior is virtually wasted in dealing only with the small temperature swings of the interior surfaces of the masonry (8.21). External insulation offers the additional advantage of protecting the building, particularly the roof structure, from extreme stresses of thermal expansion and contraction. Even in tem-

56

Interior   Wall   Exterior

Temperature variation over 24 hours

8.20

Interior   Wall   Exterior

Temperature variation over 24 hours

8.21

perate climates, the addition of thermal capacity, inside the well-insulated enclosure normally provided, helps even out wintertime fluctuations in air temperature caused by solar heat gains through windows, heat losses through windows, fireplace fires, cooking and baking, and heating plant breakdowns. In summer, the capacity helps moderate high daytime temperatures. On the other hand, buildings in hot, damp climates where night temperatures remain high are best off with as little thermal capacity as possible. They should instead be designed to reflect away solar heat and to react as quickly as possible to cooling breezes and small downward shifts in air temperature. A typical indigenous house in such a climate is elevated above the ground on wooden poles to catch the wind, is roofed with a light covering of thatch, and has walls that are open screens of wood or reeds. In the colder climates, buildings that are

8.22

occupied only occasionally during the winter ought to be low in thermal capacity but high in resistance, so that they will warm quickly for occupancy and cool quickly after the occupants have departed, wasting no stored heat on an empty interior. Thus in designing a church or a cottage for weekend use at a ski resort, we might choose a well-insulated frame construction with a wood-paneled interior.

High thermal resistance is a desirable attribute of building enclosures under nearly all climatic conditions, especially in roofs, which are subject to both heavy solar heat gains and heavy cold-weather heat losses. High thermal capacity is also desirable where cyclical daily temperature variations need to be smoothed out. The combined effects on the indoor thermal environment of thermal capacity, thermal resistance, radiant gains and losses through windows, gains and losses from ventilation, and gains from heat released within the building are often extremely complicated, especially when several of these factors vary independently with time. But even in the absence of a detailed mathematical analysis, an informed designer ought to be able to make preliminary selections of materials and design decisions that are thermally correct in at least a qualitative sense.

Because of the high thermal capacity of the soil, building surfaces that are in contact with the earth below the deepest penetration of frost, such a basement walls or walls against which earth is banked, remain at a fairly constant temperature, usually in the middle fifties Fahrenheit (13°C–15°C) throughout the year (8.22). In hot weather, such surfaces remain cool, and in cold weather, they are not exposed to the extreme temperatures of the air. Because of this, the buried portions of buildings are generally much easier and cheaper to cool in summer and to heat in winter. In order to realize these important advantages, however, underground building surfaces must be insulated to thermal resistance values approaching those considered optimal in above-ground portions of the building enclosure, and where possible, frost penetration into the ground adjacent to the building should be minimized by burying horizontal sheets of foam plastic insulation just below the surface of the soil.

Water Vapor

The effects of various building materials on water vapor and of water vapor on materials are of extreme importance to the thermal behavior of buildings. Water vapor is a colorless, odorless gas. It is universally present in the air, but in widely varying quantities. The warmer the air is, the more water vapor it can contain, but air seldom contains as much vapor as it could at a given temperature. The most

58

convenient way of defining the content of water vapor in the air is by *relative humidity*, a percentage figure representing the quantity of vapor that the air actually contains divided by the maximum quantity of vapor it could contain at the given temperature. A relative humidity (RH) of 60 percent indicates that the air contains six-tenths as much water vapor as it could at the given temperature. This RH can easily be raised in an enclosed space, by boiling water to release steam, by washing or bathing, by bringing in lots of green plants—or simply by breathing. If it is raised to 100 percent, at it sometimes is in a gymnasium shower room or a swimming pool enclosure, the air can hold no more water vapor, and so some begins to condense as fog.

Another way to raise the relative humidity is simply to reduce the temperature of the room without allowing any of the air to escape. As the temperature falls, the mass of water vapor in the air remains constant, but the capacity of the air to contain it diminishes, which means that the relative humidity rises. (You will remember that this is what happens to outdoor air as it rises up a mountain, cooling by means of expansion.) If the temperature drops low enough, it will reach the *dew point*, at which the air contains 100 percent RH. If cooling continues below the dew point, the gaseous water vapor will begin to turn to liquid, as droplets of fog. Only enough vapor will condense at a given temperature to maintain 100 percent RH, with the remainder staying in the air as a gas. If the temperature is reduced still further, another increment will condense, just enough to bring the air mass to 100 percent RH at the new temperature. The dew point is not, of course, a single fixed temperature; every mass of air has its own dew point, the exact temperature of which is determined by the absolute proportion of water vapor that the air contains. The drier the air is, the lower its dew point will be, and the more moist the air is, the higher its dew point will be.

Air in buildings is frequently cooled below its dew point by coming into contact with cold surfaces. We see this phenomenon in humid summer weather, when condensed moisture appears as "sweat" on a cool drink, a cold-water pipe, a tank of cold water on the back of a toilet, or a cool basement wall. Dripping condensation from pipes and tanks often causes water staining, mildew, and decay in buildings. In cold weather, the most visible evidence of air cooled below its dew point is on cold window panes, which become fogged and sometimes frosted from the condensation of interior water vapor. Although fog and frost on windows are often picturesque, they later collect as liquid on window frames, encouraging rust or decay.

Much more serious is the nonvisible way in which water vapor condenses in building when an insulated assembly, such as a wall, is

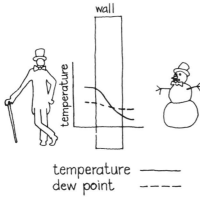

temperature ———
dew point - - - -

8.23

surface air →
plaster
gypsum
lath
insulation
wood
sheathing
wood
siding
surface air

condensation

degrees F: 80 70 60 50 40 30 20 10 0
degrees C: 27 21 16 10 4 -1 -7 -12 -18

temperature ———   dew point - - - - -

8.24

placed between the warm, relatively humid air on one side and the cool, relatively dry air on the other (8.23). Two such situations are a heated building in the winter, filled with water vapor from breathing, washing, and cooking; and a cooled, dehumidified building in a hot, humid climate.

Water vapor in air exerts a partial gas pressure known as *vapor pressure*. The higher the moisture content in the air is, the higher the vapor pressure will be. This pressure drives the water vapor to expand into areas of lower vapor pressure, seeking to create equilibrium. In a condition in which moist air is on one side of a wall and drier air is on the other, water vapor (an invisible gas, remember) migrates through the wall from the moist side to the dry side, driven by a differential in vapor pressure between the two sides. When there are air leaks in the wall, the air currents can also carry water vapor, often in much larger quantities than are carried by vapor pressure differences. Most common building materials offer only slight-to-moderate resistance to the passage of water vapor, and considerable quantities of vapor are pumped through the wall with only slight-to-moderate losses in vapor pressure from the moist side to the dry side. These losses are reflected in a progressive decrease in the dew point temperature as the vapor moves from the moist side to the dry side.

Simultaneously, however, the temperature of the wall drops gradually from the warmer surface to the cooler one (8.24). The warm-side wall surface, protected by an insulating air film, is slightly cooler than the air on that side. Through the various layers of construction, the temperature drops at different rates, depending on the various thermal resistances of the materials, until at the cool side, the surface, again guarded by an air film, is just slightly warmer than the cold air.

Problems arise within the wall whenever the temperature of the wall at a given location falls below the dew point at that location, causing the vapor to condense and wet the interior construction of the wall. Whenever moisture condenses from the air, a slight local decrease in the vapor pressure of the air is created, and vapor migrates toward the area of condensation from surrounding areas of higher vapor pressure. By this means the water vapor keeps moving relentlessly to the zone of condensation, and condensate keeps forming, unless either the difference in vapor pressure between the two sides or the difference in temperature decreases sufficiently to halt the condensation. The result is frequently a thoroughly wetted wall with insulation materials saturated and sagging under the weight of their absorbed water or frozen into ice within the wall. Under these conditions the insulating materials are almost totally ineffective, and the heating-fuel requirements of the building are correspondingly increased. Decay or corrosion of the wall framing is

60

a frequent side effect of vapor condensation, made more serious by the fact that the deterioration often lies concealed from sight until it is extensive enough to cause structural problems.

When migrating water vapor encounters an impervious layer, such as a well-applied coat of exterior paint, the vapor pressure can raise "blisters," literally lifting the paint off the wall. Peeling exterior paint on houses is most frequently seen outside kitchens and bathrooms, where interior vapor pressure are highest.

In any of these problem situations, the best remedy is to place a *vapor retarder*, also known, less accurately, as a *vapor barrier*, a continuous, vapor-tight sheet of plastic or metal foil, as near to the warm side of the construction as possible, but in any case between the main insulating layer and the warm side. Dripping pipes should be insulated well and then wrapped vapor tight with a plastic or metal jacket. The insulation keeps the jacket well above the dew-point temperature, and the jacket prevents the water vapor from entering and condensing within the insulation. Water closets are available with insulating liners of plastic foam inside the tank; the liner raises the outside surface temperature of the tank above the dew point. The porcelain tank acts as a vapor retarder. A window pane, quite vapor tight already, can usually have its temperature raised above the dew point by installing a second sheet of glass with an airspace between as insulation. In walls, roofs, and floors, a vapor retarder, carefully sealed at its seams and around openings, should be installed just inside the finish layer of construction on the warmer side (8.25). For an artificially cooled building in a tropical climate, the warm side is the outside. For cold-climate buildings, the vapor retarder should go just under the plaster or paneling inside the building. In older buildings with vapor problems, it is often not feasible to install a proper vapor retarder. The best that can be done is to plug air leaks in the walls, apply a good coat of paint to the warm-side surface, and provide frequent ventilation openings on the cool side to help clear moisture from the interior of the construction. Special vapor-retarding interior paints are available for this purpose.

Membrane roofs have always presented a particular problem with respect to water vapor in cold climates, for the membrane, vapor tight in itself, is quite naturally installed on top of the entire roof construction, on the cold side, to protect the construction from rain and snow (8.26). Thus if no additional vapor retarder is provided at the warm underside of the roof, the roof membrane will be subject to blistering from internal vapor pressure, and the insulating and structural materials of the roof deck will be exposed to condensation. If a separate vapor retarder is provided on the warm side, any residual moisture from rains or concrete work during construction will be trapped between the two layers and also be likely to cause prob-

vapor retarder

temperature ———   dew point ----

8.25

gravel
membrane
insulation
structure

Conventional Roof

8.26

gravel
insulation
gravel
membrane
structure

8.27   Inverted Roof

lems. Until recently there was no adequate cure for this problem, but with the introduction of water-resistant rigid foam insulating materials, *inverted roof* construction has become possible (8.27). The roof membrane is laid directly on the structural deck. The boards of insulation are then laid over the membrane, protected by a layer of gravel. The result is a roof in which the membrane is near the warm side, safe from high vapor-pressure differentials, maintained at a temperature well above the dew point, and, as a side benefit, protected from the extremes of outdoor temperature and sunlight that attack and eventually destroy membrane roofs.

Thermal Feel

We must discuss one more important thermal characteristic of building materials: how the various materials feel to us when we touch them. This is of no consequence in ceilings roofs, and outside walls, which are unlikely to be touched by people, but it is an important factor in selecting materials for floors, interior walls, tables, chairs, benches, and beds. Most of us instinctively make correct judgments that certain materials used in certain ways will feel either cold or warm. Seeking a bench in a park on a chilly day, does one select the granite bench or the wooden one? Does one prefer to step from a warm bath onto a ceramic tile floor or onto a deep-pile bathmat? Should the door handle in a 200°F (90°C) sauna be of steel or redwood? Should a child's playroom have a concrete floor or a wooden one? The answers are obvious, yet designers in similar situations often make mistakes.

Materials that are warm to the touch—wood, carpeting, upholstery, bedding, some plastics—are those that are low in thermal capacity and high in thermal resistance. By means of conduction, the body quickly warms a thin surface layer of the material to a temperature approaching the temperature of the skin, and so the material feels warm. Materials that feel cold against the body have the characteristics of high thermal capacity and low thermal resistance. When one touches a room-temperature surface of metal, stone, plaster, concrete, or brick, heat is drawn quickly from the body for an extended period of time by a relatively large bulk of cooler material, and a cold feeling results. An excellent example of this is the difference between a 72°F (22°C) room and a bath of 72°F water. The room feels pleasantly warm, but the bath feels unpleasantly cool. Air is a poor conductor of heat and has a low thermal capacity, whereas water is exactly the opposite. The body gives off heat to 72° air at a comfortable rate but loses heat much too quickly to 72° water. Similarly, a 72° plaster wall feels cool, and a 72° upholstered chair is quite cozy. A 72° carpeted floor feels comfortable to bare feet, but a concrete floor needs to be heated to a higher temperature from within by electric resistance wires or hot-water pipes or from without by exposure to sunlight, to achieve the same degree of comfort.

Further Reading

B. Givoni. *Man, Climate, and Architecture.* New York, Elsevier, 1969, pp. 96–155.

9
Controlling the Radiation of Heat

9.1

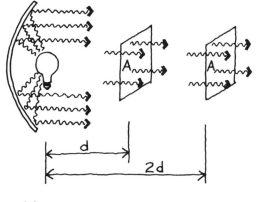

9.2

One essential role of a building in providing thermal comfort is controlling the flow of thermal radiation to and from the human body. Sometimes a building must protect the body from an excessive influx of radiant heat from the sun or from sun-warmed objects. At other times, protection is needed to prevent an excessive radiation of heat from the body to a cold outdoor environment. Exchanges of radiation also continually take place between the body and the surrounding interior surfaces of the building, requiring that the temperatures of these surfaces be regulated sufficiently to ensure comfort. In many situations the active manipulation of radiation is appropriate as the major mechanism in a scheme for achieving thermal comfort for the occupants of a building.

We have already noted that thermal radiation consists of electromagnetic energy in the infrared range of wavelengths and that it behaves very much like visible light. A point source, such as the incandescent filament of a lightbulb, radiates heat to a nearby object at a rate that is inversely proportional to the square of the distance between the filament and the object (9.1). (The sun operates according to this inverse-square law in heating the earth.) It is therefore possible to receive a very high influx of infrared by placing one's hand close to the bulb, whereas if the hand is withdrawn to a point several feet away, the heating effect is scarcely noticeable. If the same bulb is placed in front of a parabolic reflector, however, most of the diverging rays of the filament can be focused into a parallel beam of moderate radiant intensity (9.2). Within this beam, the rate of radiant flow is constant without respect to distance, except for the energy absorbed by dust particles in the air and by the air itself and for losses caused by inaccurate focusing of the beam. A surface of infinite extent also radiates to a point object at an intensity independent of distance. A bird flying five hundred feet (150 m) above the middle of the Sahara receives just as intense radiation from the hot sands as a traveler on foot does.

Usually we are surrounded by objects of differing surface temperatures. Suppose that you are sitting in a high-backed upholstered chair, facing a cozy fire to your right and a large window framing a view of a frozen lake to your left (9.3). The chair serves as a barrier to radiation, so no significant quantity of radiation is being given or received through the back surfaces of your body. The flames and glowing coals of the fire are high-temperature objects, larger than point sources but smaller than infinite surfaces, which radiate heat fairly rapidly to your body. The window is a cold object of moderate size, to which your body radiates heat. Above is a ceiling, fairly large in extent and somewhat cooler than your body, resulting in another net outflow of your body heat. The floor and walls exert similar cooling effects. In such a situation, it is not immediately apparent whether your body is, overall, gaining or losing radiant heat. In order to assess the net overall radiant flow, we must measure the temperature of each surface (the fire, window, ceiling, walls, and floor) and the solid spherical angle subtended by each surface with respect to your body. The *mean radiant temperature* (MRT) to which you are exposed is an average of the temperatures of each of the surrounding surfaces, weighted according to the spherical angle subtended by each and the thermal emissivity of each. In our example, perhaps 40 percent of your body is shielded by the chair, and your body "sees" the intensely hot fire as 3 percent of its spherical field of thermal "vision" (9.4). The large, cold window surface might constitute 15 percent, and the ceiling, walls, and floor the remainder. The fire is the only source of net radiant heat flow to your body in this example. Because it subtends an angle of only 3 percent of a sphere with respect to your body, it must be very hot if it is to overcome the cooling effect of the cooler surfaces occupying 57 percent of your body's field of thermal "vision."

MRT is not, in itself, a sufficient measure of the thermal comfort that may be expected in response to the radiant conditions in an environment. Everyone is familiar with the experience of being roasted on one side by a bonfire while being frozen on the other by radiation to a cold night sky. The MRT may be appropriate for comfort in this case, but the distribution of heated surfaces around the body is not (9.5). A certain balance is required among the temperatures of the surfaces to which the body is exposed, to prevent excessively rapid gains or losses from any one area of the body. A balance is also required among heat gains and losses through radiant flow and among heat gains and losses by convection, conduction,

9.3

9.4

9.5

9.6

9.7

and evaporation. One may be uncomfortable in cold weather in a building with uninsulated walls or very large windows, regardless of the temperature to which the air is heated and in spite of a warm fire in the fireplace, because of the excessive radiant flow from the body to the large, cold surfaces of the building. Similarly, the frigid air from an air conditioner will not be sufficient to produce comfort in hot weather if the body is exposed to direct sunlight coming through a window or skylight. If the indoor MRT is high in winter, air temperatures can be somewhat lower, thus cutting heat losses through the enclosure of the building and saving heating fuel. In summer, a building of high thermal capacity is likely to have cool interior surface temperatures, allowing comfort at higher air temperatures.

If we wish to raise the mean radiant temperature in a given interior location, we can pursue any or all of the following strategies:

1. We can allow the sun to penetrate to that location. The sun is a fickle heating device, but a pleasant and economical one. We use it almost instinctively, as does a dog or cat who dozes happily in a shaft of sunlight in the winter.
2. We can allow the building's heating system to warm the interior building surfaces to a higher temperature, by installing better thermal insulation in the walls and ceilings and multiple layers of glass and / or insulating curtains or shutters in the windows. Good thermal insulation of a building pays off in increased radiant comfort, as it pays off in every other respect.
3. We can install highly reflective surfaces in such a way that they reflect body heat back to the body. (This is how a reflective-foil emergency blanket works.) Reflective surfaces are rarely used in buildings to bounce back body heat, but they may be so used as fuel becomes more scarce, especially if they can be incorporated into furniture.
4. We can heat very large surfaces, such as floors or ceilings, to temperatures a few degrees above the skin temperature of the body.
5. We can heat small surfaces, such as electric filaments, gas-heated ceramic tiles, metal stoves, or fireplaces, to temperatures hundreds of degrees above the skin temperature of the body.

We will discuss these last two strategies in greater detail. Schemes for heating floors or ceilings are fairly commonplace, usually employing electric resistance wires, warm air circulating through multiple ducts, or warm water circulating through coils of pipe to warm surfaces of concrete or plaster. (Heating of walls is not usually attempted, because we tend to drive nails and screws into walls for hanging pictures and shelves.) Floor systems are attractive because they warm the feet by conduction and set up convection currents that heat the air in the room quite evenly. But they have several limitations: Tables and desks, for example, cast infrared shadows that hamper the ability of the warm floor to heat hands and arms (9.6). Unless a building is well insulated, such systems are incapable of furnishing all the heat required to maintain a comfortable air temperature in a cold climate without operating at surface temperatures that are uncomfortably warm to the feet. Their efficiency is greatly reduced by rugs and carpets. They are incapable, because of the considerable thermal capacity of the floor slab, of reacting quickly to small or sudden changes in the demand for heat inside a building. And if anything goes wrong with heating wires or pipes inside the floor, repair can be messy and expensive.

Ceiling systems have few of these problems. They can run at high temperatures because people seldom come in contact with ceilings. Tearing down a plaster ceiling for repairs is much easier than tearing up a concrete floor, and some ceiling heating systems are made up of snap-together metal components allowing for easy maintenance. Ceiling systems can usually react fairly quickly to changing demands for heat, because of their relatively low mass. Downward convection from a warm ceiling is poor, however, leading to lower overall efficiencies and a stratum of cool air at floor level, a defect made worse by the infrared shadows that tables and desks cast on people's legs and feet (9.7).

Small, high-temperature infrared heat sources with focusing reflectors are highly effective if installed so as not to cast shadows. They are especially useful where high air temperatures cannot be maintained, as in large industrial buildings or even outdoors, where they can produce heat instantaneously when it is needed and beam it precisely to where it is needed (9.8). Open fires and stoves are less efficient radiant heat sources because of their omnidirectional, inverse-square radiation and because of the relatively large amount of fuel that they convert to warm air rather than radiant energy. Because of its thermal similarity to solar radiation, infrared heat from either low- or high-temperature sources feels very pleasant on the bare skin. Swimming pools, shower rooms, and bathrooms are particularly appropriate locations for such systems.

Our means for lowering the mean radiant temperature of an interior location are somewhat more restricted than our means for raising it. We cannot, for example, cool our bodies by exposing them to a small surface at a very low temperature. Whereas we can easily heat an electric filament or gas flame to a temperature a thousand or more degrees above body temperature, there are only a

9.8

few hundred degrees with which to work between body temperature and absolute zero, and devices for producing very low temperatures are expensive to build and operate. Furthermore, a very cold surface quickly frosts over with moisture condensed from the air, thereby losing most of its effectiveness because of the insulating properties of the frost. Even a moderately cold surface becomes moist and unpleasant in warm summer weather, which is why we do not actively cool floors and ceilings except in rare cases when we can control the humidity at a level low enough to eliminate condensation. What we can do instead is to shade roofs, walls, and windows against the summer sun, surface them on the exterior with highly reflective coatings whenever practical, insulate them well, and provide enough thermal capacity in the interior surfaces of the building to ensure the maintenance of cool temperatures throughout the day. We can also, in some cases, open a building to the night sky, allowing our bodies and the warm surfaces of the building to radiate heat into space.

To implement many of these strategies for manipulating mean radiant temperatures upward or downward, we must operate through the medium of the building's enclosure and take into account its interactions with outside thermal forces. Among these, the most important are the inflow of solar and terrestrial radiation and the outflow of radiation at certain times when the sun is not out.

The roof of a building is a major barrier against excessive summertime solar radiation, especially in the tropical latitudes where the sun passes directly overhead. The roof surface itself is of extreme importance. A surface that is highly reflective of solar infrared heats very little in the sun, whereas an infrared absorptive roof surface can reach extremely high temperatures. The transmission of solar heat from the roof to the interior of the building, where it produces high ceiling temperatures, can be reduced by the use of thermal resistance, thermal capacity, and/or ventilation of spaces within the roof structure (9.9). Under inclined roofs, the convective draft of the heated air can provide the ventilating force to remove the heat, if the roof is so designed (9.10).

In tropical latitudes, north and south walls receive relatively little solar radiation, but east and west walls need protection of the same general sort as that for roofs described in the previous paragraph (9.11). In more northerly locations, the south wall may also require protection against the summer sun. For low buildings, deciduous shade trees and vines are a preferred method of sun control, especially because they shed their leaves and allow most sunlight to penetrate during the cold months. A roof overhang or horizontal shading devices at each floor can block the high summertime sun

9.9

9.10

from south-facing walls but admit the lower winter sun (9.12. 9.13).

In cold weather, of course, such solar radiation as can be absorbed by roofs and walls is a welcome addition to the heat content of the building. Some designers have gone so far as not to insulate the south-facing sides of buildings. This is a misguided effort, for cloudy weather and short hours of daylight bring relatively few hours of sunshine in winter, with the result that for about three-quarters of the winter hours in a typical northern climate, a south-facing surface is losing more heat than it gains. A more productive strategy is to insulate such surfaces well and to utilize large windows to trap solar heat, closing them off with insulating shutters or heavy curtains or shades (preferably reflective of long-wave infrared) when the sun is not out, to retard losses. The well-insulated wall surfaces do not gain appreciable heat when the sun is out, but their heat losses are reduced or eliminated by the solar heating of their exterior layers.

The same highly reflective exterior surfaces that are useful in reducing solar heat gain in the summer can also help reduce building heat losses in winter, through their limited ability to emit radiant heat. Polished metals are the only common building materials that are inefficient emitters of low-temperature infrared. White paint, excellent as a barrier against solar radiation, is of little use against the emittance of building heat in cold weather.

In warm weather, the sunlight entering through windows can produce an undesirable heating effect on the interior of the building, warming interior surfaces that in turn warm the air of the room and radiate heat to its occupants. Where possible, it is best to intercept the sunlight outside the glass, with trees, vines, roof overhangs,

9.11

9.12

summer

winter

9.13

9.14

louvers, or awnings (9.14). In this way the heat absorbed by the shading device is reradiated and convected largely to the outdoor environment rather than the interior. Outdoor shading devices are difficult to adjust from inside the building, however, and they are subjected to the destructive forces of Nature. Some designers, moreover, are unwilling to accept the appearance of exterior shading devices on their buildings. For these reasons, interior shading devices such as roller shades, blinds, and curtains are often used instead. The effect of these interior devices is largely to absorb solar radiation and convert it to convected heat in the interior air while preventing solar radiation from impinging directly on occupants and furnishings inside the building. Interior shading devices are therefore relatively ineffective in reducing the solar heating of air inside a building, but they are effective in protecting individuals from high radiant heat gain from the sun, and in reducing visual glare from direct sunlight.

Ordinary window glass passes more than 80 percent of solar infrared radiation but absorbs the majority of the longer-wave infrared from sun-warmed interior surfaces. In cold weather the glass loses most of this absorbed heat by convection to the outside air. The glass does serve, however, to prevent the passage of heated air from the sun-warmed interior back to the outdoors, and it is primarily for this reason that greenhouses, parked automobiles, and flat-plate solar collectors heat so dramatically in sunny weather.

Heat-absorbing and *heat-reflecting glasses* are frequently used in buildings to reduce summer air-conditioning loads. The heat-absorbing glasses, usually gray or brownish in color, are not as effective as one might first assume from published solar absorption figures. A glass that absorbs 60 percent of solar heat, for example, does not transmit only 40 percent to the interior. The 60 percent that is absorbed must ultimately go somewhere, with roughly half radiated and convected to the interior of the building and half to the outdoors, giving a net overall reduction in solar heat gain of only about 30 percent (9.15). Such a reduction may be perfectly sufficient, of course, for many applications. Of much higher efficiency are the heat-reflecting glasses, which bounce off most of the sun's heat without absorbing it. But a large wall of reflective glass can reflect enough sunlight to overheat adjacent buildings and outdoor areas quite seriously and to cause severe visual glare problems in neighboring streets and open spaces. A designer using reflective glass thus must exercise restraint and good judgment.

If sufficient care is given to window orientations, much of the expenditure of materials, equipment, and fuel energy to deal with problems of the passage of infrared radiation through windows can be avoided. In temperate, Northern Hemisphere locations, north-facing windows lose radiated heat in all seasons of the year, especially in the winter. East-facing windows gain heat very rapidly in summer because the sun shines into them at a very direct angle, but this gain occurs only in the mornings, when some influx of heat is often welcome after a cool night. South-facing windows receive solar heat for most of the day in summer, but at a low intensity, because the high sun always strikes the glass at a very acute angle. In winter, the sun arrives at a low angle through south-facing windows for the entire day, bringing a warmth that is usually beneficial to the occupants of the building. West windows receive heat rapidly on summer afternoons, when the building is already warm, and generally overheat the rooms in which they are located. This effect is especially unfortunate in west-facing bedrooms, which reach maximum overheating at bedtime in summer. It is further aggravated if the west walls of the house are poorly insulated, allowing the interior wall surfaces to heat up and emit radiant heat. Shade trees planted to the west, or deep awnings over the windows, can be of considerable help in correcting existing problems of western exposure. In tropical latitudes, of course, east and west windows cannot be contemplated without the use of exterior shading devices.

Radiational outflow from a building is at a maximum on clear, dry nights and is especially rapid from roof surfaces that "see" large portions of the night sky. Roofing materials frequently cool by means of nocturnal radiation to temperatures that are appreciably below surrounding air temperatures. In areas where nighttime air humidities are generally low and skies are clear in hot weather, water may be cooled by contact with the roof at night and then stored in an insulated tank for use in cooling the building during the day. Building surfaces may be cooled directly by the water if the humidity is low enough, or the water may be used to absorb heat from the coils of a mechanical air-conditioning system. A more direct use of night radiant cooling is the construction of roofs of high thermal capacity in hot, dry climates. The most direct application of all, however, is simply to sleep outdoors at night in warm weather, as is commonly done on flat rooftops in many areas of the world, thereby overcoming the heating effect of the air by radiating heat directly from the body to the infinite blackness of space (9.16).

Because of the opacity of glass and most plastics to long-wave thermal radiation, neither closed windows nor glass-covered or plastic-covered solar collectors are very efficient in radiating heat to the night sky. Open windows are more effective than closed ones, but a large proportion of what a window "sees" is usually warm trees, earth, and surrounding buildings, and not cold sky. The black plate

Clear Glass

Heat-Absorbing Glass

Heat-Reflecting Glass

9.15

9.16

of a solar collector "sees" mainly sky, but it must be left without a glass covering in order to work efficiently. Perhaps the most efficacious of all simple radiant cooling devices is water ponded on a flat roof. The water "sees" virtually nothing but sky, and the radiational cooling effect is enhanced by additional evaporative cooling from the surface of the pond.

Further Reading

J. F. van Straaten. *Thermal Performance of Buildings*. New York, Elsevier, 1967.

10
Controlling Air Temperature and Humidity

The roles of air temperature and humidity in human thermal comfort are easily grasped. In cool air the body loses heat too quickly for comfort, and in hot air, too slowly. We seek a happy medium. If the air is too humid, skin evaporation is too slow for comfort. If the air is too dry, the skin and respiratory surfaces are dried too rapidly, and static electricity becomes a nuisance. Thus we expect in our buildings that these two parameters, along with thermal radiation and air movement, will be regulated within fairly close tolerances.

The enclosure of a building, quite independently of any mechanical heating or cooling systems, does a great deal to modify the temperature and humidity of the interior air. The humidity is reduced in a well-designed building by the exclusion of both ground dampness and precipitation. Beyond that, the humidity is dependent on the admittance of exterior air at a humidity different from that of the existing interior air, the generation of atmospheric moisture by the building's occupants, and the raising and lowering of air temperature within the building enclosure. A rising air temperature automatically results in a lower relative humidity, and a falling temperature results in a higher humidity. At times, water vapor is taken from the air by a cold building surface that condenses it, such as a window pane, a water pipe, a basement wall, or a concrete floor slab.

Air temperatures in an unheated, uncooled building are affected by a number of factors. Heat enters the building through the metabolic heat of its occupants (a considerable quantity in auditoriums, classrooms, and crowded stores), the heat generated by their activities (cooking, bathing, running machinery, operating lighting devices; all these are potentially large sources), direct solar radiation,

10.1

10.2

terrestrial reradiation of solar heat, inward conduction of heat from outside air, and entry of warmer air from outside through windows, doors, and ventilating systems (10.1). Heat leaves the building through the exhaust or leakage of heated air to the outdoors, outward conduction of heat to outside air, radiation of heat to cooler outdoor surroundings, and the discharge of heated waste water into sewers (10.2).

The effects of these sources and flows of heat on the interior air temperature of the building are highly dependent on the thermal characteristics of the building enclosure. Consider the effects of just two parameters of an enclosure, thermal resistance and thermal capacity. We can construct from these two parameters four extreme combinations of thermal characteristics (10.3):

1. High resistance, high capacity
   (a heavy concrete building wrapped in insulation).
2. High resistance, low capacity
   (a well-insulated wooden building).
3. Low resistance, high capacity
   (an uninsulated concrete building).
4. Low resistance, low capacity
   (an uninsulated wooden building).

A building based on combination 1 heats up slowly in response to its internal sources of heat and reaches an equilibrium temperature that fluctuates rather slowly and belatedly as these sources change. It is relatively little affected by outdoor conditions. A building built according to combination 2 also is relatively little affected by outdoor conditions but heats up rapidly and fluctuates fairly quickly. The air temperature in a building whose thermal characteristics match combination 3 is heavily affected by outdoor conditions, but its responses are sluggish and somewhat attenuated. The uninsulated wooden building, corresponding to combination number 4, has but a small advantage with respect to air temperature over a wind-protected outdoor space. Its interior air temperature adjusts to a value rapidly approaching the outdoor temperature at any given time. These are oversimplified cases, of course. Designers control many more parameters of interior air temperature, although these two, thermal resistance and thermal capacity, are among the most potent.

It is worth our while to examine what happens over the span of a cold but sunny winter day to interior air temperatures in a hypothetical, unheated building of moderately well insulated wooden construction with a large south-facing window of double glass (10.4). At midnight, the outdoor temperature is lower than the indoor temperature and the interior surfaces, particularly the glass, are therefore cooler than the indoor air. As air approaches these surfaces, it is cooled and becomes more dense. It falls along all four walls, losing more heat as it goes, to collect as a cold stratum along the floor. Warmer air rises in the center of the room to replace it, but it, too, is cooled in turn by the ceiling and walls and sinks at the perimeter toward the floor. The air near the ceiling is warmer than the air near the floor; if the room were taller, this stratification would be even more pronounced. Toward dawn, the heat stored in the air of the room and in the interior materials of the building enclosure is largely exhausted, and the interior temperature slowly approaches the outdoor temperature.

As the sun rises in the sky, the outside air temperatures rise slightly, and the eastward- and southward-facing exterior surfaces of the building are slightly warmed by direct solar radiation. Most of this new warmth is convected from the surfaces into the still-cool outdoor air, but it does help, along with the increased outdoor air temperature, to slow down the rate at which interior heat is conducted outward through the walls and roof. This situation prevails

10.4

10.3

10.5

10.6

10.7

throughout the day, with continuous but moderate losses from the interior to the outdoors.

Meanwhile, sunlight is entering through the window, striking and warming parts of the interior walls and floor. These warm surfaces heat the adjacent air, which rises to be replaced by cooler air, which is then also heated. A new pattern of convection is set up, with an upward flow over the sun-warmed surfaces and a downward flow where heat is lost through the walls, especially on the cooler sides away from the sun, and down the warmer but still-cool glass. The interior air temperature rises, reaching a peak in the early afternoon, after which the setting sun, falling outdoor temperatures, and the night sky radiation combine to begin a net cooling of the interior that is most rapid in the early evening, and is already growing slower by midnight.

There are several ways in which the thermal performance of this building enclosure could be improved considerably. The enclosure could be better insulated, of course, to cut down its rate of heat loss, using either permanent insulating materials or rugs, tapestries, and curtains. Heat losses could be further reduced by minimizing the building's ratio of exposed surface area to enclosed volume. This could be accomplished by reproportioning the building until it more closely resembled a cube or, better yet, a sphere, but severe re-proportioning might force an offsetting reduction in the area of glass that could collect solar heat. It could also be accomplished by tightly sandwiching the building between other heated buildings on any or almost all of its surfaces (10.5). A heavy curtain could be drawn across the window, or the shutters closed, when the sun was not in the sky, to slow the outward conduction of heat through the glass. This would make it profitable to enlarge the window still further, to gain still more solar heat, but such an enlargement might result in gross overheating of the space at midday—unless the thermal capacity of the building interior were increased to absorb some of this daytime heat gain and hold it until evening. By these means, a considerably different daily cycle of temperatures can be achieved on those days when the sun shines. On cloudy days, some heat is gained through the window from the diffuse light penetrating the clouds, but the heating effect is weak. The building therefore remains rather cool throughout the twenty-four-hour cycle.

When a heating device is added to this simple building, a warm updraft, usually of considerable strength, is added to the convective circulation pattern. If the device (some coiled tubing filled with circulating hot water, let us say) is placed in the center of the room, where a weak updraft already exists, it will accelerate the existing pattern of circulation while gradually raising the temperature of the air, especially near the ceiling (10.6). Cool downdrafts from the window and wall surfaces will cross the floor before being warmed by

76

the coils. A better location for the heating device would be under the window, to counter the strong downdrafts and prevent them from reaching the floor (10.7). By this means, the rapid rise of the warm air is also slowed somewhat, and a gentler pattern of circulation is set up that avoids excessive accumulations of warm air in the unoccupied zone near the ceiling, or of cold air in the zone around the feet and ankles of the occupants.

The heat-producing capacity of the device has a great deal to do with the level of comfort that can be achieved in the room. If we know that the room will lose 5000 BTU (5000 kJ) per hour to the outdoors at a given indoor temperature and under a certain set of weather conditions, we also know that we must add 5000 BTU (5000 kJ) per hour to the interior air to replace this loss. If this is done with a heating device that can produce heat only at the rate of 10,000 BTU (10,000 kJ) per hour, we will want to operate the device only 50 percent of the time to achieve the necessary output, using some time pattern such as ten minutes on, ten minutes off, and so forth. During the ten minutes the device is on, the average room temperature will rise from slightly below optimum to slightly above optimum, and the cold drafts will be effectively stopped. During the ten minutes the device is off, the temperature will fall to slightly below optimum before the device goes on again. This in itself may be of very small consequence to the occupants' comfort; of greater seriousness is the loss of the circulating action of the heating device during the time it is off. The warmer air in the room will migrate toward the ceiling, and the more dense cool air will flow to the floor, chilling ankles, feet, and children who are playing there. It is preferable to have a continuously operating heating device whose output can be adjusted to 5000 BTU (5000 kJ) per hour, so that its stirring and mixing action can continuously prevent cold drafts and uneven temperature distributions.

10.8

10.9

Heating Fuels

A wide variety of heating devices and systems are used today. The most primitive and psychologically nourishing is the open fire of wood or coal, but its heating effect is mainly radiant, and most of its warmth, along with considerable quantities of inducted room air, is lost up the chimney (10.8). The enclosed stove of metal or ceramic is considerably more efficient with respect to both radiation and convection, and some modern thermostatically controlled stoves are of very high efficiency indeed (10.9). Heat losses up the chimney are relatively low in stoves, but as with open fires, considerable heat is lost through the room air that is drawn into the flame for combustion, unless an outside combustion-air supply is piped directly from outdoors to the base of the flame. If a room has neither a separate supply of combustion air nor enough leakage around windows and doors to supply combustion air through the room, an open fire or stove is apt to become smoky, and the oxygen in the room air may become seriously depleted.

Electric resistance heaters are in many ways a favorable alternative to combustion devices. They are unobtrusive, cheap to buy and install, easy to control, can produce (in various models) any desired mix of radiated and convected heat, and cause no loss of heated air to the outdoors. They convert electricity to heat with complete efficiency. Their overriding disadvantage is the cost of electricity as a fuel. In monetary terms, except where cheap hydroelectric power is available, electricity is several times more expensive than any other available fuel. In terms of resource utilization, when electricity is generated from fossil fuels or nuclear energy, for every unit of heat released through electrical resistance into a room, two or three units are discarded into waterways and the atmosphere because of losses in electrical generation and transmission, making electric heat, overall, roughly half as efficient in terms of fuel consumption as is the direct combustion of fuel in heating devices inside the building.

Coal was once the preferred fuel in central heating systems. It is relatively difficult to distribute from the mines to the buildings, however, and difficult to handle within the buildings. Its combustion produces a heavy, dusty ash that must be transported away for disposal. Coal is also relatively difficult to burn efficiently and cleanly. For these reasons, coal as a heating fuel has been largely supplanted in the United States by oil and gas.

Oil fuel is much easier and cleaner to handle than coal because it can be pumped from delivery trucks directly into a building's fuel tanks and from the tanks automatically to the burner. Gas is the cleanest and easiest fuel of all, for it is usually piped directly to the burner, under pressure from mains under the street. Originally most fuel gas was produced locally by distilling coal and was distributed through purely local networks of piping. Today natural gas is much more common than locally produced artificial gas and is often piped for thousands of miles directly from the wellhead to the consumer.

Solar energy is attractive as a source of heat because it is free of cost, nonpolluting, and, unlike any other fuels except wood and wind, renewable. Its disadvantages are several: It arrives at the building site at a very low intensity. It is available for only a fraction of the time during the heating season, because of short hours of daylight and frequent cloudiness. And for the majority of existing buildings and a large proportion of potential building sites, its availability is severely limited by the surrounding buildings, trees, and geographic features and by an unfavorable orientation of the building or building site with respect to the sun.

Summer sun

Winter sun

Heavy curtains for nighttime closure

Typical Passive Solar Heating System

Dark floor surface absorbs solar radiation

Insulation

Concrete floor slab stores excess heat

10.10

Because of the relatively low intensity of solar radiation, large areas of building surface must be devoted to its collection in a solar energy system. Focusing collectors, which must move to track the diurnal motions of the sun, are generally too cumbersome and expensive for use on buildings. Instead, we use either large areas of windows to catch the sunlight or *flat-plate collector* panels. Although neither windows nor flat-plate collectors can produce the high efficiencies and high output temperatures of focusing collectors, either is capable of gathering useful quantities of heat at temperatures adequate for the comfort heating of buildings.

If windows are used as the basis for a solar heating system in the Northern Hemisphere, they should be oriented within a few degrees of south, to catch a maximum of winter sunlight (10.10). To avoid wintertime overheating during sunny periods and to store heat for nights and sunless periods, thermal storage capacity must be provided within the enclosure of the building, using large volumes of masonry, concrete, or water, or smaller volumes of chemical salts. The system will work best if the storage materials are directly exposed to the sunlight entering the windows. Nighttime heat losses through the glass must be minimized by the use of insulated shutters, heavy curtains, or special window glazing that is highly reflective of long-wave infrared. A suitably designed roof overhang or exterior sunshade serves to block the high summer sun from entering and heating the building while admitting the full rays of the low winter sun. Window-based solar heating systems usually have no moving parts and are therefore classifed as *passive* systems.

Active solar heating systems generally pump either air or liquid

Glass

Metal tubing
Black metal sheet

Insulation

Flat-plate collectors

Fan and coil

pump

pump
Insulated
storage tank
for hot liquid

<u>Typical Active
Solar Heating
System</u>

10.11

return
riser (water)

convector

steam trap

valve

steam header

steam
riser

fire boiler

vacuum
pump

<u>Steam Heating System</u>
10.12

through flat-plate collectors to carry away the absorbed heat (10.11). The heat is then stored in liquid, rocks, or salts in an insulated container inside the building, from which it may be withdrawn as necessary by the building's heat distribution system. The collectors are usually installed at an angle that is calculated to lie approximately perpendicular to the midwinter noontime rays of the sun. The construction of the collector is usually quite simple: One or two cover plates of glass or plastic admit the sunlight and trap its heat; a dark-colored metal surface absorbs the heat; air or liquid traverses interior passages to carry away the heat; and an insulated back prevents the waste of heat.

It is virtually impossible to design a solar system, either active or passive, that can provide all the heat required by a building under all weather conditions. A series of cloudy days in midwinter can exhaust the useful heat from even the largest storage container. A backup heating system is required, therefore, using fossil fuel, wood, or electricity. The backup system must have sufficient capacity to heat the building during a prolonged sunless period. This means that it is as expensive to install as is a heating system in a similar building with no solar heating system. Thus it is inherently much more expensive to construct a building with an active solar heating system than without it.

Wind energy, though it is most abundant in the cold months of the year and is often available at night, is unlikely to be a feasible alternative to solar or fossil-fuel heating in most buildings. Aside from its sporadic nature, wind is simply too diffuse an energy source and too difficult to capture. Even a small, well-insulated dwelling requires a very large windmill, difficult to maintain and subject to storm damage, to generate enough energy for wintertime heat in a temperate climate. The cost of the mill would be of the same order of magnitude as the cost of the dwelling.

Heat Distribution

Heat can be distributed from a central source to the various spaces in a building through several media. Steam was once popular and remains in use in many buildings today. It is produced in a boiler, circulated under pressure through insulated pipes, and condensed in cast-iron "radiators" (in reality, their effect is largely convective), in which the latent heat of the steam's vaporization is released to the air of the room. The condensate is then pumped back to the boiler through a network of return pipes (10.12). Steam heating systems are reasonably efficient, but they are difficult to control as precisely as is desirable because of the rapidity with which the condensing steam gives off heat. Hot-water distribution, commonly called *hydronic* heating, is much easier to control (10.13). It involves the circulation of much greater quantities of water than a steam system provides, because only the sensible heat of the water is transmitted to the air, not the copious latent heat of vaporization. But by regulating both the temperature of the water and its rate of circulation, a very even and controlled release of heat to the air can be achieved, resulting in a high degree of comfort for the occupants. Hot-water systems also are silent when properly installed and adjusted.

Warm-air systems for the distribution of heat are not as quiet as hot-water systems are, especially if high air velocities are used, and unless constantly maintained, they can circulate dust as well as air through a building. Their ductwork is bulky and difficult to house, compared with piping. But warm-air systems have strong advantages: Control of comfort conditions can be at least as good as with hot-water systems, through the simultaneous control of air temperature and air volume, and especially through the greater ability of the moving stream of air to stir and redistribute the air in a room. This is particularly important in tall spaces where excessive stratification might otherwise be a problem. Air systems have the further attribute of being able to incorporate filtration, humidification, ventilation, and cooling functions, using the same ductwork. Any desired proportion of fresh outdoor air can be added at the furnace, and in hot weather, the burner can be shut off and cooling coils activated for the circulation of cold air.

The central warm-air system originated simply as a large stove in the middle of the basement, with grilles in the floors above to

Hot-Water (Hydronic) Heating System

10.13

Warm-Air Heating System

10.14

Compression Cycle

10.15

allow the heat from the stove to convect to upper levels of the building. The uneven temperatures and airflows of this system were improved by the addition of supply-and-return ductwork, by means of which convecting air could be directed to the places where it was most needed. By the further addition of a fan to drive the air, however, ducts are reduced to a more manageable size and bulk; filters can be installed at the furnace to clean the air as it circulates; and better mixing of room air is possible (10.14). With the fan as part of the system and the addition of cooling coils, both cool and hot air can be circulated.

Cooling Systems

Two basic systems are employed to produce cool air in buildings. One is the *compression cycle*, in which a gaseous working fluid, most commonly a chlorofluorocarbon, is compressed and liquified so that it releases heat (10.15). The released heat is absorbed by water and is pumped from the building, or it is absorbed by fanblown air and wasted to the outdoors. The heated water may be dumped into the sewers. More commonly, it is trickled over a latticework against a current of fan-blown air inside an outdoor *cooling tower* to release heat through evaporation and convection and then is recirculated to cool the fluid emerging from the compressor. The compressed, cooled working fluid is now released through an expansion valve into coils of tubing where, changing to a gas, it derives its latent heat of vaporization from the surrounding water or air. It then returns to the compressor to begin the cycle again. The water or air that is cooled by the expansion coils is distributed throughout the building, where it absorbs heat from occupants, machinery, lights, and building surfaces before being returned for another cycle of chilling.

As an alternative to the compression cycle, an *absorption cycle* may be used (10.16). A concentrated solution of a hygroscopic chemical, usually lithium bromide salt, absorbs water by evaporating it from a vessel. The water in the evaporator vessel cools rapidly as a result of the evaporation, and it may be tapped through a heat exchanger as a source of chilled water. The diluted salt solution must be continually drawn off from the absorber vessel and reconcentrated by boiling before it returns to renew the cycle. The steam that boils off condenses with cool water or air and then returns to the evaporator vessel.

Notice that both these systems have a "hot" side and a "cold" side. For cooling we tap the cold side of the system. But it is equally possible to harness the hot side as a source of heat in cold weather, and this is often done. In this application such a system is known as a *heat pump* (10.17). A relatively small amount of energy is used to

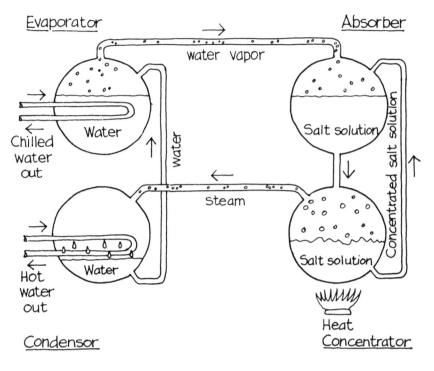

Evaporator — Absorber

water vapor →

Chilled water out

Water

water

← steam

Salt solution

Concentrated salt solution

Salt solution

Hot water out

Water

Condensor

Heat Concentrator

Absorption Cycle
10.16

Air to building

Hot side

Compressor or Absorber

Summer Cooling

fan

Cold Side

Air to building

Hot side

Compressor or Absorber

Winter Heating

Cold side

Principle of the Heat Pump
10.17

Solar collector

Air to building

Hot side

pump

Compressor
or
Absorber

10.18

Electric generator
driven by diesel engine

Air to building

Hot side

Compressor
or
Absorber

10.19

"pump" a relatively large amount of heat from a colder substance (usually water, the ground, or the outdoor air) to a warmer substance, the air inside the building. A heat pump is particular effective and economical for utilizing low-temperature heat sources, such as jacket water from an internal combustion engine or warm water from a flat-plate solar collector, to produce higher-temperature water or air for space heating (10.18, 10.19). It can often be found in a *total energy system*, which concentrates the waste heat from an electric generating system to heat the same buildings that are served by the generators.

When humid summer air is cooled, it usually reaches a temperature below its dew point. This raises two problems: Condensed moisture must be removed from the cooling coils, and the cooled air has an uncomfortably high relative humidity of 100 percent. Condensed water is removed as it drips from the coils, by a metal pan and drainage piping. The humidity of the air may be reduced by simply cooling it to a lower temperature than is desired and then reheating it to the desired temperature, thus lowering its relative humidity. The required heat may be furnished by a hot water or steam coil, but in most systems it comes simply from mixing the chilled air with the warmer air of the room.

The simplest central air-conditioning system is a *constant air volume* (CAV) system, in which a fan circulates air past heating and cooling coils through a system of ducts that deliver it to all the rooms in the building (10.20). The heating coils are activated only when the building requires heat; in a small system, they often are replaced by a firebox in which gas or oil is burned. The cooling coils in a residential-scale air-conditioning system are cool-side coils of refrigerant connected directly to the compressor. In a larger building, the cooling coils carry water that has been chilled by refrigerant coils from a nearby compression or absorption chiller. Electrically controlled flaps called *dampers* exhaust a percentage of air from the return ductwork and admit an equal percentage of fresh air from outdoors to ventilate the building.

In larger buildings, a CAV system, which is controlled by a single thermostat, is usually incapable of maintaining comfortable temperatures simultaneously in parts of the building that are exposed to different amounts of sunlight and that contain differing amounts of heat-producing machines such as computers. One way of overcoming this problem is to divide the building into zones, each of which has similar needs for heating and cooling, and to install a separate CAV system for each zone, delivering hot and chilled water to all the CAV fan rooms from a central boiler and chiller plant.

Another way is to install a *variable air volume* (VAV) system. A VAV system closely resembles a CAV system, but each zone of the

Cooling tower

Smoke →

← Cool water

Hot water →

Supply ducts

Return ducts

Fan

Exhaust air

Fresh air

Filter

Dampers

Coils

Pump

Chiller

Chilled water

Hot side

Cold side

Pump

Pump →

Hot water

Boiler

Schematic Diagram of a Constant Air Volume (CAV) System

10.20

Coil of heated
or chilled water

Condensate pan

Fan

Drainage
piping

Outside air

Room air

Fresh air
control damper

Unit Ventilator Schematic
10.21

Hot side
outdoors

Compressor

Cold side
indoors

Window air
conditioner
10.22

building has its own thermostat that operates a damper to control the amount of conditioned air that is admitted to the local ductwork in that zone. If a zone needs more cooling, its damper will open, and more cool air will be circulated. If it needs less, the damper will close partway, and less air will be circulated. The fan, coils, and main ductwork are identical to those for a CAV system.

In buildings whose temperatures must be closely controlled in a large number of zones or rooms, still other types of systems may be installed. A *dual duct* system circulates both heated and cooled air to a control box in each zone, where a thermostat regulates the relative proportions of the two that are mixed and delivered to the rooms. A *terminal reheat* system circulates chilled air and hot water to each zone. The air is delivered through a thermostatically controlled hot-water coil that heats the air to the desired temperature. Dual duct and terminal reheat systems are more expensive to install and operate than are CAV or VAV systems, so their use is usually restricted to such demanding environments as laboratories, electronics factories, and hospital operating rooms.

An alternative system allows individual temperature control in each room of a building, by circulating only chilled or heated water from the central unit to the rooms. In each room, a *unit ventilator* on an outside wall circulates the room air plus a percentage of fresh air from outdoors through a filter and a water coil (10.21). When chilled water is circulated through the coil, condensate forms on the coil and drips off. A metal condensate pan and drainage piping are provided to remove the water thus produced.

Small, electric-powered *unit air conditioners*, mounted in windows or in exterior walls, are widely used to cool both new and existing rooms and buildings (10.22). They are easy to select, easy to install, and easily to service or replace. They are unlikely, however, to be as efficient as a large central unit, particularly if the central unit is powered by a fuel other than electricity. And they are generally noisy and cause unpleasant drafts in the room because of their high velocities of air distribution.

In moderate climates, unit air conditioners are commonly configured so that room air may be circulated through either the cold-side or hot-side coils. This allows each unit to act as a *heat pump* that can cool the room in hot weather and heat it in cool weather. In very cold weather, the heating cycle cannot operate economically because not enough heat can be "pumped" from the cold outdoor air to the warm interior of the building; in this case, electric resistance coils must be activated to take over the heating function.

In dry, hot climates, a simple and inexpensive *evaporative cooler* is often sufficient to maintain comfortable conditions in a building. Air is circulated through a wet pad, from which it absorbs moisture

86

in the form of water vapor (10.23). The air is cooled by the latent heat of vaporization that it furnishes to the water. In humid climates, unfortunately, the moist outdoor air is capable of absorbing little additional water, and so evaporative coolers are not effective.

Evaporative cooling can also be used to cool exterior roof surfaces and thereby slow or prevent the flow of solar heat through to the rooms below. Sprays of water above the roof are most effective in reducing roof temperatures, but a shallow pond on a flat roof is nearly as effective.

Evaporative Cooler

10.23

Humidity Control

Some active control of the air's humidity is often needed in conjunction with its heating or cooling. In winter, heated air becomes extremely dry, to the point that wood components of buildings and furniture shrink and crack excessively, leaves of plants wither, static electricity causes unpleasant shocks, our skin becomes uncomfortably dry, and the mucous membranes of our nose, throat, and lungs are dehydrated and made more susceptible to infection. By introducing additional moisture into the air, these conditions can be alleviated, and air-temperature levels can be reduced slightly without affecting thermal comfort, because of the slower rate of evaporative heat loss from the skin. Thus the higher humidity in winter can lead to lower heating fuel expenditures. If a warm-air heating system is used, moisture can be added to the air as it passes through the furnace, by means of water sprays or absorbent pads or plates that are automatically and continuously supplied with water. With other heating systems, containers of water can be placed on convectors, or electric humidifying units can be installed in rooms to boil or atomize water into the air. Excessive indoor humidity can lead to serious condensation problems in the building, however, unless the building is provided with double-glazed windows, adequate insulation, and a tight vapor retarder; particular caution must therefore be exercised when humidifying older buildings.

In summer, the air humidity is often so high as to reduce skin evaporation to uncomfortably low levels and occasionally to cause various types of mildew and fungus growth in buildings. When air is chilled by a cooling device, its humidity is raised, often to the point that water condenses on the cooling coils and drips off. This is the principle on which an electric dehumidifier works. The same phenomenon occurs, as we have seen, in an air-conditioning system in which moisture must be continually cleared from the cooling coils and the air is initially chilled to a temperature somewhat below the desired distribution temperature and then is warmed slightly to decrease its relative humidity.

Air moisture can play an important role in the habitability of outdoor spaces. A splashing fountain or a lawn sprinkler can perceptibly chill dry outdoor air, by vaporizing water into the air. Golf courses and other inhabited outdoor areas in desert climates are sometimes cooled with nozzles that generate mists. On the other hand, in areas where mosquitos are a problem, a warm, dry, sunny lawn or courtyard furnishes an environment that does not appeal to mosquitos, whereas a sprinkled lawn or damp garden brings them in swarms.

Further Reading

Benjamin Stein and John Reynolds. *Mechanical and Electrical Equipment for Buildings* (8th ed.). New York, Wiley, 1992, pp. 281–473.

11
Controlling Air Movement

Clean, oxygen-rich air for breathing is the most pressing environmental requirement for human life. Continuously moving air is also a primary requirement for thermal comfort, to convect away excess body heat and to evaporate perspiration. Although the air in a rural outdoor environment in fact contains such natural pollutants as odors, bacteria, pollens, spores, molds, and dust, all but the most allergic persons can find optimum breathing conditions. Air movement in the outdoors varies over a broad range. On the occasional summer day when there is little or no wind, a sweltering, suffocating, claustrophobic sensation is felt. A light breeze has a pleasant, exhilarating, cooling effect. With increasing wind velocity, convective and evaporative heat losses from the skin can become excessive, particularly in the colder range of outdoor air temperatures. At very high wind velocities, chilling of the body is extreme; respiration may become difficult; solid objects are picked up and carried by the wind; and structural damage to trees and buildings is likely.

In cities, manufactured pollutants crowd the air: carbon monoxide, carbon dioxide, nitrogen oxides, hydrocarbons, sulfur dioxide, hydrogen sulfide, soot, ash, dust, and odors. Most of these substances are generated by the combustion of fuels in vehicles and heating plants, and others are given off by industrial processes. In the confined spaces of buildings, air loses some of its oxygen and gains carbon dioxide through repeated respiration by human lungs. Bacteria and viruses accumulate. Odors build up from sweating, smoking, toilet functions, cooking, and industrial processes. Gaseous pollutants such as radon and formaldehyde may be given off by building materials. The vapor content of the air is raised by breathing, sweating, bathing, cooking, washing, and drying and by unven-

11.1

tilated, gas-burning appliances. Dust and dirt particles float suspended in the air. The temperature of the indoor air may rise above comfortable levels, through solar heat gain, electric lighting, body heat, or the incidental heat given off by industrial processes, cooking, or washing. Air movement is restricted by the walls, floors, and ceilings of the building and may become uncomfortably sluggish. Thus buildings require ventilation systems to ensure an optimum velocity of air movement inside and to dilute and replace contaminated air with new air of acceptable temperature, dryness, and cleanliness.

At the same time, the air in buildings often contains odors that we find pleasant, such as the aroma of baking bread, the scent of a vase of flowers, or the evocative pungency of incense in a cathedral, and too-rapid ventilation can spoil the experience. But in buildings that are especially prone to dampness or natural overheating or in rooms that house such heat- and odor-generating functions as restaurant kitchens, gymnasium locker rooms, bars, chemistry laboratories, livestock barns, auditoriums, or foundries, rapid rates of air replacement are necessary. Lower rates are usually sufficient for most residential occupancies, lightly occupied offices, warehouses, and light manufacturing plants. Regardless of the volumetric rate of ventilation, however, indoor air speeds must not be so high as to blow belongings about the room (11.1).

Natural Ventilation

Any building ventilation system, from the simplest to the most complex, has four basic components:

1. A source of air of acceptable temperature, moisture content, and cleanliness.
2. A force to move the air through the inhabited space of the building.
3. A means of controlling the volume, velocity, and direction of the airflow.
4. A means of recycling or disposing of contaminated air.

The simplest, almost inadvertent ventilation system in buildings is one that utilizes the outdoor air as its source, the wind as its motive force, the cracks and seams on the windward side of the building as orifices that introduce the fresh air at a controlled velocity and volume, and the leeward cracks and seams as orifices that leak stale indoor air back to the outdoors (11.2). In tightly constructed buildings, this infiltration ventilation is slow, but in buildings with loose-fitting windows and doors, it can become excessive under windy

11.2

outdoor conditions, causing drafty rooms, and wasting energy in cold weather through the leakage of heated air to the outdoors. In general, infiltration should be minimized by the weatherstripping of doors and windows and the airtight sealing of construction seams. Even when such measures are employed, some air leakage is inevitable, but it functions as a useful, minimum-level air replacement system for a simple building.

Most schemes for the natural ventilation of buildings use windows to control the volume, velocity, and direction of airflow. For this reason, most types of windows are designed to be capable of being adjusted to any degree of openness. In most areas, an insect screen must be incorporated into windows, to keep out bugs, birds, and small animals while still admitting air and light. Where security is a potential problem, as in banks, jails, mental hospitals, and buildings in high-crime areas, steel bars or heavy metal screens may also be fitted to the openings. Various patterns of window operation have particular advantages: A *casement window* opens fully, and its swinging sash can function to divert passing breezes into the room (11.3). A *double-hung window* can open to only half its total area, but the half can be at the top, the bottom, or a part of each (11.4). An *awning window* or *hopper window* admits air while keeping out rain, a function that other window types can perform only if protected by a broad roof overhang or a separate awning (11.5).

Either or both of two motive forces may be employed for natural ventilation: One is wind and the other is convection. Air flows through a building because of the migration of air from a higher-pressure area to a lower-pressure one. In convective ventilation,

Casement
11.3

Double-hung
11.4

Awning
11.5

91

11.6

Wind-powered ventilation
11.8

Convective Ventilation
11.7

11.9

differences in pressure are created by the difference in density between warmer air and cooler air (11.6, 11.7). In wind-powered ventilation, the air flows from a higher-pressure area in one side of a building to a lower-pressure area on another. For wind-powered ventilation, it is most efficient to have windows on at least two sides of a room, preferably in opposite walls (11.8). Where only a single wall abuts the outdoors, a casement window can be helpful in creating a pressure differential that induces interior airflow (11.9). The building should be sited and configured in such a way as to best intercept the winds prevailing in the seasons when ventilation is most necessary. For convective ventilation, the rate of ventilation is proportional to the square root of both the vertical distance between

92

openings and the difference in temperature between incoming and outgoing air. Openings must be relatively large, as convective forces are not usually so strong as wind forces, and impediments to airflow, such as insect screens, should be eliminated wherever possible. It is often desirable to design for both wind and convection, placing some openings low on the windward side and some high on the leeward side of the building, to allow both sources to work together.

Openings other than windows are often used for natural ventilation. *Roof ventilators, roof monitors,* and opening *skylights* are especially useful (11.10). Some types of roof ventilators are designed to be spun by the wind, activating a centrifugal flow of air drawn from the room below. Others rely on convective flow, or the creation of a low-pressure area of dynamic wind flow that is filled by interior air. In any of these devices, however, control dampers are necessary to reduce or close off the opening as required. A door ought not to be relied on for essential building ventilation, unless it is provided with a dependable mechanism to hold it open at any desired angle. An ordinary door is incapable of controlling the amount of air flowing past it.

Fuel-burning devices such as stoves, furnaces, and fireplaces require oxygen for combustion. This oxygen is often drawn from the room in which the device is located. If the device has no flue or chimney, products of combustion will replace the oxygen consumed from the room air. A gas cookstove works in this way, consuming oxygen and releasing carbon dioxide and water vapor into the air of the kitchen. Devices that consume larger quantities of fuel—especially fuels other than natural gas, many of which produce toxic gases as combustion products—must be provided with chimneys. The *chimney,* a convection-driven, vertical ventilation tube powered by heat of the combustion products, exhausts these products to the outside air. Thus the room that furnishes the oxygen for the flame is left at a reduced air pressure with respect to the outdoors, a differential that causes outdoor air to be sucked through any available cracks or openings and into the room. The result is a continuous and often surprisingly large draft of outdoor air through the room. In warm weather this draft may be welcome, but in cold weather it negates a considerable portion of the heating effect of the fuel-consuming device on the room. If the air leaks in the room are plugged, the fire will become sluggish and smoky, and the chimney will refuse to work properly, leading to a depletion of oxygen and a buildup of smoke in the room itself, a situation that is both uncomfortable and dangerous. The solution is to provide a duct or grille that allows sufficient outdoor air for combustion to be drawn directly from the outdoors to the fire, without passing through the room.

11.10

11.11

Outside a building, a designer's concern with natural air movement is usually one of reducing the speed of the wind. In streets, on sidewalks, or in courtyards, yards, plazas, gardens, playgrounds, parks, or patios, wind must often be reduced if the area is to be habitable, even in warm weather (11.11). In winter in northern climates, drifting snow frequently presents problems where wind blows around and between buildings. Wintertime heat losses from a building are greatly increased by wind, partly through the greater infiltration of air and partly through the more efficient transfer of heat between the exterior skin of the building and the rapidly moving outdoor air. When for any of these reasons wind speeds around buildings must be reduced, the most effective protective device is a long, high barrier erected perpendicular to the direction of the wind and upwind from the building or outdoor area to be sheltered (11.12). A solid barrier such as a wall creates a small area of relative calm in its wake, but a somewhat more porous barrier is much better (11.13). *Shelter belts* of trees are especially effective, allowing through just enough low-velocity air to fill the low-pressure area behind and divert the full force of the wind for a considerable distance. *Snowfencing* creates an area of low-velocity air in which blowing snowflakes can settle in drifts rather than obstructing roads or buildings.

Tall buildings create particularly severe wind problems. Natural wind velocities increase rapidly with height above the ground, exposing the upper stories of a tall building to strong forces that may disrupt the cladding of the building and that require careful consideration when bracing the building against lateral structural loadings. At ground level, exceptionally strong wind currents are created by the rapid escape of air from the high-pressure windward side of the building to the low-pressure areas behind. If an open space is provided beneath a tall building at ground level, the flow of air through the opening will be so rapid as to make walking difficult when winds are moderate to strong, and doors in the opening either will not open or will open with destructive force when unlatched (11.14). Ground-level wind problems can be largely avoided either by providing very large openings completely through the building a story or two above the ground or by using projecting horizontal surfaces at this level to direct the strongest wind currents around the building before they can reach the ground (11.15). Neighboring buildings, of course, create local anomalies in wind flow that make extensive wind-tunnel testing advisable before constructing any tall building, in order to determine the full structural loads that must be resisted by the skin and skeleton of the building as well as any ground-level wind problems that could bedevil pedestrians and drivers.

94

11.12

11.13

11.14

11.15

Mechanical Ventilation

The use of fixed fans for room ventilation is common when reliable, positive airflow is required (11.16). In residential kitchens and baths, simple fans dump interior air directly or through a short run of ductwork to the outdoors (11.17). This air must be replaced by air leaking in from outdoors in various parts of the house. When the house is being heated or cooled, this means a considerable loss of energy, and such fans should therefore be used as little as possible.

Fans in more elaborate ventilation systems are connected to systems of ductwork for better distribution throughout the building (11.18). One system of ducts pulls away stale air while another distributes clean air. Such systems are usually coupled with heating and cooling systems in such a way that the clean air is distributed at a proper temperature for thermal comfort (see Chapter 10). Except in buildings where high hazards of chemical, bacterial, or radioactive contamination exist, such systems filter and recirculate most of the interior air they take in, continuously adding a predetermined fraction of outside air and exhausting a similar fraction to the outdoors. Energy can be recovered from the exhaust air by means of a *regenerative wheel*, a rotating device made of metal mesh that uses its large thermal capacity to transfer heat from one duct into another, or by means of an air-to-air heat exchanger with a very large surface area (11.19).

An alternative scheme for the ventilation of buildings employs one or more unit ventilating fans at the outside wall of each room to

11.16

11.17

11.18

96

circulate the room air and replace a fraction of it with outdoor air. A window or through-the-wall air conditioner works in this way, as do central heating or cooling systems that use coils of hot or chilled water to temper the air in room ventilation units (see Chapter 10).

Air is usually filtered in a building's ventilating devices by means of a thin, porous pad of fiber through which the air is blown, leaving dust particles trapped among the fibers. Much better dust filtration can be achieved by passing the air between electrically charged metal plates, resulting in the precipitation of most particles. Most odors can be absorbed by activated charcoal filtration. The air may also be "scrubbed" with jets of water to remove dust from the air in some large ventilation systems. Many bacteria can be killed by employing ultraviolet lamps to irradiate the air. Such lamps need not be in the ductwork but are often placed directly in the rooms they serve, particularly in institutional kitchens, sickrooms, and overcrowded dwellings, where they are effective deterrents to airborne disease. Because the susceptibility of the eyes and skin to damage by ultraviolet light, ultraviolet lamps must be mounted high in the room and shielded from sight.

Nature renews outdoor air in many ways. Sunlight kills bacteria in the air. Green plants remove carbon dioxide and replenish oxygen. Rainfall washes the air, and gravity draws out the heavier particulate contaminants. Wind mixes and transports the air, diluting and distributing contaminants. The microscopic hairs on the surfaces of plant leaves catch and hold airborne dust. But there is a limit to the efficacy of these processes, especially when climatic conditions are not ideal. It is important that we not ask too much of the atmosphere as a converter of air contaminants. Fuel burning must be minimized through energy conservation and through as much use as possible of nonpolluting sources such as hydroelectric and solar energies. Combustion devices must be made and maintained in such a way as to burn cleanly and thoroughly. Fuels that do not burn cleanly must be preprocessed to remove contaminants, or filters must be installed in the chimneys to trap the contaminants after combustion. Industrial air exhausts should be filtered for chemicals, and kitchen exhausts for grease, so that only easily biodegradable gases reach the atmosphere. Exhaust and inlet openings in any group of buildings need to be located so that they work with prevailing winds and do not mix outgoing air with incoming air. City streets must be kept broad and open enough so that they are continually flushed by the wind. It is of utmost importance, too, that we maintain and increase our inventory of lawns, gardens, forests, meadows, cultivated fields, and clean waterways, in which reside the green plants that are the fundamental producers of our atmo-

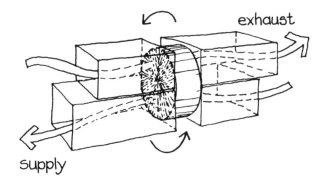

Regenerative Wheel
11.19

spheric oxygen. Air and sunlight are the only necessary substances that enter our buildings free of charge, but even they are not totally free. That is, they are obtained at the cost of human vigilance to ensure that they will always be available.

Further Reading

Victor Olgyay. *Design with Climate*. Princeton, N.J., Princeton University Press, 1973, pp.94–112.

Benjamin Stein and John Reynolds. *Mechanical and Electrical Equipment for Buildings* (8th ed.). New York, Wiley, 1992, pp. 334–341.

12
Keeping Water Out

Elaborate and expensive precautions are taken in buildings to prevent the entry of even a drop or two of water. It is tempting to believe that a good deal of money could be saved in construction by designing buildings to a slightly lower standard of watertightness. But as one experiences more and more of the consequences of water leakage in defective buildings, any such belief disappears. Water has unique thermal properties: It chills the skin, destroys the insulating value of clothing and building fabric, and raises the moisture content of the air in buildings to unhealthy levels. Water is the universal solvent, dissolving or at least staining many materials used in building interiors and encouraging the corrosion of others. Most important, water is a necessity for all forms of life, including bacteria, molds, mildew, other fungi, plants, and insects. A leaking building is not only uncomfortable and unsanitary, but it is also destined for an early death through corrosion, decay, and insect attack.

In order for water to penetrate the enclosure of a building, three conditions are necessary:

1. Water must be present at the surface of the enclosure.
2. There must be an opening in the enclosure through which the water can pass.
3. There must be a force to move the water through the opening.

These conditions are so simple as to be self-evident, yet they constitute the complete basis for the systematic exclusion of water from a building. Unless all three conditions are satisfied, water cannot enter. By eliminating any of the three conditions at a given location on the building enclosure, a watertight condition can be ensured.

Water is present in and around a building in many guises. Rain and snow impinge directly on the skin of a building and collect on the ground around it, bringing surface runoff and subsurface water into contact with its foundations. Water can be tracked into a building by people or vehicles. Inside a building, atmospheric moisture can condense on cold surfaces and drip onto the floor. Piping, plumbing fixtures, cooking, washing, bathing, and industrial processes may cause the leakage or spillage of water. Building materials that are put in place wet, such as concrete, brickwork, tile work, and plaster, release large amounts of water vapor as they dry, frequently causing the engorgement of wood fibers and copious condensate running from windows and cold-water pipes.

Buildings are amply provided with openings through which water can pass. Some, such as expansion joints, joints between pieces of cladding materials, and cracks around doors and window sashes, are intentional. Other openings are unintentional but inevitable: shrinkage cracks in concrete, defects in workmanship, defects in materials, holes for pipes and wires, and cracks and holes created by the deterioration of building materials over time.

Water can be driven to penetrate a building by any of a number of forces. Gravity is a force that constantly pulls water downward and causes hydrostatic pressures where water is allowed to accumulate to any depth. Air pressure differentials caused by wind action can drive water in any direction, including uphill. Capillary action can pull water in any direction through porous materials or narrow cracks. Even the kinetic energy of a falling raindrop is sufficient to exert a significant pressure when the drop hits a surface or to drive the drop or its spatter deep into an opening.

The problem of preventing water penetration is aggravated in many cases by the wintertime freezing of water into ice. The ice itself is usually incapable of penetrating the enclosure, but it may clog normal drainage paths and cause ponding of water on roof or ground. The expansion that occurs during the transformation of water into ice is a common factor in several kinds of building deterioration.

Let us examine a building, starting from the top and moving to the bottom, to see what sorts of strategies are employed to prevent water penetration. The most secure strategy is keeping water away from the surface of the enclosure, and we see this approach used in many parts of a building, but some components, such as roofs, cannot be shielded from water, and many others can be protected only in part. Eliminating the openings through which water can pass is the most difficult and least secure alternative open to building designers and is employed only as a last resort. Neutralizing the forces that can move water through openings is relatively easy, and we see it used in many different fashions in many different parts of a building.

Roofs

A roof that is dead level or that rises at a slope of less than one in four sheds water slowly and therefore offers maximum opportunity for water penetration. Such roofs are commonly covered with a continuous impervious *membrane*. This may consist of layers of mineral felt bedded in tar or asphalt, metal sheets soldered together, sheets of synthetic rubber cemented tightly together, a synthetic rubber compound applied in liquid form, or, in primitive buildings in relatively dry climates, a thick layer of clay soil. These continuous roof membranes, seemingly the simplest and most foolproof way to keep out water, constitute in reality the least reliable roofing mechanisms that one can employ. They are highly susceptible to puncture, especially from materials or tools dropped during construction. They are exposed to extreme thermal stress from summer sun, winter cold, daytime–nighttime temperature shifts, and air temperature differentials between indoors and outdoors. Sometimes they crack from the resulting thermal movement. They are incapable of passing water vapor, which sometimes leads to blistering and rupture of the membrane. A slight hole in the roof caused by any of these mechanisms is likely to pass prodigious quantities of water, because water drains slowly, if at all, from a flat roof, presenting maximum opportunities for gravity and capillary forces to do their work. Nevertheless, there is often no alternative to a membrane roof, and if care is taken during construction, thermal movement joints are provided at appropriate intervals, and steps are taken to avoid problems of vapor pressure, a membrane roof can give long and satisfactory service.

A roof that slopes at a substantial angle is much easier to waterproof than a flat or nearly flat one is. The steeper the slope is, the faster the water will run off, the less likely it is that the wind will drive water up the slope of the roof, and the easier it will be to keep out water. Almost any material will shed water if it slopes steeply enough, as can be proved by holding a washcloth or flat sponge under a water faucet at various inclinations. Whatever material is used on sloping roofs, it is usually installed in small units known as *shingles*.

Shingles of many materials—slate, limestone, wood, asphalt-impregnated felt, fired clay, sheet metal—are used in different parts of the world. Each shingle is a small unit, easily handled and applied by the roofer, easily replaced later if defective, and free to adjust to thermal or moisture stresses in the roof structure. Each shingle allows water to pass off three of its four sides under the forces

Felt

Length of shingle

Exposure to weather

Nails

Wood Shingle Roof

12.1

12.2

of gravity and wind, but the shingles are laid in such a way that the next lower shingles catch and drain the water quickly in turn, and so on to the lower edge of the roof (12.1). The weakness of a shingle roof is its susceptibility to water driven up the slope or across the slope by a very strong wind. This is countered by a twofold strategy of providing a sheet material beneath the shingles, usually a light sheet of asphalt-impregnated felt, to block the passage of air through the roof plane, and by sloping the roof steeply enough that a larger component of gravity is brought into play against the upward flow of water. Through experience, safe minimum roof slopes have been determined for shingles of various materials under various wind conditions, and leakage is unlikely even in a heavy storm if these criteria are satisfied. In windswept locations—seashores and mountaintops—it is often wise to use even steeper slopes or to increase the overlap of the shingles.

The adhesive force of water is utilized as the major water-resisting mechanism of a *thatch* roof (12.2). If a thick layer of straw, leaves, or reeds is held horizontally under falling water, it quickly becomes saturated and begins to leak. But if the same layer slopes at a sufficient angle, the drops of water adhere to the fibers and run downward along them to the eave, just as water can be transferred from a beaker to a test tube in the laboratory by pouring it along a glass rod. A thatch roof absorbs considerable water and must dry out between storms to minimize decay. Thatch is therefore never laid over a solid roof surface but instead is tied to spaced, horizontal poles or strips of wood over a well-ventilated attic. The sheer thickness of the layer of tightly packed stalks is sufficient to dissipate wind energy that might otherwise drive rain through, without the use of a sheet material beneath.

On one- and two-story buildings, broad roof overhangs can greatly protect walls and windows from rain. The walls of all but the top story or two of taller structures are attacked directly by rain, making roof overhangs superfluous unless they are supplemented by similar protective devices for the walls of the lower floors.

Edges of roofs are particularly problematic. Water may creep under the roofing material or penetrate the tops of parapet walls. The problem is worse on sloping roofs and some flat roofs because all the water gathered by the roof drains to the edges of the roof for disposal. In most cases, sloping roofs are simply lapped over the walls and projected beyond, so that the roof water drips free of the wall structure, a simple and effective expedient. The dripping runoff considerably erodes the soil below, however, often enabling water to penetrate into the basement, washing away soil from around and beneath foundations, and spattering earth onto the building walls. At a minimum, a trench filled with gravel should be provided be-

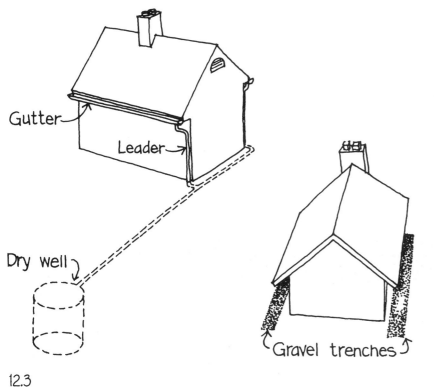

Splash block

Gutter

Leader

Dry well

Gravel trenches

12.3

neath the eave to prevent erosion and provide drainage (12.3). An alternative system is catching the runoff in *gutters*. The gutters are sloped slightly to drain into vertical pipes called *downspouts* or *leaders*, which in turn discharge onto splash blocks, into a municipal storm sewer network, or into dry wells (gravel-filled pits) to be absorbed by the ground. But such systems tend to clog with leaves, dirt, pine needles, and other debris and are a nuisance to clean, a problem that can be alleviated somewhat by installing coarse screening over the gutters.

Snow causes particular problems at the edges of sloping roofs in cold climates. One problem is caused by snow's tendency to slide off, tearing away gutters and endangering people and objects below. It is better to hold the snow on the roof with small metal or wood fences installed for that purpose (12.4). Not only is the danger reduced, but snow is a fairly good thermal insulator, and heating fuel can be saved by retaining it in place. The supporting roof structure must be designed to hold a considerable depth of snow without distress.

A second problem is caused by the melting of snow on sloping roofs, especially where the thermal insulation of the building is inadequate. Heat passing from the warm interior of the building gradually melts the snow from beneath. The snowmelt water runs

Snow logs on
Alpine barn roof
12.4

12.5

12.6

down the roof until it reaches the overhang and the gutter, which are much cooler than the roof over the interior spaces, in many cases colder than the freezing temperature of water. The water refreezes into ice, clogging the downspout and gutter and mounting the overhang, and a pool of water collects above this *ice dam* (12.5). Unfortunately, shingled roofs are not resistant to standing water. The water penetrates around and under the shingles and is often first noticed when it discolors the interior wall surfaces and drips from the window heads just under the roof. The remedies for ice dams are improved attic insulation and ventilation openings under the eaves and at the roof ridge, to carry away quickly any heat that gets through the insulation (12.6). If for some reason these measures are impossible, the last few rows of shingles at the lower edge of the roof may be replaced by an impervious membrane, or electric melting cables may be installed at the eaves.

Edges of flat or nearly flat roofs may or may not overhang the walls, or they may join a *parapet wall* (12.7, 12.8). In any case, it is important that the edge of the roof membrane be raised at least a few inches (100 mm or more), in order to keep water from spilling over it and down into or onto the structure beneath. The membrane is turned with a *cant strip* to avoid having to make a crack-prone 90° fold. The vertical edge is protected with overlapping sheet metal *flashings* or is tucked into a *reglet*. Rainwater may be carried away by interior roof drains evenly spaced across the expanse of the roof or by *scuppers* and downspouts around the exterior walls.

Walls

Walls, being vertical, are not subject to water pressures induced by gravity. Gravity, moreover, works to the advantage of walls, stripping water off them before it has much time to penetrate. But wind forces on walls are usually much greater than on roofs, driving the raindrops hard against wall surfaces, moving water sideways and sometimes upward across the surfaces, and pumping water through even the most minute openings where the air pressure is lower on the inside than on the outside. We often build walls of more porous materials than roofs, and we invariably riddle our walls with cracks or joints between pieces of material and with holes to accommodate windows and doors, so that water penetration problems are frequently encountered.

Masonry materials, especially the less dense varieties of brick and stone, all absorb and transmit water to some extent. Mortar joints that have deteriorated over the years afford particularly easy paths for water to pass. Water adheres to the walls of the pores of the materials, and if, as in most cases, the adhesive force between the water

Coping

Flashings

Parapet

Scupper

Alternative detail using reglet block instead of flashing

Reglet

12.7

Edge flashing

Cant strip

Roof membrane

Fascia

←Overhang→

No overhang

12.8

Outer wythe

Inner wythes

Cavity

Metal tie

Sheet metal flashing

Weep holes between bricks in bottom course

12.9

molecules and the wall material is greater than the cohesive force between the molecules themselves, the water will be drawn in by capillary action. A strong wind can increase the rapidity of absorption. A possible solution to this problem would be to apply an impervious coating, such as a heavy paint or a synthetic rubber, to the outside face of the masonry. This would repel rainwater quite effectively, but it would also stop the outward migration of water vapor, thus leading to rupture of the coating and subsequent peeling and leaking. The coating would also be susceptible to tearing because of thermal movement in the underlying wall.

A more reliable solution is to assume that some water will penetrate the outer layer of masonry, but to provide a continuous gap just behind the outer layer to break the capillary path to the interior of the building. This is the logic of the masonry *cavity wall*, with the outer *wythe* of stone or brick held a couple of inches (50 or 60 mm) from the inner wythes by means of stiff metal ties (12.9). The effectiveness of the cavity depends on keeping it free of mortar droppings during construction and providing *weep holes* at frequent intervals to drain water from the bottom of the cavity. Careful flashing work with sheet metal or plastic must be carried out around window and door frames to avoid capillary paths across the cavity. An incidental benefit of the cavity wall is that it transmits heat much more slowly than does a solid wall, and in most cases foam plastic thermal insulation can be installed in the cavity to enhance this effect.

If the penetration of water into brick, stone, or concrete is followed by subfreezing air temperatures, it can lead to *spalling*, the chipping off of flakes from the surface by the expansion of water as it freezes inside the material. Spalling was a major force in the destruction of concrete walls and pavements until it was discovered that concrete deliberately produced to contain microscopic air bubbles provides expansion space for the water as it freezes and so virtually eliminates spalling. Obviously, spalling can also be eliminated by keeping water off the wall with roof overhangs or other protective devices.

Although masonry walls, as we have seen, need to be treated as porous, we often clad walls with relatively nonporous materials such as painted wood siding, slabs of dense precast concrete, or sheets of metal or glass. With these materials, the problem is not one of stopping an overall slow seepage but of preventing leakage at the joints between pieces. With horizontal wood siding or shingles, horizontal overlapping, when it is backed up by a barrier to the passage of air (such as asphalt-impregnated felt or bonded plastic fibers), is sufficient to make the wall watertight except under unusually severe conditions of wind-driven water. When larger sheets or slabs are used as wall materials, however, the problem is more difficult. Such large panels cannot be fitted tightly together because of their relatively large amounts of thermal movement and because of the unavoidable inaccuracies in their manufacture and installation. Quarter-inch to three-quarter-inch (6 mm to 19 mm) gaps must be provided on all sides of each panel, and these gaps must somehow be made resistant to the passage of water. The easiest, but not the most reliable solution, is to fill each gap with an airtight, watertight *sealant*, a liquid synthetic rubber that is injected against a foam plastic backup strip and hardens into a continous elastic plug that adheres to both sides of the gap. Alternatively, a molded synthetic rubber *gasket* can be tucked into the gap (12.10). In theory the sealant or gasket expands and contracts readily with any movement of the panels, all the while maintaining its tight seal against wind and water. In practice, even the best sealant or gasket joints will deteriorate over a period of years, particularly if they are exposed to the weather, and will ultimately crack or lose their grip on the panels. Joints sealed with anything but the finest workmanship will fail much sooner; often they leak from the moment they are installed.

More reliable joints between wall panels are produced by reducing or eliminating the joint's dependence on a sealant material for its water resistance. This means that either water must be kept away from the joint or the forces that can move water through the joint must be neutralized. It is nearly impossible to keep water completely away from vertical joints in walls, although horizontal joints can be given a large measure of protection by overlapping components. Thus we must turn our attention largely to neutralizing the forces that might move the water.

The three primary forces that move water through wall joints are the momentum of impinging raindrops, capillary action, and differential air pressures. The momentum if raindrops can be effectively stopped by means of a simple *labyrinth* consisting of interleaving baffles arranged in such a way that a drop cannot be thrown through thr joint without striking a surface that blocks its passage (12.11). Notice that the baffles in a labyrinth do not touch one another. Rather, they are spaced far enough apart that a drop of water cannot bridge between them, thus preventing capillary entry as well as kinetic entry. It is important that labyrinth joints drain freely, to get rid of the water that they normally trap in the performance of their function. Corners and intersections of panels must be designed especially carefully, to drain the vertical joints without flooding the horizontal ones.

Air pressure differentials are created wherever wind strikes a building surface. The windward exterior face of a building is often at a higher air pressure than are the interior rooms just behind. Under

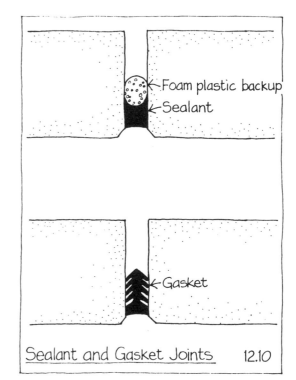

Foam plastic backup
Sealant

Gasket

Sealant and Gasket Joints   12.10

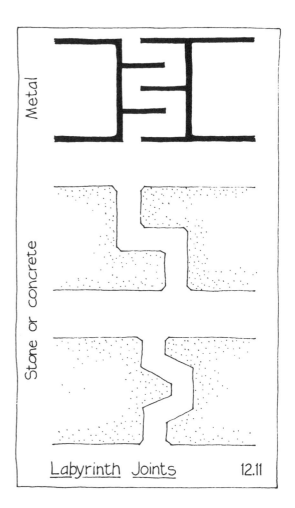

Metal

Stone or concrete

Labyrinth Joints   12.11

Sealant outside

defect

water

wind

Sealant inside

defect

water

wind

12.12

Wind

P_1 P_2

Rainscreen panels

Pressure equali-
zation chamber
(p.e.c.)

Air barrier

Principle of the Rainscreen

Wind pressure $P_1 = P_2$, pressure in p.e.c.

Therefore wind cannot force water
through joints in rainscreen.
12.13

this condition, water present in a joint in the wall, even a labyrinth joint, can be carried into the building by the force of moving air. In order to stop the movement of air through the joint, we could apply a sealant to the exterior edges of the joint, but any imperfection in the sealant would allow a stream of moving air to carry water into the building (12.12). If instead we apply the sealant to the interior edges of the joint, the sealant will be exposed to air but not to water, which is excluded by the labyrinth. Even if the sealant is defective, for example, if it does not adhere perfectly to one side of the joint, only small volumes of air are likely to pass, not enough to transport water through the labyrinth. Furthermore, the sealant joint in this case is protected from the deteriorating effects of sunlight and water and , if suitably detailed, is accessible from inside the building for inspection and maintenance. A reliably waterproof joint is thus achieved with a minimum of means.

The same effect can be achieved without the use of sealant, by providing a continous layer of air behind a facade of unsealed, labyrinth-jointed exterior panels. The backup wall behind the airspace must be more-or-less airtight, must be sealed to the panels around the edges of the facade, and must be strong enough structurally to resist the expected wind pressures on the building. In this case, very small amounts of air passing back and forth through the joints serve to maintain the air pressure in the airspace at exactly the same level as the wind pressure outside at any instant, effectively eliminating any air-induced movement of water through the joints. In this arrangement, the panels form a *rainscreen* to divert raindrops. The backup wall forms an *air barrier*. The space between is a *pressure equalization chamber* (*p.e.c.*) that prevents the formation of air pressure differentials between the inside and outside of the joints in the rainscreen (12.13). The backup wall can be made very simply— of concrete blocks surfaced with an airtight mastic, for example, or of light wood or steel framing with sheathing panels covered by an air barrier of asphalt-impregnated building paper cemented together at the seams.

In the example of rainscreen cladding shown here (12.14), a multistory building is faced with panels of aluminum sheets. No joint sealant is used. The open joints between the panels are configured so that they systematically neutralize all the forces that might move water through them. Gravity is defeated by sloping the horizontal surfaces of the joints toward the outdoors. Capillary action is eliminated by keeping the panels a sufficient distance apart at the joints. Labyrinth joints keep out water that is carried by momentum. Air pressure differentials are neutralized by the pressure equalization chamber behind the panels. The p.e.c. is divided into compartments by the horizontal aluminum components at each floor line

Rainscreen

p.e.c.

Air barrier

Structure and insulation

Vertical Joint

Building With Rainscreen Wall
(after Anderson and Gill)

12.14

and by the aluminum ribs that support the vertical edges of the panels. This compartmentation is desirable because wind pressures vary considerably across the face of a building, particularly near the corners and the top edge. If the p.e.c. were not compartmented, air could rush through it from an area of higher pressure to one of lower pressure, drawing water through the joints in the higher-pressure area.

Exterior Side

Wood

Aluminum

Window Sill Profiles

a   Drip
b   Capillary break
c   Weatherstripping (air barrier)
d   Wash

12.15

The rainscreen principle can be applied effectively even to very small exterior details such as door and window frames (12.15). The exterior sill should have a sloping top surface, or *wash*, to divert water away from the door or sash, and it should project over the wall below, with a *drip* to prevent clinging water from working its way back into the wall beneath the sill. A *capillary break* should be provided where the sash meets the sill, to keep water from being drawn through the crack by capillary action. If the sash is weatherstripped on the interior side of the capillary break, the capillary break will also serve as a pressure equalization chamber, making it very difficult for wind to drive water through the crack. The weatherstripping is the air barrier that maintains pressure in the p.e.c.

Floors and Basements

Splashing mud from the drip line of a roof poses only a problem of unsightliness in the case of concrete or masonry walls, but soil microorganisms can cause severe decay problems in wood siding. A wise precaution is never to allow wood closer than six inches (150 mm) to the ground. A clearance of eight inches to a foot (200 to 300 mm) is even better. Moisture from the soil may rise up through foundation walls of masonry or concrete by capillary action, to cause dampness and decay in ground floor rooms. A flashing through the wall just above the ground line cures this problem.

The strategy of keeping water out of a building by keeping it away from the building surfaces is nowhere better applied than to the portions of a building that reach into the ground. A building constantly exposed to standing or running water must rely on expensive and inherently unreliable methods of preventing the water from penetrating, whereas a building on a well-drained site needs only a minimum of precautions in order to stay dry. An adequate roof drainage system is required to carry runoff a safe distance from the building before discharging it. The ground should be graded in such a way that surface runoff is directed away from and around the building, rather than against it. Perforated piping should be laid in a gravel-filled trench outside the foundation, just below the level of the basement floor. Water that might otherwise build up around the foundation seeps through the gravel and the perforations into the pipes (12.16). If subsurface water conditions are severe, more perforated pipes should be installed at intervals beneath the basement floor slab. From the system of perforated pipes, water is conducted away by a nonperforated pipe. If the site is a large, sloping one, this pipe can slope gently downhill until it exits from the slope, to drain the away by means of gravity. On a small or flat site, the pipes drain by gravity into a *sump*, a small, cylindrical pit in the floor of the basement. An automatic electric pump in the sump discharges accumulated water back to the surface of the ground or to a storm sewer.

If the water table is low and drainage is good, a simple coating of asphalt on the exterior of the basement wall is sufficient to keep moisture out. Under more severe conditions, a continuous membrane must be installed around the entire basement and must be maintained free of defects while the excavation is being backfilled. A built-up membrane of asphalt and felt, similar to that used on a flat roof, or sheets of synthetic rubber cemented carefully at the seams may be employed, ar a continuous layer of clay may be placed against the walls. When using the felt or rubber membranes, particular attention must be paid to the junctions between floor and walls, and to joints in the walls, in order to avoid real or potential leaks.

If no basement is constructed, either a crawl space or a concrete *slab-on-grade* is built instead. The soil level in a crawl space should be high enough that it will not collect water that may seep in from outside, and a sheet plastic membrane should be installed to keep ground moisture from being released into the air in the crawl space. A system of generously sized foundation-ventilation openings keeps air moving through the crawl space to remove any moisture that may accumulate there (12.17). In the case of a concrete slab-on-grade, a thick drainage layer of crushed rock beneath the slab will prevent water from building up, and a continuous membrane between the crushed rock and the slab will block the upward migration of water vapor from the soil.

When moist soil freezes, it expands slightly. Although this expansion is not severe, it is sometimes enough to crack pavings, slabs, or foundations when the soil underneath freezes. Much more serious damage is possible when soil moisture migrates toward the surface because of a vapor pressure differential between the air in the pores of the soil and the free air above the surface of the ground. In general, once below the surface layers of soil, the deeper one digs, the higher the soil temperature will be because of the outward flow of heat from the earth's core. Thus moisture vapor moving upward during subfreezing weather encounters cooler and cooler soil until a level is reached at which the soil temperature is equal to the freezing point of water. Ice crystals form and grow vertically, pushing against the soil with enormous force as they grow. Upward soil movement of several inches (50 mm or more) is quite common under these circumstances, and pavements and foundations can be severely damaged. This phenomenon is known as *frost heaving*. In a foundation, it is usually prevented simply by placing the bottom of the foundation below the level to which the soil freezes in winter. With pave-

12.16

12.17

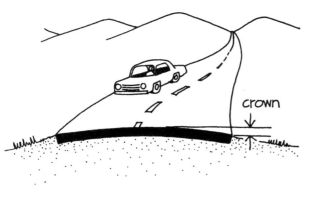

12.18

ments, a generous layer of uniform-sized stones beneath the slab generally suffices to carry away moisture and allow for any freezing expansion. In subarctic climates this is not always sufficient, but pavements laid on plastic foam thermal insulation, which maintains the underlying soil temperature above freezing, sometimes are satisfactory.

Flat outdoor areas of any kind—roadways, tennis courts, dead-level roofs, athletic fields, sidewalks, patios—can never be made perfectly plane. Because of the limitations inherent in tools, measuring devices, and materials, low spots and high spots always occur in the surface, even under the most carefully controlled conditions. This results in the accumulation of puddles during precipitation, leading to the premature deterioration of the material under the puddled areas. For this reason we seldom attempt to build a perfectly flat surface outdoors but instead introduce enough of a slope into the surface to drain the lower spots. A slope of about one in fifty, or one-fourth of an inch of drop per foot of horizontal run, is generally sufficient to leave a reasonably well made surface free of standing water. "Flat" roofs are usually pitched toward their roof drains at about this slope. If a dead-level roof is attempted, however, more durable and expensive roofing materials must be used to withstand the deleterious effects of the standing water that must be expected. Symmetrical surfaces such as roadways and athletic fields are not usually sloped in a single direction but are gently *crowned* in the center and fall off equally toward both sides (12.18).

Interior Sources of Water

Unwanted water can originate inside a building from leaking plumbing or heating systems, splashover from sinks and baths, and condensation on cold surfaces. Leaky pipes can be prevented only by careful installation. Plumbing installation that tend to develop leaks, such as interior roof drains and built-in shower drains, are provided with underlying metal or plastic sheet membranes to gather stray water and funnel it into the drain pipes. Where splashover is expected, impervious surfaces and, if necessary, floor drains should be installed to keep water out of the fabric of the building. Condensate dripping off water tanks and cold-water piping is a frequent cause of building damage in humid climates Piping and tanks should be insulated and provided with a vapor retarder, as described in Chapter 8.

Condensate running down the interior of window panes results in a decaying or rusting sash. Double glass has an interior surface temperature sufficiently high to avoid condensation under most circumstances. The metal frames of windows and doors sometimes

Thermal Break Window Frame Profile

12.19

accumulate condensate in cold weather. If such frames have hollow internal spaces, condensate may form inside and cause damage unless it is drained continually to the outdoors through drain holes or unless the hollows are completely filled with sealant or mortar to prevent moist air from occupying the space. Condensation on the exposed indoor surfaces of metal frames can usually be avoided by providing a *thermal break* in the frame section, to enable the indoor surface to be maintained at a temperature above the dew point (12.19).

Further Reading

J. M. Anderson and J. R. Gill. *Rainscreen Cladding.* London, Butterworths, 1988.

J. K. Latta. *Walls, Windows and Roofs for the Canadian Climate.* Ottawa, National Research Council Canada, NRCC 13487, 1973, pp. 66–87.

13
Seeing and Illumination

We gather most of our information about the world by means of our eyes. Eyes are organs capable of sensing a portion of the spectrum of electromagnetic radiation that we call light. We perceive the longest visible wavelengths as red in color, and progressively shorter wavelengths as orange, yellow, green, blue, and violet (13.1). "Colorless" light, which we perceive as white, is in reality a balanced mixture of all the wavelengths, whereas black is an absence of light.

Light and Seeing

Useful light originates from either the sun or artificial sources. Because eyes evolved for the purpose of seeing in sunlight, they perceive sunlight as being normal in color. Most artificial sources generate light that is perceptibly different in color from sunlight. *Incandescent* sources, such as an open fire, a candle, an oil lamp, or a glowing filament in a lightbulb, emit light that is deficient in the shorter wavelengths and is therefore more reddish than sunlight. *Fluorescent* light is created by a sealed glass tube filled with mercury vapor. An electrical discharge between the ends of the tube excites the mercury vapor into discharging energy to a coating of phosphor on the inner surface of the tube, causing the phosphor to glow. The color of light emitted by a fluorescent tube depends on the chemical composition of the phosphor. Most commonly, the light is somewhat deficient in the longer, "warmer" wavelengths and appears bluish, but fluorescent lamps also are available with phosphors that emit "warmer" light.

For the most part, the role of these primary sources of light is to radiate light to objects in the environment. Each object absorbs a

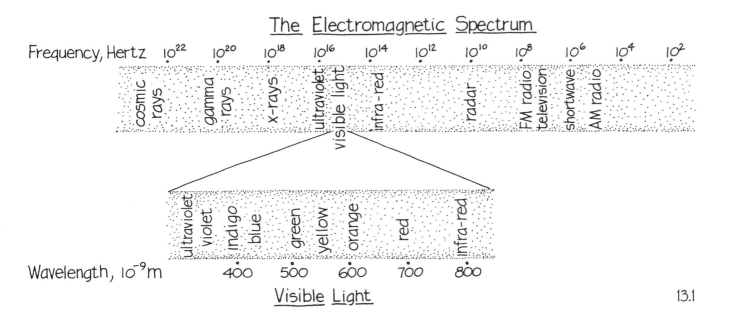

The Electromagnetic Spectrum

Frequency, Hertz 10^{22} 10^{20} 10^{18} 10^{16} 10^{14} 10^{12} 10^{10} 10^{8} 10^{6} 10^{4} 10^{2}

cosmic rays · gamma rays · x-rays · ultraviolet · visible light · infra-red · radar · FM radio · television · shortwave · AM radio

ultraviolet · violet · indigo · blue · green · yellow · orange · red · infra-red

Wavelength, 10^{-9} m 400 500 600 700 800

Visible Light

13.1

part of the light that falls on it and reflects the rest back into the environment. Our eyes gather a small portion of this reflected light, organize it by means of lenses, and convert it at our retinas to nerve impulses that our brains translate into visual images. The color of objects is caused by the selective manner in which they absorb light (13.2). An object that absorbs more of the shorter wavelengths than the longer ones reflects light richer in the longer wavelengths; that is, it has a warm color. Our eyes perceive objects as shaped areas of various colors.

At very low levels of object brightness, the eye can see only large, simple shapes and cannot distinguish colors from one another (13.3). At a slightly higher level, it can see somewhat smaller shapes, but it still cannot distinguish colors. With a bit more light, colors begin to be discernible but are still very muted and grayish. We can read large black print on white paper, but not easily. As the intensity of object brightness is further increased through progressively brighter illumination, we can read finer print, faster and with greater accuracy. Colors appear progressively brighter, and we can distinguish increasingly finer gradations of hue. As intensities become very high, however, visual efficiency increases only marginally. Our eyes begin to be more and more dazzled by intensely bright objects. We begin to feel pain and squint in an attempt to cut down on the amount of light entering our eyes. We can look at brilliant light for only short periods of time before our eyes close from visual fatigue. If we are forced to view objects of painful brightness, our retinas may be damaged.

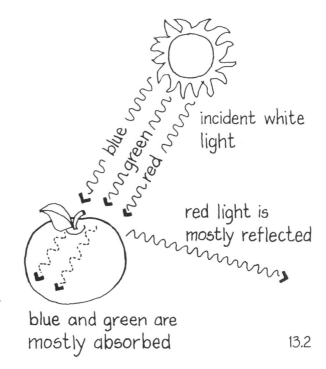

incident white light

red light is mostly reflected

blue and green are mostly absorbed

13.2

115

average illumination on subject of .01 footcandles (0.11 lux)

100 footcandles (1076 lux)

1 footcandle (10.8 lux)

10,000 footcandles (107,600 lux)

13.3

Our eyes adjust automatically to changes in light intensity. Eyelids, eyelashes, and eyebrows constitute an external system of adjustment. The pupils change size quite rapidly in response to varying lighting conditions, regulating the amount of light gathered by the eyes. The major adjustment mechanism is much slower, however, and occurs in the retina. Eyes adapt quickly to small changes in brightness by changing the pupils but need an adaptation time measured in minutes for large changes. In Nature, where changes of illumination are gradual, this causes few problems. When walking from bright sunlight into a dark theater or basement, however, we experience a condition of "night blindness" for a period of some minutes.

Eyes can adjust to only a single level of brightness. That is, if a very bright object and a dark object are placed side by side, the bright object will be seen as being very harshly lit and may be too bright to look at for very long, and the dark object will be difficult to discern and will at best be seen as a silhouette (13.4, 13.5). Yet when the same dark object is placed against a still darker background in the absence of the very bright object, it appears quite bright and is legible in considerable detail, because the eye has adjusted to its level of brightness. When we look at a person or an object next to a bright object such as the sun, a lightbulb, or a portion of the daytime sky, our eyes adjust to the glare of the bright object insofar as they are able, and we see the remainder of the visual field as a gray blur. We

116

13.4

13.5

see best when the object we wish to see, termed the *visual task* by lighting designers, is the brightest thing in our field of vision and everything else is less bright, although still within the same general range of brightness.

Daylighting

Until quite recently in history, people went to bed when the sun went down. Fires, candles, and oil lamps were very weak sources of illumination and too expensive for most people to afford. Under these conditions, the role of natural light in buildings came to be rather well understood in an intuitive way. Building orientations and configurations, the configuration of window openings, and interior finishes often were selected in such a way as to ensure sufficient levels of daylighting in interior spaces. Buildings were also developed with architectonic devices such as overhangs, pediments, string courses, quoins, niches, and various moldings to create pleasing, shifting patterns of shade and shadow on their facades as the sun moved across the sky, an art that lies largely forgotten at the present time (13.6).

We are forced to adopt an ambivalent attitude toward the sun in the daylighting of buildings. The sun is, of course, the source of daylight, and a shaft of sunlight entering a window, particularly in winter, exerts a very cheerful influence, brightening interior colors and bringing both psychological and physical warmth. Yet we cannot look directly at the sun itself, and the finer visual tasks such as reading and sewing are almost impossible to carry out in the intense

Rome, Santa Susanna 1597–1603
Carlo Maderno, Architect
13.6

117

13.7

13.8

glare of direct sunlight. Even the sky, brilliant with scattered light from the sun, is often bright enough to distract the eye. In warm weather, furthermore, we cannot tolerate the heat of direct sunlight in buildings. The bleaching effect of sunlight can be a problem at any time of year. And finally, we must face the fact that the sun is often obscured partially or entirely by clouds. For these reasons, we rely largely on diffused sunlight or on reflected, indirect sunlight to illuminate the interiors of buildings. The reflecting surface absorbs much of the heat and scatters the visible light at a much lower intensity than direct sunlight does. A large vocabulary of shading and reflecting devices has developed over the millennia. Trees, vines, overhangs, awnings, shutters of every description, louvers, blinds, shades, and curtains are among the more common (13.7–13.9). Overhead shading devices block or filter direct sunlight, allowing only reflected light from sky and ground to enter the windows. Louvers and blinds are themselves capable of converting direct sunlight to a softer, reflected light. Whitened exterior surfaces and window frames help gather more reflected light through windows. Windows and skylights that face north in the northern temperate latitudes receive little or no direct sunlight and so are useful in gathering indirect light without significant heat gain.

When the sun does not penetrate a room directly, the amount of natural light available at a given point in the room is determined by

13.9

13.10

several factors. The most important is the proportion of the total area of the sky that can be "seen" directly by that point through windows and skylights, and the relative brightness of those parts of the sky that are "seen." The sky at the horizon is only about one-third as bright as the sky directly overhead. For this reason, the nearer a window is to the ceiling, the more light it will gather, assuming, of course, that no trees or other buildings obstruct it. Skylights, which gather light from the bright overhead sky, are particularly effective sources of natural illumination (13.10). In some situations, significant quantities of light are also reflected into windows by the ground or nearby building surfaces and reach a particular indoor point either directly or after being reflected again by the interior surfaces of the room.

The shape and surface finishes of the room play an important role in daylighting. In general, tallness, shallowness, and high surface reflectances help make rooms brighter (13.11). Low rooms, deep rooms with windows at the narrow end, and rooms with dark-colored surfaces are more difficult to illuminate with daylight (13.12). The farther one moves away from the windows toward the back of the room, the smaller the segment of sky that will be "seen" directly, and the larger the number of successive reflections that will be needed to carry light to the visual task. Highly reflective surfaces absorb less light at each reflection, allowing more to reach the interior of the room. Higher ceilings reduce the number of reflections required to carry light a given distance toward the interior. Windows on a second side of the room, interior monitors, skylights, or clerestories are good at making daylighting more balanced throughout a room (13.13).

13.11

13.12

13.13

13.14

If windows or skylights are within the normal field of vision of people in a room, they are likely to be distractingly bright compared with other things the occupants want to see. A window next to a blackboard in a school, for example, is likely to be many times brighter than the blackboard and makes a glare that renders the blackboard useless. Windows should generally be placed away from interior focal points of rooms. If windows or skylights view large areas of sky, louvers or curtains may have to be installed to reduce their apparent brightness. Light-colored window frames, especially if they are splayed, help reduce uncomfortable contrasts between bright outdoor views and a darker interior (13.14).

Lighting by daylight is an appealing concept, for a number of reasons. It provides a pleasant psychological linkage between indoors and outdoors. It is "natural" in color. It varies in an interesting way with the weather and the time of day and year. It usually costs little more money to install windows and surfaces that are appropriate to a good daylighting scheme than to install them at random, and the cost of daylighting energy is forever free. Some maintenance costs are incurred in keeping glass and interior building surfaces clean, but little if any more than the normal costs of building maintenance. The chief drawback of daylighting is its inconstancy, especially its total unavailability between sundown and sunup. Artificial electric light is instantly and constantly available, is easily manipulated by a designer, and can be controlled by the occupants of the building. This suggests strongly that daylighting and artificial lighting make good partners, with artificial lighting being used mainly for nighttime illumination and as a daytime supplement when daylighting alone is insufficient.

Artificial Lighting

The total flow of light produced by three common artificial sources of light (collectively called *lamps*) is approximately as follows:

Wax candle	13 lumens
100-watt incandescent lamp	1500 lumens
87-watt high-efficiency fluorescent lamp	6600 lumens

The 100-watt lamp produces about one hundred times as much light as a candle does, at an hourly energy cost that is about a penny at current electrical rates. Its efficiency is 15 lumens per watt. The fluorescent lamp is about five times as efficient, which means not only that it can produce the same level of illumination at a much lower energy cost but also that it introduces into the room a great deal less waste heat per lumen output than does an incandescent lamp, a feature that is of considerable importance in a building that must be kept cool in hot weather.

But efficiency is not the only criterion in choosing a light source. Incandescent lamps cast a warm-colored light somewhat similar to firelight or candlelight. A person's skin looks warm and rosy under incandescent illumination; food looks appetizing; and a room takes on a pleasant glow, especially if its walls are made of warm-colored materials such as natural wood or reddish brick. The reflection of the glowing filament sparkles invitingly in glassware, china, silver, or the finish of an automobile. By contrast, people and food look a bit sickly under the bluish light of cool-white fluorescent illumination, and the low-brightness fluorescent source does not create such intense sparkles. Incandescent fixtures also are simple and inexpensive to install and maintain. Thus incandescent lighting still predominates in the home, restaurants, churches, and many retail establishments where warm color and sparkle enhance the appearance of the merchandise. But fluorescent lighting is clearly superior economically in large commercial, industrial, and institutional applications, and with the introduction of fluorescent lamps in a wider range of color spectra and shapes, the choice between the two systems is no longer so clear.

In the same range of efficiency as the best fluorescent tubes are *high-intensity-discharge* (HID) lamps, including metal halide, high-pressure sodium, low-pressure sodium, and mercury vapor lamps. Despite their high output of light, however, many of these sources give poor color renditions, limiting their use primarily to outdoor lighting. But some high-pressure sodium and metal halide lamps with acceptable color characteristics have been developed specifically as high-efficiency replacements for incandescent lamps in interior applications. Unlike incandescent sources, fluorescent and HID lamps require *ballasts*, electromagnetic or electronic components in each fixture that regulate voltage, current, and waveform to start and operate the lamps.

Tungsten halogen incandescent lamps are smaller and operate at a higher temperature than do standard incandescents. They also are more efficient (though not as much so as fluorescents and HIDs), and they provide good color rendition and sparkle.

Where to place artificial light sources in a building is a question of great importance. Sometimes a poorly placed fixture displays a person or an object "in a bad light," as when a light coming from directly above or below casts underworldly shadows across even the most pleasant of faces. Sometimes a badly located lamp can place an object in shadow, as is the case when a right-handed person tries to write in light coming from a lamp at the right-hand side of the desk.

13.15

13.16

Sometimes a source of light intrudes into the field of vision and causes distracting or damaging glare. Shielding or diffusing devices within the light source can do a great deal to counter this glare, but it usually is preferable to locate the source outside the normal fields of vision of persons using a given area.

An important objective of lighting design is to achieve an appropriate brightness (more properly called *luminance*) of the visual task. The appropriate luminance may be very dim if the visual task is a plate of food on a dining table, very bright if it is someone's appendix on an operating table, or between the two for most other visual tasks (13.15, 13.16). In order to achieve the desired luminance, an appropriate density of light flow to the surface must be provided. This light flow is achieved by selecting and arranging light sources of the required pattern and quantity of luminous output in conjunction with room surfaces of appropriate reflectances. As with daylighting, light-colored, highly reflective room surfaces help provide more illumination from the same amount of energy. Surface colors play an important role, too, in preventing glare: A white piece of paper on a black desktop causes visual fatigue, whereas a white paper on a light gray top may be viewed with comfort for long periods of time. The other essential consideration in preventing glare is to avoid sharp contrasts between the levels of light flow to the task and to the surrounding environment. It is often a good idea to have a small lamp casting a bright light on an exacting visual task, but unless the rest of the room is illuminated to an intermediate level of brightness, visual fatigue is likely to result.

The correlation between increasing quantities of illumination and increased visual efficiencies has led some designers to install systems of extreme brightness and prodigious electrical consumption in offices and factories. This correlation was established in laboratory tests. Field testing, however, has shown that once an acceptable minimum level of lighting has been established in a room, human satisfaction and performance are more likely to be based on qualitative factors than on the sheer quantity of illumination provided.

Anyone designing a lighting system for a building must begin by asking the purpose of the system: Is it to create a certain mood, to enhance the appearance of the building from inside or out, to flatter human faces, to call attention to an object or a person, to make reading or work easier, or some combination of these? How will people enter the building, move through it, and leave it, by night and by day, and how can the lighting design help their eyes and their emotions adjust to these transitions? When a person is housed for a time in an interior space of the building, how can light best contribute to the person's comfort and pleasure? Once these questions are answered, the design options can be analyzed: What role can daylighting play, and where will artificial light be preferable? What color spectra of artificial light will be most effective? How is the illumination of the building and its tasks to change between day and night? Should the light in a given area of the building be spread evenly throughout the area or largely concentrated on specific places? What types of windows and fixtures will create the appropriate patterns of illumination, and where should they be placed? These decisions are critical, for it is through illumination that the eye perceives a building from inside and outside, and it is through the luminous environment of buildings that the human eye is able to function and to enjoy the unique aesthetic experiences of sight.

Further Reading

M. David Egan. *Concepts in Architectural Lighting*. New York, McGraw-Hill, 1983.

14

Hearing and Being Heard

We enjoy enormously the sound of a favorite piece of music, the sound of a friend's voice, the songs of birds on a summer morning, and the spoken words of the players in a play. We derive great satisfaction from creating music with voice or instruments, speaking to a friend, or conveying an important message to an interested audience. Under such circumstances, we want to hear and to be heard. But we also, under other circumstances, want the equally important options *not* to hear and *not* to be heard, the options of peace and privacy. We wish not to have to listen to continual loud traffic noise or to music that appeals to a neighbor's taste but not to ours, especially if these noises interfere with our sleep, our ability to concentrate, or our ability to hear and to be heard in our immediate surroundings. We wish not to have our secrets known to any but their intended hearers, and we may even wish to make unpleasant sounds—like learning to play the violin or cutting lumber on a power saw—without embarrassing ourselves or disturbing others.

We are sometimes frustrated in our attempts to hear and be heard by the weakness of the sound we are making or attempting to hear or by its being obscured and confused by unwanted noise or by its own echoes. Often our acoustical privacy is violated by noisy surroundings or by surroundings in which we know that every whisper is audible to a neighbor. Any building, whether or not it was designed with hearing conditions in mind, has numerous important effects on the propagation of sound. If thoroughly understood, these effects can be exploited and manipulated by a designer to create indoor acoustical conditions that are appropriate to the various human functions housed by a building.

Sound

Sound is a sensation induced through the ear by means of waves of varying air pressure emanating from a vibrating source. Within the ear, the sound waves strike the eardrum (tympanic membrane), setting up vibrations that are transmitted mechanically by tiny levers of bone to an extraordinarily sensitive inner ear mechanism (cochlea), where they are converted to nerve impulses for interpretation by the brain (14.1). The ears of a young listener are capable of detecting frequencies of vibration ranging between about 20 and 20,000 cycles per second (Hz), but with advancing age, ears become less sensitive to the higher frequencies; thus 10,000 to 12,000 cycles per second are typical upper limits of hearing for middle-aged ears.

With respect to the pressure of the sound waves, the average ear can withstand the loudest sounds of Nature while also being able to detect sounds at pressures many millions of times smaller. In order to compress this broad range of sound pressure levels into manageable scale of measurement, a logarithmic scale of *decibels* (db) is used. The accompanying diagram gives a clearer idea of how the human ear is affected by sounds of different pressures (14.2).

The sounds of human speech are produced by vibrations of the vocal cords, which are then modified by the actions of the throat, nose, and mouth. The various sounds range in duration from about one-fiftieth to one-third second. Their fundamental frequencies lie mostly between 100 and 600 cycles per second, but many of the consonant sounds in particular are of much higher frequency and must be heard clearly for maximum intelligibility. Between the most timid whisper and the loudest shout, there is a wide range of sound pressure levels, but the average speaker covers a range of no more than about 30 db. As one would expect, louder speech is generally more intelligible than softer speech.

Musical sounds are usually of longer duration than the sounds of speech and cover much broader ranges of both frequency and sound pressure, especially in the case of instrumental music. Some large pipe organs are capable of producing pitches whose frequencies lie close to the extreme lower end of the hearing spectrum. Very high frequencies occur routinely in the high-pitched overtones of all musical instruments. The softest passages of symphonic music are barely audible, and the loudest rock music exceeds the threshold of pain.

Noise is unwanted sound. It may be speech or music, sounds of natural forces such as wind and rain, or mechanical sounds of engines, gears, fans, tires on pavement, squealing brakes, buzzing electrical equipment, or banging pipes. The potential sources of noise in contemporary society are so diverse in their sound charac-

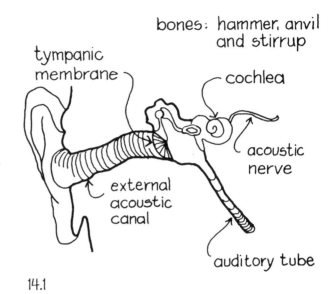

14.1

14.2

$\dfrac{watts}{cm^2}$	Decibels	
10^{-2}	140	Jet aircraft at close range
10^{-3}	130	Threshold of pain
10^{-4}	120	Elevated train close by
10^{-5}	110	Symphony orchestra, ff
10^{-6}	100	Power saw
10^{-7}	90	Downtown street
10^{-8}	80	Shouting at close range
10^{-9}	70	Inside automobile, 55 mph
10^{-10}	60	Face-to-face conversation
10^{-11}	50	Average office
10^{-12}	40	Quiet living room
10^{-13}	30	Quiet bedroom
10^{-14}	20	Rural ambient noise
10^{-15}	10	Rustling leaves
10^{-16}	0	Threshold of hearing

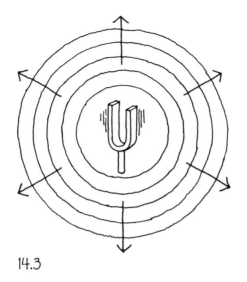

14.3

teristics that it is impossible to offer any generalizations about their properties; each noise problem must be analyzed individually to determine its source, its characteristic range of frequencies, and its sound pressure before steps can be taken to rectify it.

In theory, sound waves radiate spherically from a point source (14.3). If the source were suspended in an ideal volume of air, the sound pressure would diminish as the square of the distance from the source. In practice, sound waves originate from sources such as the human voice that radiate more strongly in some directions than in others, and the waves are invariably acted on in various ways by ground or building surfaces, resulting in the formation of sound fields that cannot be described by means of simple mathematical expressions (14.4, 14.5).

Wavelengths for audible frequencies vary from more than fifty feet (15m) for very low pitches to less than an inch (to a few millimeters) for the very high ones. When a sound wave strikes a surface that is large compared with its wavelength, a portion of the sound energy is reflected, much as light is reflected from a mirror, and a portion is absorbed. (When sound waves strike an object that is smaller than or similar in dimension to the wavelength of the sound, diffraction occurs, scattering the waves rather than reflecting them.) The harder and more rigid a surface is, the larger the proportion it will reflect. Soft, porous materials absorb a large proportion of the incident sound energy, dissipating it in immeasurably small flows of heat created by friction between the moving molecules of air and the walls of the pores. Optimum absorption is achieved for a given frequency by pores placed at a distance of one-quarter wavelength from a rigid, hard surface, where the velocity of the air molecules in both incoming and reflected sound waves is at a maximum. Greater thicknesses of porous materials are therefore required to absorb

14.4

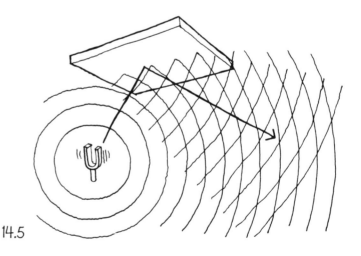

14.5

lower frequencies. A thin fabric wall covering absorbs only those frequencies near or above the top of the audible range. A padded carpet or thick drapery absorbs the majority of incident sound in the higher portion of the audible range. Deep, porous upholstery absorbs most sound from middle frequencies upward. The lowest musical frequencies cannot be absorbed efficiently by ordinary thicknesses of porous material. A window opened into free air absorbs all sound striking it and is the limiting case of total absorption. A smooth, dense, painted wall of concrete or plaster absorbs less than 5 percent of incident sound and thus comes fairly close to being a perfect reflector.

Sound is capable of inducing resonant responses in hollow constructions whose natural frequencies match that of the sound. The air within the hollow acts as a spring, oscillating at a characteristic frequency. Because a resonating body absorbs energy from the waves that excite it, resonating devices offer a means of absorbing sound energy. In practice, *resonators* are easiest to construct for the lower frequencies, which makes them a useful adjunct to porous absorbers for the treatment of rooms in which the full range of frequencies needs to be controlled. In modern concert halls, resonators are usually constructed as concealed hollows in walls.

Sound is able to travel in media other than air and can be transmitted through steel, wood, concrete, masonry, or almost any other rigid material of construction (14.6). The sound of feet is readily transmitted through a concrete floor slab into the air of the room below. A metal pipe can carry plumbing noise throughout a building. A beam can carry the vibrations of a typewriter to an adjacent room or the rumble of an electric motor through a building.

A building produces sounds of its own, such as the impact noises of rain and sleet on building surfaces; the whistle of infiltrating wind; the slamming of doors; the creaking of old wood floors underfoot; the mechanical noises of heating systems, plumbing systems, elevator machinery, garbage grinders, and various other machines; and the occasional creaks, cracking noises, and groans of a structure being pushed and pulled by wind, heat, and humidity. We can reduce mechanical noises by selecting quiet devices, installing them as far as possible from the inhabited areas of the building, mounting them with resilient fittings to eliminate structure-borne noise, and housing them in sound-isolating enclosures to cut down on the airborne transmission of their noise. We can usually reduce wind noises with better weatherstripping on windows and doors, which gives the added benefits of lower transmission of outdoor noises to the interior and lower heating and cooling costs. Rain and sleet sounds, if objectionable, can be reduced by using heavier roof and window construction. Structural noises, produced by the slippage of building

14.6

14.7

14.8

components past one another during sporadic releases of built-up stresses, are largely inevitable and difficult to remedy. Sometimes, if the source of the rubbing can be located precisely, a building component can be nailed or bolted tighter, or graphite particles can be blown into the moving joint as a lubricant.

A building conducts sound from room to room in various ways. Sound passes between rooms wherever an opening exists, even a very small one such as a keyhole, the slot at the bottom of a door, or the crack between a partition and the ceiling (14.7). Open or ill-fitting windows and doors transmit sound readily. Ductwork for heating, cooling, or ventilating systems often provides an air path from room to room that, unless lined with sound-absorbing material, readily transmits conversations and other sounds. (14.8). If we want privacy, we should weatherstrip cracks around windows and doors and close all other cracks and openings with airtight sealants. Partitions must go from the top of one floor slab to the underside of the next for maximum sound isolation and should be built in as massive and airtight a manner as possible. A thick brick partition wall makes a good sound barrier between rooms. A partition of concrete blocks is not as good as one of bricks, because the blocks are somewhat porous, allowing sound to penetrate. Plastering one or both surfaces of a block partition to make it airtight resolves this problem.

Most partitions are built of light, upright framing members to which plaster or gypsum board surfaces are attached on both sides. An ordinary partition of this type is not a very effective barrier to sound. To improve its acoustical performance, layers of gypsum board may be added to one or both sides to increase its mass. If one of these layers is attached with resilient metal clips instead of being screwed tightly to the framing, the structure-borne transmission of sound through the partition will be reduced substantially. Still better acoustic isolation can be achieved by inserting fibrous batts to deaden the transmission of sound across the airspaces inside the partition.

"Acoustic" tiles, which are excellent absorbers of incident sound within a room, help to lower noise levels by absorbing some of the sound energy generated in a room, but because of their extreme porosity and low density, they are of no value in reducing the passage of noise from room to room through a ceiling or wall. The same is true of curtains and carpets, except for the impact-cushioning action of carpets in preventing the generation of noise. An excellent way of reducing the transmission of impact noise through floors is to add a thick carpet and pad to the floor. For more quiet, a resilient layer can be added to the floor construction, such as a layer of compressible plastic matting between the floor slab and the finish flooring material or resilient metal clips to which the plaster ceiling is mounted to the underside of the slab.

Creating Good Hearing Conditions

The effects of a room on sound generated in the room depend mainly on the shape, size, and proportions of the room and the amounts of sound of various frequencies absorbed, reflected, and diffracted by its surfaces and contents. The shape is important because it determines the geometry of the paths along which sound is reflected. In small rooms with parallel walls, *standing waves* are sometimes evident: Certain frequencies of voice or music are exaggerated as they repeatedly bounce back and forth between opposite walls. A room with parallel walls can be improved acoustically if standing waves are eliminated by slightly tilting or skewing two of the walls or by adding acoustically absorptive material to one of the walls. Rooms with concave surfaces can focus sound reflections in such a way that sound is greatly reinforced at the foci of the surfaces and is less loud elsewhere. A "whispering gallery" is a room in which two participants can stand at two related foci of curved surfaces and hear each other's whispering with startling loudness and clarity (14.9). Convex surfaces scatter reflected sound widely, helping reinforce sound levels in all parts of a room. Rooms of broken, irregular shape scatter and reflect sound in nonregular patterns, usually distributing it more or less evenly throughout the room.

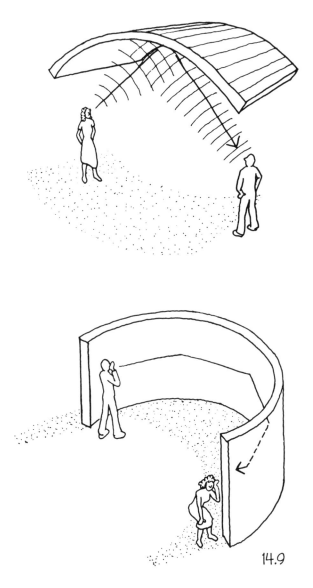

14.9

Sound *reinforcement*, the amplification of sound by its being heard from various reflections as well as directly from the source, is a very important function of the reflective properties of a room. The ceilings of meeting rooms, classrooms, and auditoriums sometimes are completely covered with sound-absorbing materials by well-intentioned but ill-informed people. This nullifies the potential for sound reinforcement offered by reflections off the ceiling, resulting in inadequate sound levels toward the rear of the room. The usual next step, the installation of an electronic sound reinforcement system, often would be unnecessary if much of the center of the ceiling had been left uncovered as a reflecting surface. On the other hand, in some very large halls a reflected sound can take so long a path that it arrives at the ears of a listener significantly later than the direct sound from the stage and so is heard as a distinct *echo*, which confuses the sound rather than reinforces it. Such long-path reflections must be eliminated through improved room geometry or the selective use of absorptive surfaces to allow reinforcement of sound along short paths while absorbing sound that would travel excessive distances.

The period of time during which a sound bounces around a room before dying to an inaudible level is known as the *reverberation time* of the room. In general, reverberation time increases with room volume, because of the longer paths that each sound wave must travel between its successive reflections, and it decreases when we add sound-absorbing materials, which intercept and swallow the waves. Reverberation is important in lecture halls, theaters, houses of worship, and concert halls because it sustains and blends the sounds, an effect that makes them much smoother and richer than the same sounds propagated in the open air. The achievement of an appropriate reverberation time for a given hall is of great importance. For speech, a short reverberation time is best, so short consonant sounds remain clear. But a certain amount of reverberation helps enrich a speaker's voice and gives a speaker some sense of how well his or her voice is carrying to the audience. For music, longer reverberation times extend and blend the sounds of the instruments or voices in a way that composers, musicians, and audiences have come to expect and demand. Music sounds dead and brittle in a hall with too short a reverberation time but will lose clarity and definition if the reverberation time is too long. A hall of optimum design imparts brilliance and color to the music, without destroying its clear articulation. Houses of worship in which preaching is of prime importance need relatively short reverberation times, whereas those with a more ceremonial service, particularly in which music is important, need longer ones. It is thought that the practice in the more ceremonial religions of chanting the liturgy grew out of the need to communicate clearly in early religious buildings with enormously long reverberation times. Liturgical music, from medieval times to the present, has often depended on large, echoing interiors for much of its emotional effect.

In order to design a hall with good hearing conditions, then, we must develop a room shape that distributes and reinforces sound evenly throughout the audience. The distribution of sound in the hall is predicted by plotting paths of sound rays and their reflections on plan and section drawings or by using computer graphics. These predictions may be sharpened and elaborated by electronically testing a scale model of the hall. In addition, we must achieve a reverberation time that is appropriate to the purposes of the hall. We also must reduce noise levels to a minimum to avoid interference with the sounds of the performance, using heavy, airtight construction in walls, roofs, and floors to keep out external noise and installing very quiet systems for ventilating, heating, and cooling the hall.

Sophisticated electronic devices have enhanced our ability to design the acoustics of performance halls. When creating a hall out of an existing building that was designed for other purposes, it is sometimes impossible to achieve the optimum configuration and proportions for good hearing conditions. When this happens, a system of speakers and amplifiers often can be designed to remedy the defects in the natural acoustics. Such a system might focus additional sound into "dead" areas of the hall, or it might add a fraction of a second to its reverberation time. It is possible to predict in advance what the acoustical characteristics of any hall will be and to model them with electronic equipment through which we can hear an accurate simulation of what music will sound like as heard from any designated location in that hall. This allows management, musicians, and designers to "try out" the hall before it is constructed, to propose changes in its acoustical environment, and to hear the results of these changes.

Controlling Noise

Where noise is a problem and we need quiet rooms for sleep or study, we begin by planning the building in such a way that the quieter rooms are as distant as possible from sources of noise—busy streets, public rooms, kitchens, workshops, or rooms housing operating machinery—and thus are shielded by the intervening rooms from much of the clamor. If the noise is coming across open land from a factory, airport, or highway, increasing distance helps reduce its intensity. Dense groves of trees can absorb some of the noise, although individual trees or single lines of trees are of little use. Ordinary wood fences are too lightweight to block noise. A heavy wall of concrete or masonry can be more effective, but it must be high and broad enough to block all direct sight lines between the quiet room and the noise, and it must be close to either the room or the source of noise. Otherwise, sound that is diffracted around the edges of the barrier negates most of its effect. The walls, floor, and ceiling of the room should be heavy and airtight, of course, including multiple glazing of windows if the noise problem is severe.

Sometimes when noise is particularly persistent and distracting, a building cannot be effectively protected from it, or there may not be enough money for treatment to reduce it. And sometimes a room is so quiet that even a whisper is distracting, and the sounds of one's respiration, heartbeat, and body movements are annoying. In any of these cases, introducing a low-level *masking noise* can help obscure the unwanted sounds. The best masking noises are the natural ones that almost everyone enjoys: waves lapping against a shore, wind blowing through trees, an open fire crackling, rain drumming on a roof, a brook or fountain splashing. None of these restful sounds has the distractive qualities inherent in music or speech. But if they are not available, a slightly noisy ventilating system may be as effective. In many commercial buildings, masking noise is introduced electronically through a system of speakers distributed throughout. Any masking noise must be strong in the frequencies that predominate in the sound to be masked.

Creating Privacy

If a building must create acoustical privacy—preventing conversations from being overheard—much the same strategies come into play: Construction must be airtight and heavy. Sound levels within the room can be lowered somewhat by the use of sound-absorbing materials. And masking noise can be invaluable. A bar room packed elbow to elbow with chattering people is in fact a very private environment for intimate conversation. There is simply so much noise generated in the frequency range of human speech that only the closest, most attentive listener can understand one's words. This is why, too, master spies and diplomats, whether fictional or real, turn up the radio or television before conducting discussions in a room that is suspected of being "bugged."

Hearing, being heard, not hearing, and not being heard are important factors that we must consider in the design of buildings. In most circumstances the ordinary materials with which we build are sufficient for the purpose. But they must be correctly and carefully used.

Further Reading

M. David Egan. *Architectural Acoustics*. New York, McGraw-Hill, 1988.

15
Providing Concentrated Energy

Until just over a century ago in America, only two forms of energy were commonly available in ordinary buildings for performing useful work: fire and human muscle power. Today, electricity is available in almost every room as a clean, reliable, exceptionally convenient form of energy for illuminating, heating, operating tools, and powering electronic communications.

Electricity is not usually generated on the building site. Small generating units, whether powered by internal-combustion engines, water, sun, or wind, are generally expensive to buy and maintain, are of limited capacity when compared with the capacity we have grown to expect of our electrical systems, and are less efficient and reliable than central generating plants. They may also be noisy and smelly; they may be unable to generate steady alternating current; and they may not be able to provide electricity when water levels or wind speeds are low, when clouds are present, or when the machinery breaks down. As fuel prices rise, as human expectations become more reasonable, and as technologies for the generation and storage of energy advance, this assessment may change, but for the moment, such private generating systems are usually either standby units to keep critical buildings electrified during power failures or generators installed in large building complexes as part of total energy systems.

Large central generating plants are powered by either water turbines fed from reservoirs or, more commonly, steam turbines (15.1). The steam is generated by coal, oil, gas, or nuclear fuel. The best steam plants are about 40 percent efficient, which is considerably higher than can be achieved in small on-site generators, but this still means that one and a half times as much heat is lost up the chim-

15.1

133

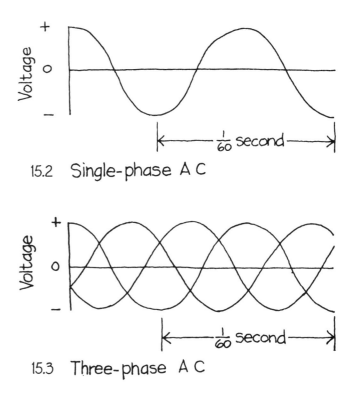

15.2   Single-phase A C

15.3   Three-phase A C

Generating Plant

Substation

15.4

neys of the power plant and into the waterways used to cool the condensors as is put into the transmission lines as potentially useful energy. Further losses are incurred in transmitting the electricity to the user, resulting in an overall efficiency for an electrical generation and distribution system of about one-third. Fortunately, electrical devices in buildings convert the electricity to useful energy at rather high efficiencies, but this does not change the fact that heat-producing appliances that can burn fuels in a building, generally at efficiencies of 70 to 90 percent, are inherently more conservative of fuel and cheaper to operate than are their electrical counterparts, except in some areas with abundant hydroelectric energy.

Virtually all electricity is generated as *alternating current* (AC). The frequency of alternation is 60 cycles per second (Hz) in the United States but is lower in some countries. The chief advantage of AC electricity over *direct current* (DC) is that its voltage is easily and efficiently changed by means of *transformers*. Generators put out current at many thousands of volts. This voltage is further increased by transformers at the generating plant before the electricity is passed to the main transmission lines, in order to reduce amperage to a minimum. When amperages are kept low, large amounts of energy can be transmitted through small wires with minimal transmission losses.

Most alternating current is utilized as *single-phase* electricity, meaning that the voltage varies as a single sine wave, reaching zero twice in each cycle (15.2). For most purposes this pattern is entirely acceptable, but electric motors, particularly the more powerful ones, are relatively large, bulky, and inefficient when designed to run on the intermittent pulses of single-phase electricity. For this reason, *three-phase* AC is distributed in industrial areas, using three sets of generator coils to superimpose three sine waves 120° out of phase, giving a steadier flow of energy and enabling the use of smaller, more efficient motors (15.3).

Before being passed to local transmission lines for distribution to buildings, electrical energy is reduced in voltage in local transformer substations (15.4). This results in somewhat higher transmission losses per mile in local lines than in main lines, but the local lines cannot be insulated or protected as heavily as main lines can and local lines are much shorter. This voltage is still too high for consumer uses, however, so each building or group of buildings is provided with a small transformer to reduce the voltage still further before it enters the building. In small buildings, service is usually provided at 230 or 240 volts. Large buildings or building complexes often buy electricity at local line voltage for more efficient internal distribution, reducing its voltage with inside transformers as needed before use.

Both copper and aluminum are excellent conductors and are commonly used as material for electric wires. Copper is a better conductor than aluminum, but aluminum wire is somewhat cheaper, even taking into account that slightly larger wire sizes must be used than in copper. A disadvantage of aluminum is that its oxide, unlike that of copper, is an electric insulator, and this has caused overheating problems and fires in some buildings where aluminum wire was improperly connected to fixtures, allowing corrosion to interfere with current flow.

The electrical system in a small building is quite simple in concept. Three wires pass overhead or underground from the transformer to the building (15.5). One is a *neutral wire*, which means that no electric potential exists between this wire and the ground. That is, one could stand on wet soil and touch the neutral wire with no danger of electric shock. To ensure that this is so, the neutral wire is connected firmly to one or more long copper-covered steel rods driven into the soil near the point at which the wire enters the building. The second and third wires are "hot," energized in such a way that they have a potential of 230 volts between them, but only 115 volts between either of them and the neutral wire. The hot wires pass through an electric meter before entering the building, driving a tiny motor at a speed proportional to the rate at which current passes through the wires. The motor advances pointers on dials by means

15.5

135

Neutral wire

Service entrance head

Drip loops prevent entry of water

Meter

black   red

Neutral wire

Main service panel

Ground bar

Circuit breakers

115V

115V

230V

Ground rod

15.6

of gears, recording in units of kilowatt-hours the quantity of energy consumed.

Inside the building, the three wires enter a main *service panel* (15.6). The neutral wire is connected to the steel box housing the panel and to a copper or aluminum bar to which all building circuits are grounded. Each of the hot wires, color-coded black and red on their insulating layers, is connected to a copper or aluminum bar fitted with connectors by means of which *circuit breakers* can be attached. These two bars, carefully insulated from the grounded panel box and from each other, are configured in such a way that a single circuit breaker connects a single wire to one or the other of the bars, and a double circuit breaker, occupying two adjacent connectors, connects one wire to one bar and one to the other. By this means, a single circuit breaker enables the connection of a single 115-volt circuit, consisting of a black-insulated hot wire connected to the breaker and a white-insulated neutral wire connected to the metal grounding bar. Depending on where the breaker is placed in the box, the hot wire for a 115-volt circuit may be connected to either the red or black wire coming from the meter; it is immaterial which. A double breaker connects to both the black and red wires and is used for 230-volt circuits. Breakers are easily installed as needed to connect the various circuits in a building. Each breaker serves as a convenient on–off switch for maintenance work on its circuit, in addition to performing the important safety function of automatically shutting off current to the circuit if for any reason more current starts flowing than the wire is capable of carrying without overheating and causing a fire. Such a condition can be caused by too many appliances being plugged in at once or by a *short circuit* created by either faulty wiring or a faulty appliance.

There usually are three wires serving any circuit, whether 115 volt or 230 volt, a black-insulated wire, a white-insulated wire, and an uninsulated wire connected to the grounding bar in the panel. These wires must be protected from damage as they pass through the structure of the building. In wood residential construction, this is usually done by means of a tough protective plastic sheath housing all three wires. In heavier types of construction, the wires are run in steel or plastic pipes called *conduits*. A conduit offers better protection to the wires than does a plastic sheath, and in a building wired through conduits, new wires can be installed by pulling them through existing conduits, something not possible with plastic-sheathed cable.

At each electrical device—a receptacle, a lighting fixture, or a switch—a metal or plastic box must be fastened securely to the structure of the building to support the device and protect its connections (15.7). The cable or conduit is clamped tightly to the box where the wires enter, thus protecting the wires from being pulled from their connections in case the cable or conduit is disturbed. The bare neutral wire is connected to the box and to the frame of the device to ensure that they will never be able to cause shocks if the device should become faulty. The black and white wires are stripped of insulation at their ends and then are connected to the device by means of screws or clips. After the circuit is tested for safe, satisfactory operation, the device is screwed snugly to the box, and a cover plate of metal or plastic is attached to keep fingers out, to keep the electrical connections free of dust and dirt, and to provide a neat appearance.

The sizes of wires used in an electrical system must be selected according to the maximum amount of current to be carried and the length of wire needed, in order to avoid excessive heating of the wire and excessive energy loss. Quite slender wires are used for light-duty circuits at 115 volts, whereas a residential service entrance often uses wires as thick as one's finger.

A safety device called a *ground fault interrupter* (GFI) is required in addition to a circuit breaker in circuits that serve areas where there is an increased hazard of accidental electric shock, such as bathrooms, kitchens, swimming pools, and outdoor receptacles. If a GFI senses any leakage of current from a circuit, no matter how small, it will disconnect the circuit completely and instantaneously.

Electrical systems in large buildings are, at their extremities, much like the small-scale system described earlier in this chapter. A large building has many service panels for its various floors and zones. When very large quantities of current must be carried at ordinary voltages, large rectangular copper or aluminum *bus bars* are used instead of wires, each enclosed in a protective metal duct. Local panels are then connected to these bars, with wires in conduits branching out from the panels to local fixtures. If the wiring is to be changed frequently, as it is in some office buildings and most computer facilities, wires may be run through special rectangular underfloor ducts supplied with numerous access boxes to which fixtures may be easily attached; or a raised floor surface may be provided, below which conduits may run at random. Designers of any building much larger than a residence must provide horizontal and vertical spaces for conduits, bus ducts, panels, and communicatons wiring, and access for electricians through doors, hatches, or removable panels.

Most electric codes specify a maximum horizontal distance allowed between receptacles in a room. This is to ensure that a lamp or appliance with a standard-length cord can be located anywhere around the perimeter of the room without requiring an extension cord. Also specified are a minimum number of receptacles per room and a maximum number of receptacles per circuit in order to avoid overloading the wires with excessive flows of current.

Neutral wire

Cable

Cover plate

Box

Wiring of Receptacle
15.7

Low voltage wiring, usually at 12 to 14 volts, is frequently used for doorbell circuits, thermostat circuits, and, through relays, for the switching of lighting circuits, especially where complex switching or remote-control panels are required. The advantage of low-voltage wiring is that it is incapable of giving severe shocks or causing fire, so it may be run through a building without using a cable or conduit. Since the required amperages also are low, the wire itself is small and inexpensive. The current is produced by means of a small transformer connected to a 115-volt circuit. Most telephone and communications wiring is also low voltage, with current provided by the communications company.

Forms of concentrated energy other than electricity are often piped into buildings. Fuel gas is the most common of these and is usually piped directly from wellhead to building. Some small users in remote locations use liquified gas delivered to pressurized tanks that are connected to the building's gas piping. For any type of gas, the piping system is extremely simple, involving a *regulator* to step down the high pressure of the main or tank, a meter to measure consumption, and pipes of appropriate size to serve the various appliances.

High-pressure steam is available from underground mains in certain urban areas and is used by many large buildings for heating and absorption cooling, thus avoiding the need to install individual boilers and chimneys. At one time steam also was used to power elevators, fans, and pumps in buildings, but it has now been replaced by electricity for nearly all these functions. The steam is usually exhaust steam from the local electric generating plant, reheated somewhat and distributed through mains and meters to users, thus increasing nicely the overall efficiency of fuel usage in the generating plant.

Compressed air is often provided through pipelines in workshops and factories, where it is used to power portable tools, clamping devices, and paint sprayers. Air-powered tools tend to be cheaper, lighter, and more rugged than their electric equivalents. The air is usually furnished by an electric-powered compressor on the premises. Vacuum piping is common in scientific laboratory buildings. In some urban localities, vacuum lines, compressed air lines, or high-pressure water mains for use in driving tools were once run beneath the streets as utility systems. Today, electricity, gas, and steam are the only energy utilities remaining in common use.

Further Reading

Benjamin Stein and John Reynolds. *Mechanical and Electrical Equipment for Buildings* (8th ed.). New York, Wiley, 1992, pp. 761–907.

16
Fitting Buildings to People

People are the true measure of all things in building. Buildings are built by people, for inhabitation by people. At both ends of the architectural process, the building and the inhabiting, the dimensions and movements of the human body are the major determinants of the shapes and sizes of things. This presents an immediate problem: People vary a good deal in size, shape, and mobility. On the average, men are larger than women, and children come in all sizes (16.1). The average human today is considerably larger than the average human of a century ago, and we grow measurably with each generation (16.2). Of course, there is no such thing as an "average" human figure. Quite "average"-appearing men vary in height over a range of at least a foot (300 mm), and many exceptionally tall or short ones fall outside this range. The same is true for women. Body builds in both sexes vary in bone structure, musculature, and fat distribution. Young children are much smaller and less physically coordinated than adults but are more active. Adolescent children are nearly as large as adults, but more active and perhaps better coordinated. Adults become progressively less agile through middle age until in later years many are quite restricted in their motions. Persons of any age, if on crutches, confined to a wheelchair, or otherwise disabled, are likely to have physical dimensions very different from those of fully mobile persons. Given this diverse clientele, then, by which of them should we measure our buildings?

The easy answer is, we should custom-design each building for the exact people who will use it. But this is not always possible, because we must often build for unknown tenants. Even when we know intimately the occupants of a building, it is likely that someday they will move elsewhere and a new group of persons of unknown

16.1

13th century   Today

16.2

16.3

16.4

sizes and shapes will move in. Children present a special problem because they grow up. In a school we can resolve this problem to some extent by scaling different classrooms and toilet rooms to different age groups (16.3) while compromising somehow for the comfort of the adult teachers, but in a residence a child often grows up in the same room over a period of many years. A room scaled specifically as a nursery will grow obsolete as the child ages.

There is no fully satisfactory answer to this dilemma. The best we can do in most cases is to size building components to accommodate the preponderance of the adult population while leaving a few people of exceptional size or shape, along with the younger children, in the position of continually having to make accommodations to the building. A good deal of their strain can be eased through the provision of appropriately scaled furnishings, as seen especially vividly in the case of children. In residences, libraries, lounges, and other buildings in which the inhabitants are free to locate themselves in any of a number of places, spaces of varying scales and degrees of enclosure may furnish important opportunities for persons of different physical and psychic dimensions to find appropriate surroundings.

Building Dimensions

The dimensions of a building grow ultimately from the dimensions of the human figure. At the most basic level, a woman sitting in a soft chair establishes certain important dimensions (16.4). The inte-

140

rior of the chair must be large enough in all dimensions to support her body comfortably in any of a number of normal sitting postures: feet on the floor, legs crossed, legs tucked under her body, sitting straight up, sitting wedged diagonally into a corner of the chair, even sitting with a leg dangling over one armrest. The distance between the seat cushion and the floor, the angle of the cushion, the angle of the chair back, and the height and angle of the armrests all are based on the size and configuration of the average human body, represented here by a woman. From these dimensions, plus the thickness of structure required to support the weight of her body and the thickness of padding required to distribute her weight comfortably across her flesh, grow the external dimensions of the chair. Around the chair, within easy reaching radius of the woman's arms, are other furnishings: a lamp tall enough to cast light over her shoulder and onto her book; a magazine rack large enough to contain ordinary reading matter, which in turn is of a size that comfortably fits her hand and eye; and a side table at a height that puts a cup of tea within easy reach (16.5).

16.5

The woman rises and walks to the dining table. As she moves, her body sweeps a volume of space that must be maintained clear of obstructions. There must be space for her to move behind her dining chair, space to pull out the chair, and space to enter between her chair and the next (16.6). The chair must support her comfortably at a height appropriate for eating, and the table must present the tableware and food at a height convenient to her hands and mouth. The plates and cups are of sizes that will serve the quantities of various foods that her stomach is expected to hold. The utensils are fitted dimensionally to her hand and mouth. The dimensions of the ta-

16.6

16.7

16.8

bletop are worked out so as to accommodate a given number of diners, together with their tableware, elbows, and knees. It is also worked out to maintain a comfortable distance between people sitting opposite each other (16.7). Even when people are sitting or standing with no table between them, they keep distances that allow sufficiently close visual and aural contact without encroachment on personal spatial territories. A dining table or a living room can be too small for comfort, thrusting people into intolerable proximity. It can also be too large, making communication difficult.

Rooms acquire their dimensions on the basis of such considerations: the dimensions and forms of human bodies, the dimensions and forms of the necessary pieces of furniture, the dimensions and forms of the volumes swept by moving human bodies, and the desired distances between people (16.8). Even the television set has its appropriate distance from its viewer.

In a kitchen, a bathroom, or a factory, machines acquire at least equal status with people in terms of spatial requirements. The machines are arranged in a convenient sequence. Each has its own dimensions, the dimensions swept by its working parts or moving workpieces, and the dimensions swept by the moving bodies of its operator and its maintainers. The room must provide amply for all these volumes and furnish other volumes to conduct pipes, hoses, wires, or ducts to and from the machinery as required.

Some very simple sorts of mechanisms are universal in buildings and also demand space for their operation. Sliding drawers and swinging doors are two good examples, in which both the operator and the mechanism must have space to move freely.

In general, the larger a building is, the more it will cost to build.

Consequently, we usually attempt to make rooms as small as is consistent with comfort. By relegating specific activities and pieces of furniture to specific places, we can often create a workable room within remarkably small dimensions. The modern residential kitchen is compact and efficient and has become an integrated unit of entirely built-in components. But a compact, carefully worked-out room arrangement has little or no flexibility. Any change in furniture locations would require enlarging the room. This is a choice that designers constantly face: A larger room allows for more subsequent choice and variety in its furnishings, but a smaller room is generally less costly.

The height of an ordinary room is determined, at minimum, by the height of the tallest person normally expected to move through the room, plus a bit to allow for his hat and a small safety factor (16.9). But there is much more to it than this. A ceiling may be quite high enough to clear the hat but still feel uncomfortably low and oppressive, particularly if the room is large in horizontal extent. In general, the larger the room is, the higher the minimum height of a ceiling must be so as not to appear to bear down on the occupant. Ceiling height has important effects on air convection and the propagation of natural light; these factors also tend to indicate higher ceilings for larger rooms. Primitive houses in subarctic regions are commonly built with very low ceilings, to minimize heat losses to the outdoors and give a snug, cozy feeling during the cold winters. In warm climates, high ceilings allow warm air to drift to the ceiling and comfortably cooler air to pool closer to the floor, where the occupants are. In churches, concert halls, and sports arenas, high ceilings allow clear lines of sight from all spectators to the performance and achieve a better distribution and reverberation of sound.

The heads of ordinary windows are usually placed at least high enough that a standing person can see comfortably to the horizon (16.10). Where natural light is important, windows often are placed

16.9

16.10

143

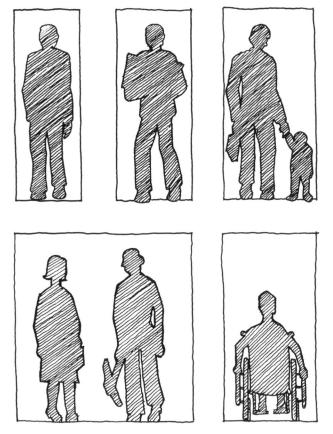

16.11

as close to the ceiling as possible, allowing only for the necessary lintel to support the wall and floor above. Sill height is much more variable. For ordinary purposes, it may be sufficient that the window reach low enough that one can look out from a sitting position, or perhaps a bit higher so that one can lean out the window while resting one's forearms on the sill. It often is important that a table, chair, or countertop fit against the wall beneath a window. In a room high above the ground, a higher sill may offer a welcome feeling of security against tumbling out. In a private room at ground level, a very high sill keeps out prying eyes. In a window opening onto a garden, a sill set into the floor allows one to walk directly outside in pleasant weather.

In the absence of other factors, the perimeter of a building is shaped by the outermost walls of the most convenient internal aggregation of rooms. When combining rooms, certain proximities are important to maintain. A bedroom should be near a bathroom, without an intervening bedroom or living room. The kitchen should be near the dining room. Such simple relationships are basic to the design of any building.

Doorways are necessary to allow access to and from rooms. They are scaled to accommodate a walking figure, plus a bit more to allow for carrying a bundle of groceries, a suitcase, or a young child (16.11). In public buildings, doorways become exitways whose ca-

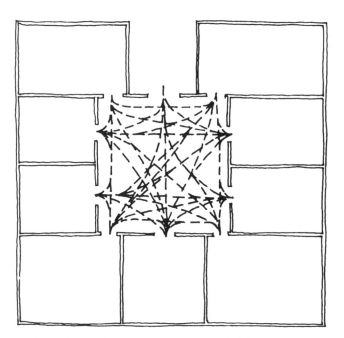

Natural paths through a lobby
16.12

144

pacity must be calculated to pass the entire occupant population of the building in a specified minimum time, and both widths and numbers of doors increase accordingly.

Corridors are useful for facilitating complex circulation paths among a number of interrelated rooms. A corridor width of three feet (900 mm) is quite sufficient for a single person, but two people will find it difficult to pass one another. Another foot (300 mm) of width makes passing easy for two but will not permit the comfortable passage of two parallel files of people. Corridors must be sized like water pipes, to accommodate the expected flow. The pipelike character of many unimaginatively designed corridors has led many designers to do away with them, substituting instead a seemingly generous lounge or lobby. Unfortunately, the result is usually little more than a broader corridor, with circulation paths cutting across in all directions, leaving little room free for other activities (16.12). Such situations are easily foreseen by sketching on a floor plan the natural paths along which people will circulate.

Vertical Movement: Stairs, Ramps, Ladders

Designing for vertical movement of people in and around buildings requires extremely careful attention to the dimensions and peculiarities of the human body. The hazard of tripping and the effort of climbing or descending must be minimized by comfortably accommodating the feet and legs. Handrails must be provided in such a form and location that they can be easily and securely grasped, either to assist in climbing or to prevent a vertical fall over the edge of the stair. And headroom, often a scarce commodity in stairways, must be at a safe height to protect the brittle and vulnerable cranium from damage (16.13).

Architectural devices for reducing an impossible floor-to-floor vertical leap to human-sized steps exist in a range that will let us climb at any angle from the near-horizontal to the completely vertical (16.14). *Ramps* provide a smooth, slow ascent or descent that can be traversed at any length of stride, or even by a wheelchair or baby carriage. They are particularly effective in exhibit spaces, theaters, and arenas where large crowds must be accommodated. A ramp cannot be pitched very steeply, however, before our feet and ankles feel in danger of slipping, particularly on the descent. As a result, the ratio of run to rise for a ramp is very large—ramps occupy a very great deal of space in a building. *Step ramps* can rise somewhat more steeply and economically and can be very pleasant in a garden. Indoors, we get the unpleasant feeling of possibly slipping on them, as on a ramp, and also of possibly tripping, as on a stair, so they should be avoided. Fixed *ladders* and step ladders in buildings are

16.13

16.14

16.15

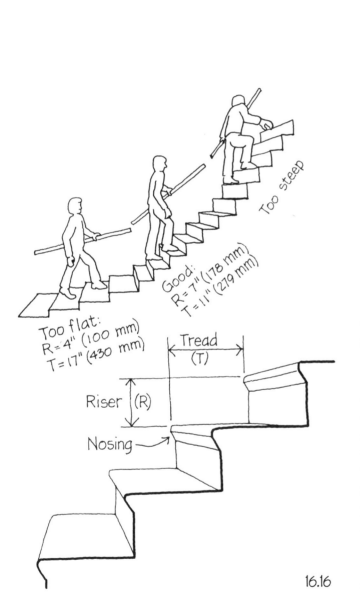

16.16

generally restricted to seldom-used access routes to attics, chimneys, boiler rooms, and bookshelves or to playful features of children's rooms and vacation cottages (16.15). Vertical and near-vertical ladders are especially hard to negotiate while carrying anything, which further restricts their usefulness.

Stairs are the safest and most useful of vertical movement devices in a designer's repertoire. *Risers* divide the total vertical climb into small increments that the legs can negotiate comfortably whether ascending or descending. *Treads* provide reassuringly level, secure footholds. The drawbacks of stairs are that they cannot accommodate people with various sorts of physical disabilities (ramps or elevators must be provided instead); they become fatiguing after only a few stories of going up or down; and a fall on a stairway can be particularly damaging because of the numerous hard edges presented by the stairs.

The danger of falling on stairs and the potential for fatigue are minimized if the proportions of the steps are both comfortable and absolutely uniform throughout the stairway. Even a fractional in-

146

crease in the height of one riser in a stair can lead to more accidents. Uncomfortably proportioned stairs are familiar to everyone: Excessively steep stairs require too much muscular effort at each riser and offer a disturbingly narrow foothold at each tread. Very shallow stairs induce a mincing gait that feels ridiculously inefficient (16.16). According to various studies of the proportions of existing stairways, those stairs whose tread (T) and riser (R) dimensions in inches fit the formula

$$2R + T = 25''$$
(or, in SI units, $2R + T = 635$ mm)

are likely to be both safe and comfortable. Limits must be placed on the application of this equation. For example, it cannot be used for the design of monumental stairs with very small risers and very broad treads; experimentation with full-scale mock-ups is required in such cases. In stairs of more usual proportions, R should not exceed 8 inches (200 mm) in private residential stairs, or 7 inches (178 mm) in other stairs. T should not be less than 9 inches (230 mm) for residential stairs, or 11 inches (280 mm) for other stairs. Residential stairs can be steeper because they carry less traffic and are used primarily by people who are familiar with them. *Nosings* on stair treads are an important detail; they broaden the foothold significantly without changing the fundamental proportions of the stair. Except in single-family residences, stair nosings must be profiled with a sloping underside so that they will not catch the toes of a person who is climbing the stairs on crutches.

Spiral and winding staircases present a special problem because even though their riser dimensions remain constant across the stair, the tread dimensions vary considerably. A person walking next to the inside of a tight spiral stair is on a near-vertical stair with tiny treads, whereas the outside of the same stair may be excessively broad. For this reason. such stairs are illegal in public buildings. In residences, it is customary to proportion the treads and risers of such stairs to legal dimensions at a distance of 12 inches (305 mm) from the inside handrail, which is the line walked by a single person on the stair (16.17).

The number of risers in a flight has an important effect on stair safety and comfort. Flights of fewer than three risers often escape the notice of unfamiliar users, who tend to tumble over them before seeing them. Flights of more than sixteen or eighteen risers become very tiring (16.18). Long flights should be broken with periodic *landings* whose minimum dimensions are equal to the width of the stair.

Headroom problems in stairs are vexing because they are so often difficult to avoid—but there is no choice to designers. People often descend stairs with a very rapid up-and-down movement while

16.17

Too long a flight

Too short a flight

16.18

watching their feet to avoid tripping. Tall people are painfully familiar with the damage that may result.

Making Buildings Work

When laying out any of the circulation spaces in buildings—doors, corridors, stairways—designers have to keep in mind that furniture and appliances occasionally must pass through the building. That is, doorways cannot be made so narrow as to exclude refrigerators, sofas, desks, or pianos. Tight turns in corridors and stairways may be impassable for such objects unless additional maneuvering space is provided.

Lobbies serve several important human functions in the circulation systems of buildings. Entrance lobbies let people entering or leaving a building slow down, button or unbutton outer clothing, think about where to go next, adjust their eyes to the new lighting level, fiddle with umbrellas, comb windblown hair, or wait for taxis or friends. Theater lobbies serve these functions, and they also let members of the audience exercise their legs between parts of a performance. A lobby is really an expansion chamber in an otherwise linear flow network, a place at which people can step out of the moving stream and stop for a moment or two.

Outdoors, designers work at a different scale. People are still the measure, but now they are walking more rapidly or riding in vehicles. They need more room to allow for this more rapid movement and for expanded spatial expectations. Space between buildings must let sunlight penetrate. Air must circulate freely. Acoustical and visual privacy must be protected by the distance between buildings and by the buildings' configuration. Comfortable walking distances and times become the yardstick for planning local facilities, and driving times or public transport times measure the convenience of places in an urban region. At this new scale, unfortunately, the small-scale necessities of people's bodies are often overlooked by designers. Who has not yearned for a drinking fountain, a comfortable bench, or a public rest room while in the midst of a shopping or sightseeing expedition? Who has not felt personally betrayed by a nameless designer of a city who forgot that people are human?

Both outside and inside buildings, human safety is an important design consideration. Buildings can cause accidental damage to the body in an alarmingly diverse number of ways, some of which are enumerated in the accompanying chart (16.19). Thousands of Americans are killed in accidents in buildings each year, and tens of thousands are injured, many seriously. Many of these deaths and injuries could be prevented by more careful design and better building maintenance.

Some Accidents Caused by Buildings

Bumping, Catching, Pinching

  Low headroom
  Uncontrolled door swings
  Unprotected door edges
  Doors that open into traffic
  Blind corners in busy corridors
  Projecting doorknobs, railing ends

Cutting, Scratching, Puncturing, Skinning

  Sharp edges and corners
  Floor-to-ceiling glass
  Projecting nails, screws, bolts
  Splinters
  Rough surfaces

Falls

  Tripping: Low obstacles, uneven floors,
  edges of rugs, objects left on floors
  Poorly proportioned stairs or ramps
  Railings too low or nonexistent
  Poor illumination
  Slippery floors or stairs
  Loose rugs

Scalding, Burning

  Confusing hot-water taps
  Unprotected steam or water pipes
  Unprotected heating appliances
  Stove too close to circulation path
  Building fires

Electrocution

  Faulty appliances
  Faulty wiring

16.19

Disabled people are entitled by law to access to most buildings that is equal to that provided for able-bodied persons. The disabilities covered by this guarantee include loss of sight, loss of hearing, loss of function in legs or arms, and a host of other physical and emotional incapacities. The rationale behind the law is compelling: About one American in six is disabled in some way, and nearly all of us will experience disability at some time in our lives, perhaps a broken limb as a teenager or failing eyesight or decreasing muscle function as a senior citizen. The consequences for designing circulation spaces in buildings are far reaching, beginning with tactile and audible signals of various types for those with sensory disabilities. Those with physical disabilities need special parking spaces; ramped access through curbs and other minor changes in level; a convenient, linked system of ramps and elevators for moving vertically through a building; wider doors; larger vestibules; special drinking fountains; more ample toilet facilities with grab bars; special telephone facilities; lower counters for banking and shopping—the list goes on and on. An architect must learn to design accessible buildings as a matter of reflex. Circulation paths and facilities for the disabled must flow from his or her pencil as gracefully and naturally as does any other feature of a building design.

People as the Measure

As a coda to this chapter, we might do well to recall how people literally became the measure of buildings through the English system of measurement. In each medieval English village, measurements were standardized to a village pole, the length of the pole being derived from the right feet of sixteen randomly selected men placed toe-to-heel after church on a Sunday morning. A common house of that period measured one pole by two. A cord of pole length could be folded and was therefore useful in subdividing the pole into four smaller units called yards; a yard was four feet long (1.2 m) at that time. The same cord served to measure a cord of firewood, a pile four feet by four feet by eight feet (1.2 m × 1.2 m × 2.4 m), the sum of these three dimensions being equal to the length of the cord.

As textile trade became important, the Anglo-Saxon yard of four feet had to be abandoned in favor of the continental cloth yard of three feet (915 mm), measured along the edge of the cloth between the tip of the nose and the outstretched arm. The pole, by now called a rod, was increased to 16.5 feet (5.03 m), or 5.5 cloth yards. The mile, which originated as one thousand double steps (*mille passus*) of a Roman soldier, was standardized at 320 rods or eight furlongs (furrow-lengths) of forty rods each, and the acre (a day's plowing for a yoke of oxen) at 160 square rods. Later, the mile-square section of 640 acres (259 ha) became the standard of land subdivision in the central and western United States, and a quarter-section farm of 160 acres (65 ha) was the standard homestead grant.

Meanwile, a curious progression of circumstances grew out of the ancient cord measure of firewood. It became standard practice in England to saw each four-foot log into three pieces, each sixteen inches (400 mm) long, for easy handling. Fireplace and stove dimensions were standardized accordingly. When wooden lath came into use as a base for plaster, it was split from firewood, and so sixteen inches became the standard spacing for light framing members in buildings. From this spacing came, in time, the four-foot-by-eight-foot (1219 mm × 2438 mm) sheet of plywood or gypsum wallboard, which spans three or six framing modules, and from these sheets came the standard eight-foot (2.44 m) ceiling of today's tract house.

The common building materials became, in the course of history, rather more directly related to human scale. The brick, despite many small local variations in size, was standardized in medieval times within a range of sizes and weights that could be easily manipulated by the left hand of a mason, leaving the right hand free to operate the trowel (16.20). When wood joinery suddenly became cheap with the introduction of machine-made nails early in the nineteenth century, carpenters quickly adopted the easily handled "two-by-four" as the standard unit of framing (16.21). The heavy timber frame, which required a large crew simply to handle and fit its large components, was quickly abandoned, and the standard building crew was reduced to two or three carpenters working only with small, inexpensive hand tools. Hand-size elements are the traditional standard in many areas of small building construction, including shingles, wood siding, wood paneling, window glass, and paving blocks and tiles.

16.20

Today we often handle building materials in bulk rather than by hand, using mobile mechanical lifting and transporting devices of impressive capacities. It is often most economical to build using large-scale materials such as factory-built, room-size housing modules. There is nothing inherently wrong with these practices, but designers should be aware that the finished product will not automatically display the human-scale texture that hand-sized components have and that occupants often subconsciously identify with. Designers must also be wary of being forced into unnatural decisions about sizes and proportions of things by the limitations of cranes and trucks of superhuman or subhuman scale.

The metric system of measurement is not directly related to human scale. Its basic unit is the meter, originally defined as one ten-millionth of the distance from the North Pole to the equator. Its unit

16.21

of volume is the liter, a cube one-tenth meter on a side. Its unit of mass, the kilogram, is the mass of a liter of water. The second is retained as a measure of time, and the Celsius scale, which divided the range between the freezing and boiling points of water into one hundred degrees, is the measure of temperature. All other units are derived from this basic group. Because of its logic and simplicity, the metric system has been adopted by almost every country of the world outside the United States. Even in the United States, although most private projects are designed and built in conventional English units, since 1993 all federal government buildings have been built according to metric units of measurement. A refinement and rationalization of the metric system, the Système International d'Unités (abbreviated SI), is finding increasing acceptance and is used in this book as an alternative system of units to the English.

Careful designers work always from a mental catalog of sizes and proportions of things. Sketches and models from the very earliest stages of building design include representations of people, furnishings, and groupings of furnishings. Room proportions and window and door locations are constantly juggled during the design process to facilitate a variety of appropriate furniture placements in a finished building. Patterns of human circulation are progressively refined into paths that are short, smooth, logical, and pleasant and that pass to one side or the other of the different nodes of human activity within the building, instead of cutting through the middle. Materials are chosen partly for the scale of the texture they will give to the surfaces of the building. Whenever possible, future occupants of the building are made party to its design. If through these processes, the building is molded well by its designer and occupants, then the occupants are more likely to be molded well and happily by the building.

Further Reading

Julius Panero and Nino Repetto. *Anatomy for Interior Designers*. New York, Whitney Publications, 1962.

Charles G. Ramsey and Harold Sleeper. *Architectural Graphic Standards* (9th ed.). New York, Wiley, 1994.

17
Providing Structural Support

Loads and Stresses

A building is constantly being pushed and pulled by various forces. The most constant force of all is that of gravity exerting its downward pull on the fixed components of which the building is constructed—the roofs, walls, windows, floors, partitions, stairs, fireplaces—a force referred to as the *dead load* of the building. The *live loads* of the building include the less constant forces—the shifting, varying weights of people, furnishings, goods, and vehicles, the weight of any snow on the roofs, the pressures (predominantly horizontal) that may be applied by wind. Earthquakes, which cause rapidly fluctuating horizontal displacements of the ground on which a building stands, also cause horizontal live loads. Designers must configure the building in such a way that it will always support its own dead load and a live load equal to the worst combined total of people, furnishings, snow, wind, and earthquake that may reasonably be expected.

To do this, designers first estimate the magnitude of these loads, which is usually an elementary arithmetical chore, although buildings of unusual height or in unusually windy locations may require extensive measurements on the site and in a wind tunnel to determine what the actual wind loads will be. Next, designers select a combination of related structural devices—a structural system—appropriate to the site, the uses to be made of the building, and the expected loads. Last, they determine the exact configurations and necessary strengths and sizes of the components of the structural system, including all the fastening devices used to hold the larger components together. A glance at any building under construction is likely to lead to the conclusion, largely correct, that the detailed design of a structural system is a rather involved process. At its roots, however, structural design springs from some very simple concepts. No structure is built that does not stand, fundamentally, on these concepts. The depth and complexity of structural design processes lie in the skill with which designers select, combine, and proportion structural devices and translate them into buildable form, not in the basic behavior of the devices themselves.

Consider a block of material—building stone, let us say—and what happens to it as a downward load is applied uniformly across its upper surface (17.1). The load pushes down on the block from above, and the surface below the block pushes upward with an equal force. The block is being compressed. The *compressive stress* on the block is equal to the load divided by the horizontal cross-sectional area of the block:

$$\text{Compressive stress} \;=\; \frac{\text{load}}{\text{area}}$$

If the load is 3,000 pounds and the block is 10 by 15 inches, the compressive stress will be equal to 3,000 pounds divided by 150 square inches, or 20 pounds per square inch. In SI units, this exam-

17.1

ple would translate as a force of 0.0133 meganewtons divided by 0.0968 m², which equals 0.1374 megapascals (MPa). This concept of stress is a most useful one because it allows us to compare the intensity of structural actions in blocks of differing sizes and shapes under differing loads.

Suppose now that the load on the block is gradually increased by piling more weight on the top. The compressive stress will rise in proportion to the weight. Simultaneously, if we have extremely accurate measuring equipment, we can observe that the height of the block is gradually diminished by very small but finite amounts as the load is increased. If we plot a graph of the compressive stress versus this diminution (which is called *strain*), it will be a straight line, telling us that stress is directly proportional to strain (17.2). The slope of the line—the ratio of stress to strain—is known as the *elastic modulus* of the material. Elastic moduli have been determined experimentally for all the common structural materials, giving us a ready means of predicting how much a wall or column will compress under a given load (17.3). The term *elastic* also implies a property that we normally expect of any material that has a linear stress–strain curve: that if the load is removed from it, it will spring back to its original size, without loss of dimension.

As the load on the block continues to mount, however, the material within the block will ultimately be squeezed beyond its capacity to resist. The material will crush and will not return to its original size after the load is removed. The stress at which this occurs is known as the *yield point* of the material. In a brittle material such as stone, the yield point is also the point at which the material disintegrates and becomes incapable of carrying any substantial load. It is dangerous to design a building structure to be stressed to the yield point, because any tiny additional load, any minute flaw in the material, or any slight miscalculation will make the building collapse. To account for these factors, we normally design structures with a *factor of safety*. A factor of safety of two means that we design to a stress that is just half of the yield point. A factor of three means we use one-third this stress, and so on. We use lower factors of safety for materials that tend to be relatively consistent in quality, such as steel, and higher factors for materials, such as wood, that are naturally inconsistent and flawed. We use factors of safety in combination with laboratory load-test data to calculate standard *safe working stresses* for various structural materials.

Suppose that our stone block has crushed at a stress of 3600 pounds per square inch (24.82 MPa). To allow for possible flaws and inconsistencies in the stone, we will adopt a factor of safety of three, which results in a safe working stress of 1200 pounds per square inch

17.2

17.3

Average Elastic Moduli of Some Common Structural Materials

	lb/in²	MPa
Steel	30.0×10^6	20.7×10^4
Aluminum	10.0×10^6	6.9×10^4
Concrete	3.0×10^6	2.1×10^4
Wood	1.5×10^6	1.0×10^4
Brick	1.5×10^6	1.0×10^4

17.4

(8.27 MPa). If we are now asked to design a stone block to support a load of 60 tons (54,480 kg), we can do so as follows:

$$60 \text{ tons} \times 2000 \frac{\text{pounds}}{\text{ton}} = 120,000 \text{ pounds}$$

$$\text{Required cross-sectional area of stone} = \frac{120,000 \text{ lbs.}}{1200 \text{ lbs./in}^2} = 100 \text{ in}^2$$

(in SI units: $54,480 \text{ kg} \times 9.8 \text{ m/sec}^2 = 0.5334 \text{ MN}$

$$\text{Required cross-sectional area} = \frac{0.5334 \text{ MN}}{8.27 \text{ MPa}} = 0.0645 \text{ m}^2)$$

A stone 10 inches square (254 mm × 254 mm) will do the job. This may seem to be a trivial example, but this simple procedure is the basis for all structural calculations. The design of even the most complicated structure ultimately comes down to a question of whether a given piece of material can safely carry a direct stress.

Vertical Support

We can do a great deal, architecturally, with simple blocks of stone, concrete, or brick. A vertical stack of blocks forms a *column*, capable of supporting a corner of a floor or roof. A column translated in a horizontal direction becomes a *bearing wall*, which can support the load of an entire edge of a floor or roof (17.4). Provided that such columns or bearing walls are not too slender in relationship to their

17.5
Columns

Stone Brick Concrete Wood Steel

17.6
Bearing Walls

Cut Stone Rubble Stone Brick Concrete Wood

height, their thicknesses can be computed in the same simple manner as in the preceding example (17.5–17.7).

If a column or wall is too slender—or in some cases if the load from above is not applied squarely to the top of the column or wall—it will *buckle*, even though the stress in the material may be well below the safe working stress (17.8). Buckling is a lateral displacement whose causes and mathematics are still not completely understood, especially in columns that are neither extremely slender nor extremely thick. Short, squat columns and walls crush before buckling, and very tall, slender ones consistently buckle before crushing, but ones of intermediate length and slenderness may fail either way. Consequently, we rely largely on formulas derived from laboratory test data when designing columns of intermediate slenderness.

A column or wall that tends to buckle can be made safe by being thickened sufficiently or by being braced laterally with compressive *struts* or tensile *guys* (17.9). A laterally braced column has the ad-

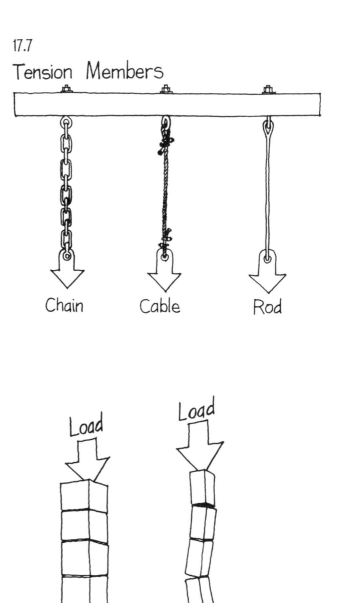

17.7

Tension Members

Chain Cable Rod

Load Load

17.8

Guys

17.9

vantage of using considerably less total material to support the same load as a thick, unbraced column does and therefore is used frequently in buildings, radio towers, and many other types of structure.

Buckling is a problem only in structural elements that are under compressive stress. Elements under *tensile stress*, such as ropes, cables, rods, and chains, have no tendency to buckle and may be made very slender in most structural applications. Consider a chain hanging vertically with a weight attached to its lower end (17.10). The tensile stress on the chain is equal to the applied weight divided by the cross-sectional area of steel in any single link. The strain, up to the yield point of the steel in the chain, is proportional to the stress. The chain will never buckle.

Horizontal Spanning: Tension Devices

Vertical loads in buildings, then, can be supported in compression by columns or bearing walls or in tension by chains, rods, or cables. Except in some cases of column buckling, the behavior of these structural devices is well understood and easily computed. The greater structural problem in most buildings, however, is to span horizontally over space, to support roofs and floors. How do we do it?

17.10

17.11

158

Suppose we hang a chain across a narrow canyon and suspend a very heavy weight from its center (17.11). The two halves of the chain become very nearly two straight lines, converging at the point where the weight is applied. The ends of the chain will pull on the cliffs at either side at an angle (a), which is determined by the length of chain we have provided (17.12). Now, as we examine what happens at the center of the chain, we note that the two halves of the chain cannot be exerting a direct upward pull against the weight; a chain can pull only along the axis (centerline) of its links. Therefore it must be resisting the downward pull of the weight with two diagonal pulls at angles (a) from the horizontal. The diagonal pulls, T_1 and T_2, each must have a vertical component, $T\text{sin}a$, equal to half the pull of the weight. At each cliff, this vertical component is transferred into the rock. But so is an accompanying horizontal component, $T\text{cos}a$. The chain cannot support a load across a span without exerting a horizontal as well as a vertical pull on its supports. We can see this more easily if we support the ends of the chain on two slender poles instead of two cliffs (17.13). The poles bend inward under the load. A common way of dealing with this horizontal pull, in suspension bridges or tents, is to run the chain (or cable or rope) over the poles or columns at each end and down to anchors in the ground some distance outside each column. The chains outside the columns provide a horizontal pull equal to the pull of the chain between the columns. They also, unavoidably, add a substantial vertical load to each of the columns, and so the columns must be strengthened accordingly.

Let us go back again to the problem of spanning the canyon and observe what happens if we use a longer chain. The angle (a) is increased. The vertical pull on the cliffs stays the same, but the horizontal pull is diminished, and so are the pull and the stress in

17.12

17.13

159

17.14

17.15

Catenary

Weight
of link

17.16

160

the chain. Conversely, if the chain is shortened, the horizontal pull on the cliffs will be increased, and the chain will be tensed much more tightly (17.14). Designers must decide, not only in a hanging chain but in *any* horizontal spanning device, *how deep* the device should be. A deep device, such as a deeply sagging chain or a deep truss or beam, generally has lower internal structural stresses and thus needs less material to carry the same load than does a shallow device that has higher internal stresses and needs more material. In practice, however, we often choose the shallower devices because they require less vertical space in a building, thus saving money on columns, exterior walls, and other components.

What happens if we add more loads to the chain? As second and subsequent loads are added, the chain adjusts its shape to maintain a line of pure tension along its axis at every point. The loads may be unequal in weight or unequally distributed along the length of the chain; the chain changes shape automatically to place each of its links in equilibrium under any loading short of its breaking point (17.15). One cannot force a chain to take an arbitrary shape but must work with the shapes a chain is capable of taking. The most familiar shape of all is the *catenary*, the graceful curve taken by a chain hanging freely under its own weight (17.16). Each link represents a resolved trio of forces in equilibrium, two exerted at an obtuse angle to each other by the two adjacent links, and the third exerted downward by the weight of the link itself.

The curve of the cable in a suspension bridge differs slightly from a catenary because the weight of the bridge is distributed evenly over the horizontal plane of the roadway that hangs from the cable, not over the curving length of the cable. The resulting curve is a *parabola*.

The important thing to remember about a chain or cable is that when it is subjected to any pattern of loads, it always assumes a shape such that it acts only in tension. The shapes taken by a hanging cable or chain are called *funicular* shapes, after the Latin word for "string." For each pattern of loads, there is a family of funicular shapes, the shapes that a piece of hanging string would take when subjected to that load pattern. For a cable hanging under its own weight only, the funicular shapes comprise an infinitely large family of catenaries, because the cable can sag a little, a lot, or anything in between. For a suspension bridge, the funicular shapes make up a family of parabolas. Over the past several pages and in the accompanying drawing (17.17), we also see shapes that are funicular for a single load and several random loads. Some of these shapes are on level supports, and others are on uneven supports.

Tents represent the principle of the funicular in a three-dimensional form, using cloth on a small scale, or networks of steel cables

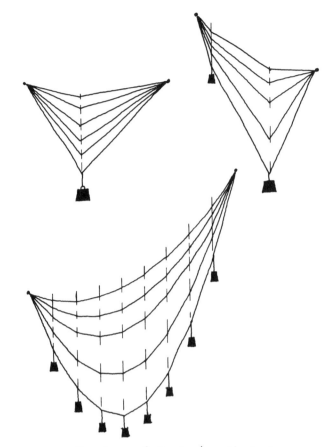

Some families of funicular shapes
17.17

161

17.18

Hammock

Cable-stayed

Cable net (anticlastic)

Bicycle wheel

Some Rigid Hanging Roofs   17.19

162

on a large scale, to cover space (17.18, 17.19). Extremely long spans between supports are possible if the poles are high enough to accommodate the necessary depth of sag in the fabric and if the fabric is sufficiently tense to prevent billowing or fluttering in the wind. Such tension can be provided by ropes or cables that pull the fabric down at various points, by applying sufficient weight to the fabric or by giving an *anticlastic* curvature (convex along one axis and concave along the other) to the fabric.

Arches

What happens if we abandon the chain and instead try to support the weight in the middle of the canyon with stone blocks? We could do this by leaning the blocks against each other, upward and across the chasm in just the right configuration so that each block would be in equilibrium with its immediate neighbors. With a series of trigonometric computations, starting from the weight we wish to carry in the center and proceeding block by block to the rims of the canyon, we could work out an ideal shape to do the job in this way. There is also an easier way to determine the shape: modeling it to scale with a length of watch chain or key chain suspended over a piece of paper that is attached to a vertical surface. Remember that in a chain, each link is in equilibrium, its own weight and the forces from the link on either side just being equal. This is exactly what we want in each block of our stone device, the only difference being that a chain can carry only tension, whereas we want our stones, which are weak in tension, to carry only compression. The solution, then, is to model the situation on a small scale with a weight suspended from a chain, taking care that the proportion between the weight of the chain itself and the weight being supported is the same as the expected proportion between the weight of the stones of the arch and the weight they will support. We need to attach a number of small weights to the chain to simulate the weight of the stones (17.20). The chain and weights in our hanging model will quickly reach equilibrium. We

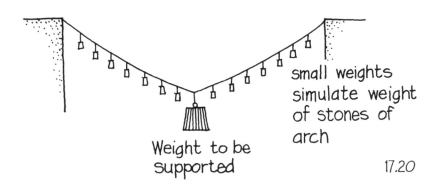

small weights
simulate weight
of stones of
arch

Weight to be
supported

17.20

163

1. Trace curve of chain model

2. Invert tracing, lay out arch

3. Construct arch

17.21

then can trace the form taken by the chain onto a sheet of paper, invert the sheet of paper, and lay out a series of stone blocks whose centerline assumes the same form as the chain (17.21). The result will be a *funicular arch* perfectly formed to carry the given load by means of pure compression within and between the stones.

If you have never seen an arch of exactly this shape, it is because few arches are built to take a single, concentrated load. Most are built to carry uniformly distributed loads and should, therefore, take the form of a parabola, as we see in many concrete arch bridges. (17.22). In buildings, most arches are not parabolic but circular, for arches are much easier to lay out as arcs of circles. If the stones of the arch (the *voussoirs*) are deep enough to contain a parabolic curve, and the arch is stiffened by containment within a wall, such simpler arches are quite stable (17.23). Furthermore, it was not known until Renaissance times that the parabola was the ideal shape for a uniformly loaded arch, so all the classical arches of Roman civilization, which we have copied so faithfully through subsequent epochs, are of simpler form (17.24). The Romans even used a *flat arch*, a form so apparently wrong that one is tempted to doubt its stability until one sees it carrying a load without apparent distress. Then one is forced to visualize a rather flat parabola superimposed on its stones.

It is important to note the mirror-image similarity between the forms developed previously with hanging chains and the funicular arch forms illustrated here. The arch to support each loading condition differs slightly from its chain analogue in that the greater deadweight of the arch itself with respect to the superimposed weight or weights may require a slightly different curvature of form. Notice also that every arch exerts a horizontal force, exactly as a chain does, but in the opposite direction (17.25). The amount of horizontal thrust and the amount of compressive stress within the stones of the arch depend on the amount of rise given to the arch. The flatter the arch is the higher the horizontal thrust and the higher the internal forces in the voussoirs will be. Once again we encounter the principle that deeper structural devices have lower forces.

In important respects, the arch is not an exact analogue of the chain. The arch is rigid and cannot self-adjust to changing load patterns. Being in compression, an arch can fail by buckling. For both these reasons, an arch cannot be made nearly as slender as can a chain or cable. A relatively thick arch is not only more resistant to buckling but also can carry comfortably within itself the stress patterns of loadings that vary a good deal from the exact loading for which it was designed. For these two reasons, also, the arch form does not have as great an ultimate spanning capability as does the hanging cable, although it is runner-up to the cable as the best long-span device in the designer's structural vocabulary.

Parabolic Arches

17.22

parabola

Semicircular Arch

parabola

Flat Arch

17.23

17.24

17.25

Arches

Semicircular

Segmental

Flat

Pointed or Gothic

Four-Centered or Tudor

Vaults

Barrel Vault

Cloister Vault

Groin Vault

Domes

Dome

Pendentive Dome

Pendentive Dome with Half Domes

Pendentive Dome with Barrel Vaults

Dome on Pendentives

17.26

The arch form underwent enormous development and elaboration in Roman and medieval times and today exists in many useful forms, both two dimensional and three dimensional, some of which are illustrated here (17.26). Most arched forms of construction need some sort of temporary support (called *centering* or *formwork*) during construction. Many materials, including all the masonry materials, concrete, cast iron, steel, and wood, are suitable for arches, vaults, and domes.

The need to resist the horizontal thrust of arches and vaults has given rise to many ingenious architectural devices. The simple, heavy masonry *buttresses* of early times became the breathtaking *flying buttresses* of the Gothic era, in which the downward gravitational thrust of heavy stone pinnacles inexorably diverts the outward thrust of the vaults until it safely enters the ground through the foundations (17.27, 17.28). In Renaissance times, as wrought iron became available, metal tie rods or chains came into use as an inexpensive (but usually less handsome) alternative to buttresses for all kinds of vaults and domes (17.29).

The availability of new and stronger structural materials in the nineteenth and twentieth centuries brought a new wave of development in vaulting techniques. Vaults and domes of metal trusswork can span vast amounts of space, using little more material than

Buttresses
17.27

Flying buttresses
17.28

Tie rods or tie chains
17.29

17.30

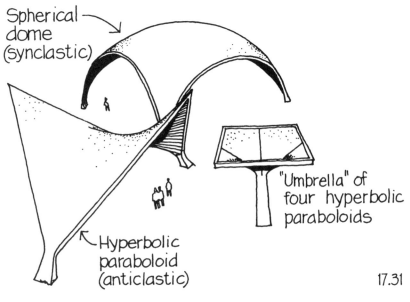

Spherical dome (synclastic)

Hyperbolic paraboloid (anticlastic)

"Umbrella" of four hyperbolic paraboloids

17.31

suspension structures of equal expanse (17.30). Vaults of reinforced concrete or clay tiles, often proportionally thinner than the shell of an egg, have become commonplace, and their designers have exploited not only the *synclastic*, spherical geometry of traditional vaulting but the anticlastic curve of the hyperbolic paraboloid as well (17.31).

Thrust-Free Spanning Devices: Trusses

We have developed so far the concepts of the hanging chain, the arch, and the tie chain. Let us now see if we can assemble from these components other devices to span the canyon, trying especially to develop devices that exert no horizontal pull or thrust on the canyon walls. Such devices would be particularly useful in buildings, allowing the columns and bearing walls to support only vertical loads.

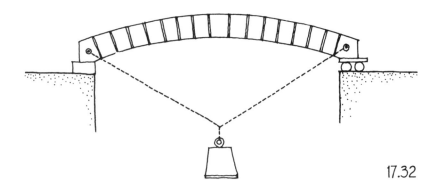

17.32

168

We will begin again with the hanging chain supporting a single load in the center, but this time we will connect the ends of the chain to the ends of a very shallow arch whose only function, besides supporting its own weight, is to counteract with its outward thrust the inward pull of the chain (17.32). If this device is properly designed, we can prove that it exerts no horizontal thrust by mounting one end of it on rollers, so it is free to move back and forth. If the rollers do not move, our design is a good one.

If we wish to support the load at a point above the arch, rather than have it hang down into the canyon below the arch, we can do this by transmitting the load down to the chain through a column of stone blocks. In order to avoid any concentrated loading at the center of the arch, where the column intersects, it is advisable to make the single arch into two shorter ones, thus providing a crude hinge point to allow for slight movement between members as the device deflects (17.33). Though we could actually make this device of stones and chain, it would be somewhat clumsy, and in practice it would be easier to replace the stones with short compression struts of wood, bolted loosely together at their junctions (17.34). It can now be seen more easily that what we have invented is a simple *truss*.

We could make a simple truss to support *two* concentrated loads, as shown (17.35). Its equilibrium is somewhat precarious, however, because the withdrawal of one of the loads will allow the upper line of struts, called the upper *chord*, to buckle upward. The addition of two chains in the center panel eliminates this possibility (17.36).

Ideal truss
17.37

Tension diagonals
17.38

panel   panel   panel   panel

Compression diagonals
17.39

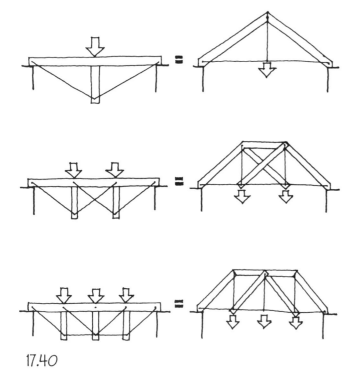

17.40

An ideal truss for three concentrated loads can be developed similarly (17.37). The truss would be easier to build if all the vertical struts were the same length. We can do this by inserting diagonal ties or struts in each *panel* of the truss to ensure equilibrium (17.38, 17.39). Notice that we can use *either* tension ties or compression struts, but one must be placed on the opposite diagonal of each panel from the other. By this means we can now produce stable trusses of any desired number of panels, although an even number of panels has the advantage of producing a symmetrical truss without the need for two diagonals in a center panel.

We can also invert all these trusses, by changing compression struts to tension ties, and vice versa (17.40).

Many different types of trusses have been developed (17.41). Trusses are easy to design and to analyze mathematically, can be made up of short pieces of material, are relatively light in weight, and can be built of wood, steel, aluminum, or concrete with equal

King Post

Queen Post

Town or Lattice

Warren

Bowstring

Pratt

Flat Pratt

Howe

Flat Howe

Fink

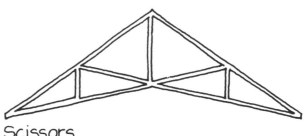

Fan Fink

<u>Some</u> <u>Forms</u> <u>of</u> <u>Trusses</u>

17.41

Scissors

Space Frame
17.42

17.43

17.44

17.45

17.46

ease. Their three-dimensional counterpart, the *space frame*, has also come into common use in recent decades (17.42). Trusses and space frames are theoretically capable of spans almost as great as those of arches and vaults, though not approaching the very long spans that are possible with hanging structures.

With trusses, as with arches and hanging structures, greater depth means lower stresses and, in general, greater economy of construction. But again, we may choose to use shallower trusses to economize on other costs of building. Let us investigate what happens as the depth of a simple truss is progressively diminished.

In the wooden truss shown in 17.43, we note that the weight of the load is carried through the vertical strut to the chain. The chain carries the load to the end supports, and the horizontal struts serve only to resist in compression the horizontal thrust of the chain.

If we shorten the vertical strut (17.44), the angle (a) of the chain will decrease, and both the horizontal pull of the chain and the tension in the chain will increase. We must use a thicker chain and thicker horizontal struts, but the vertical strut still will carry only a force equal to the superimposed load, so it can stay the same. If we shorten the vertical strut still further (17.45), the chain must become still thicker, as must the top struts. As the truss gets very shallow, forces rise extremely rapidly with each successive reduction in depth. A useful limiting case is reached when the depth of the wooden top struts required to resist the thrust of the chain without buckling is about the same as the overall depth of the truss (17.46). Internal forces in the truss are high, but within the capability of good structural materials to resist. The vertical strut can be eliminated entirely, with the center of the chain being bolted directly to the wood of the horizontal struts. What we have arrived at is a truss of minimum practical depth. It is not very efficient structurally because it uses far more steel and wood than a deeper truss would, but it is compact, and in a building it would produce both a flat floor above and a flat ceiling below, resulting in a maximum economy of space. What we have produced is, in fact, a form of *beam*, one designed specifically for the purpose of carrying only a single, concentrated load at its midpoint.

Beams

In order to arrive at a beam configuration that would be appropriate for a uniformly distributed load, the sort of load for which we normally design in the floor or roof of a building, we start with a truss that consists of two ideally shaped members for uniform loadings, a parabolic arch above and a hanging chain below. We make the arch an exact mirror image of the chain. If the two are connected at all points by a very large number of ties, each will carry half the load, and the horizontal pushes and pulls will balance each other exactly, so that no horizontal thrust will be imparted to the supports. (17.47).

As expected, both the arch and the chain thicken as the depth of the truss is reduced and the horizontal forces grow (17.48). Ultimately, reaching the useful limiting case, the arch can become flat and still support itself and its half of the load (17.49). The chain, however, must retain some sag if it is to carry directly its portion of the load. The form we have arrived at is exactly the form taken by a *post-tensioned* concrete beam, in which tightly tensioned steel cables pull against the ends of a concrete beam, following a flat parabolic curve between (17.50).

We know from everyday experience, of course, that a beam can be much simpler than either of the types we have developed here. A length of wood of the appropriate depth and thickness does the trick quite nicely, without the need for fussing with chains or stone blocks (17.51). What is interesting about a plain beam of wood or steel, however, is how the forces of tension and compression operate within it. Analysis of the principal stresses in beams shows that a beam functions by means of both compressive stresses that follow lines similar to arches and tensile stresses that follow lines similar to hanging chains. The two sets of lines are mirror images of each other and are symmetrically arranged so that the horizontal pushes of the

17.47

17.48

17.49

17.51

Post-tensioned concrete beam   17.50

— — — tension
———— compression

17.52

17.53

17.54

"arches" are exactly balanced by the horizontal pulls of the "chains" (17.52). Notice how the lines bunch together at the top and bottom of the beam in the middle of the span—the tension and compression stresses are highest in these areas, and the material in these areas of a well-designed beam is fully tensioned and compressed to the safe working stress. In the rest of the beam, however, stress concentrations are lower. The material is not working to its full structural capacity and in this sense is being partially wasted. For this reason, a beam is not nearly as efficient a structural form as a hanging cable, an arch, or a truss is, in which most or all of the material is fully stressed. But a beam is compact and convenient to work with, exerts no external horizontal thrust, and easily produces flat ceilings and floors.

The lines of principal stress in a beam indicate another phenomenon that is of interest to designers. Notice that whenever a line of compression and a line of tension cross, they do so at right angles. If we examine a small block of material taken from one of these intersections, we see that it is compressed across one diagonal and pulled across the other (17.53). By breaking each of these forces into components parallel to the faces of our block and simplifying them, we see that the block is subjected to parallel but opposite forces on its four faces. Such a condition subjects the block to *shear stress*, just as the parallel but opposite forces exerted by the blades of a pair of scissors shear a sheet of paper. When we examine the diagram of the beam again, we see that shear stress is highest at the ends of the beam, where the lines of principal stress intersect at an angle of 45° to the horizontal, and progressively lower toward the middle of the beam. Thus a beam must be designed to resist not only heavy tensile and compressive stresses at its upper and lower faces in the middle of the span but also heavy shear stresses at the ends. Shear is seldom a problem in steel beams because steel is relatively strong in shear, but wood and concrete are weaker in shear, requiring special care in design and construction.

The part of a beam where compressive stresses are highest is also subject to buckling, like any structural device that carries compression. As one would expect, the longer and more slender the beam is, the higher the risk of buckling will be (17.54). Empirical formulas have been developed to predict this risk, and where a risk of buckling is present, either the beam must be made thicker, or lateral bracing must be provided, much as for a column. Such bracing can often be furnished conveniently by the floor or roof deck that is carried by the beam.

In beams, as in all spanning devices, it is important that we be able to predict how much the beam will *deflect* under its expected loading. Rather exact formulas have been developed for this pur-

17.55

pose. By knowing in advance what the *deflection* will be, we can design beams that are stiff enough to feel solid underfoot and that will not bend so much as to crack plaster ceilings affixed to them or to apply force to windows, partitions, and other building components beneath them that are not designed to carry major structural loads. We can also *camber* a beam—that is, we can build into it an upward curvature equal to the expected deflection under load, so that it will be flat when in use (17.55).

We use beams in many different ways. We have been discussing what is called a *simple span*, which bends downward under a gravity load. Frequently, a single, *continuous* beam is run across two or more adjacent spans, or is *cantilevered* beyond its supports at one or both ends (17.56). Such configurations introduce a bending in the

Deflection of continuous beam
(Greatly exaggerated)

17.56

No horizontal thrust

Horizontal thrust

Tie resists horizontal thrust

17.57

stirrups

hooks anchor rods to concrete

Reinforcement in simple concrete beam

17.58

stirrups

Reinforcement in continuous concrete beam

17.59

opposite direction over the supports. By efficiently stressing more of the beam material to its maximum, continuity of a beam across two or more spans generally allows the use of a smaller, less expensive beam than would have to be used if only simple spans were employed.

Beams are used on an incline as roof *rafters*. If a rafter is supported vertically at both its ends, it will not exert any horizontal thrust (17.57). If two rafters are set against each other without a center support, however, they will constitute a simple arch. Each thrusts the other horizontally, and so a tie or buttresses must be provided.

In *reinforced concrete* construction, most or all of the compressive forces are carried by the concrete, with round steel bars located where they can resist the tensile forces. Reinforcement against shear failure is provided by vertical *stirrups* of steel bars near the ends of the beam (17.58). For maximum economy, continuous spans are almost always used in concrete construction, with the heaviest concentrations of steel bars alternating in location between the bottoms and tops of the beams as the direction of bending changes. Wind and earthquake loadings can cause the directions of bending in the beams of a building to reverse, so in most cases at least some of the

176

One-way concrete joist system (ribbed slab)

One-way solid slab

Two-way concrete joist system (waffle slab)

Two-way flat plate

17.60

steel reinforcing bars run the full length of the beam at both the top and the bottom (17.59).

A concrete *slab* is a very broad, shallow, reinforced concrete beam (17.60). If a concrete slab spans between two parallel beams or walls, it is reinforced primarily in the direction of spanning and is termed a *one-way* slab. If a concrete slab spans between columns arranged in a more-or-less square pattern, it is reinforced in two directions (both north–south and east–west) and spans in two mutually perpendicular directions at the same time. This *two-way* slab needs less concrete and reinforcing steel to support a given load and is therefore used whenever possible. For longer spans in either one-way or two-way concrete slabs, further economies can be gained by leaving out much of the concrete between the reinforcing bars in the bottom of the slab, to form a *one-way concrete joist system* (also known as a *ribbed slab*) or a *two-way concrete joist system* (*waffle slab*).

For maximum economy of concrete and steel, slabs and beams are often post-tensioned rather than being merely reinforced. High-strength steel cables in plastic tubes are placed in the formwork, and the concrete is poured around them. After the concrete hardens, hydraulic jacks are used to tighten all the cables to very high stresses. Because the cables were given funicular curves at the time they were placed, they support the loads on the beams and slabs very efficiently (17.61). The concrete around them acts in compression to resist the horizontal pull of the cables.

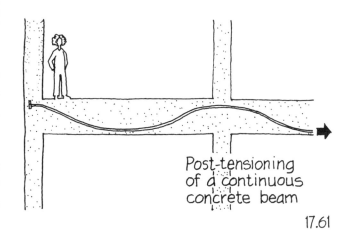

Post-tensioning of a continuous concrete beam

17.61

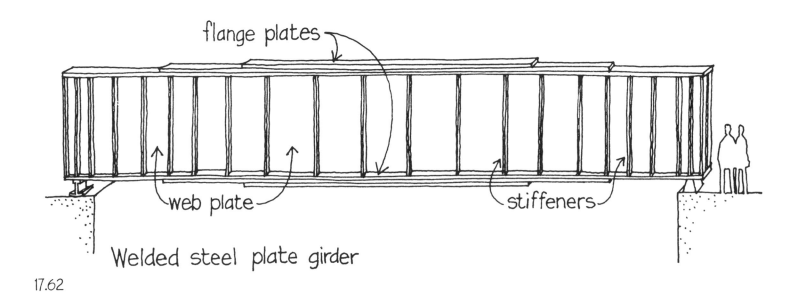

flange plates

web plate

stiffeners

Welded steel plate girder

17.62

Rigid frame

17.63

Large beams for heavy loads and long spans are often manufactured of concrete, steel, or laminated wood, in such a way that more material is provided where stresses are highest. A welded steel *plate girder*, for instance, has extra top and bottom plates to resist peak values of tension and compression at midspan, and extra vertical *stiffeners* to reinforce against shear at the ends (17.62).

A beam is not always straight. For longer spans, it is frequently advantageous to make a bent beam called a *rigid frame*, a combined column and beam with a stiff joint between (17.63). The joint (the point where the frame changes from vertical to sloping) carries very high stresses and is usually thickened to compensate. A rigid frame behaves like both a beam and an arch and must therefore be tied together at the base. This is usually done by means of a steel rod buried in the concrete floor slab.

Concrete folded plate

17.64

Concrete barrel shell

Rigid frames are capable of spans approaching those of trusses. Beams generally are restricted to shorter spans. The deeper the beam is, the longer the span can be, but beams become cumbersome and uneconomical to build at spans well below those that are easily constructed using lighter, more efficient structural forms.

If a flat plane of structural material, usually reinforced concrete, is folded or scalloped to increase its overall depth, it will be capable of spanning fairly long distances and will act in much the same manner as a deep beam does (17.64). The structural behavior of such forms is easily modeled by folding or scalloping a sheet of paper, supporting it across two books, and loading it with other sheets of paper or books.

Corbels

The *corbel* is a structural device composed of a number of stones or bricks, each of which acts as a small, stubby cantilever beam (17.65). For its stability, it depends on having the total leverage of the weight that bears on the inside portion of each block exceed the total leverage of the weight bearing on the projecting portion of the same block. The simple corbel is sometimes used to span window openings in walls or to form projecting brackets for the support of beams by bearing walls (17.66). It is frequently used in decorative brickwork. Translated into the third dimension as a linear corbeled vault, it was used by the Mayas and other ancient cultures to span narrow rooms (17.67). Its spanning capacity is the most limited of any structural form, however, because the heavy stone or brick of which it is built is weak in tension and because it uses large quantities of material, compared with other devices carrying equal loads over equal spans.

Corbel
17.65

17.66

Corbeled vault
17.67

179

Tholos
17.68

Trullo – Italy
17.69

Air-inflated

Air-supported

Air-supported

Air-supported

17.70

Considerably greater spans are possible, with somewhat more efficient use of material, if the simple corbel is rotated about its vertical centerline to form a *tholos* (17.68). The tholos employs more than just the corbel principle, however; each of its horizontal rings of stones or bricks acts as a full-circle horizontal arch to resist its own tendency to fall inward under the weight coming from above. Thus the tholos, unlike the other corbeled forms, does exert a thrust that must be resisted in its foundations or supporting walls, but it retains the advantage of all corbeled forms in that it can be erected without the use of temporary support or formwork, and it is superior to its corbeled cousins in its absence of need for a massive counterbalancing weight. It need be only one stone thick. In ancient Mycenaean tombs the tholos spans as much as 47 feet (14.3 m) while supporting a heavy load of earth from above. Spans of 10 to 20 feet (3 m to 6 m) are commonplace in other Mediterranean areas, particularly southern Italy, where the form is used for roofs (17.69).

Pneumatic Structures

A diverse group of spanning devices whose potential has only begun to be tapped are the *fluid-filled structures*. Air is the fluid most widely used, and the two categories most often constructed are *air-inflated structures* and *air-supported structures* (17.70). In air-inflated structures, structural members are made of fabric tubes or lenses braced against buckling by internal air pressure. The fabric itself carries the structural load. Only relatively short spans are possible before buckling failure occurs in the thin fabric of air-inflated structures. Air-supported structures, on the other hand, are theoretically capable of unlimited spans because each square foot of fabric is supported directly by air pressure against its under surface. Air-supported structures are often used to cover tennis courts and stadiums. The only stress in the fabric is the tensile stress, usually low, induced by the slight excess of air pressure needed to keep the fabric taut. Air-supported structures pose a unique foundation problem: Each must be held *down* to the ground by a total force equal to the product of its internal air pressure and its ground area.

Lateral Support

So far we have discussed only the basic devices for supporting vertical loads and for supporting loads over horizontal spans. In order to support the loads generated by even a simple building, a number of such structural devices must be combined to support the surfaces of the building, gather these surface loads and conduct them to columns or bearing walls, and then carry these vertical loads to the earth, to which they will be transferred by a system of foundations. In addition, we must provide devices to maintain the entire structure in a vertical position against the lateral forces of wind, earthquake, and compressive buckling that would otherwise topple it.

We can provide lateral support in three ways (17.71). One is to make the joints between columns and beams very rigid. This is easily and economically done in concrete building frames. In steel frames it is a little harder, usually requiring the connections to be welded. In wood frames, rigid joints are very hard to make because of the difficulty of making secure fastenings near the ends of pieces of wood.

Another way of providing lateral support is to insert diagonal bracing in various locations around the building, effectively creating vertical trusses within the frame. A third method, akin to diagonal bracing, is to use *shear panels* of steel, plywood, or concrete instead of braces. Both diagonal bracing and shear panels are easily constructed in wood frames, as well as in steel or concrete. Masonry walls are also good shear panels, especially if reinforced with steel bars.

With all three methods of providing lateral support, the support devices (rigid joints, diagonal bracing, or shear panels) must operate in both the north–south and east–west directions of the building, and they must be arranged, as seen from above, in a more-or-less symmetrical fashion about the centroid of the building. The floor and roof planes of a building also play a role in its lateral stability; they must be provided with braces or shear panels, the latter often being provided automatically by the material of the structural floor or roof deck (17.72). In any case, lateral loads on buildings must be carefully computed, and devices of sufficient strength provided to resist them, just as vertical loads are computed and resisted with the greatest of care.

Foundations

Where the columns or bearing walls of a building meet the ground, the vertical and horizontal loads of the building must be transmitted safely into the earth. In order to do this, some sort of transitional

17.71

Roof and floor transmit load to bracing

Wind load on wall panel

Bracing transmits load to ground

17.72

Building load

Steel column

Steel base plate

Soil pressure

17.73

Isolated footings

Strip footing

Grade beam

Mat foundation

17.74

device usually is required. A steel column, for example, carries its load at a stress of some hundreds of tons per square foot (tens of megapascals). No soil or rock is capable of carrying such an intense pressure, and if the column were allowed to rest directly on the ground, it would sink immediately and uncontrollably, carrying a portion of the building with it. If a steel column carries its load at a stress of 500 tons per square foot (47.88 MPa) and it must rest on soil that can carry safely only 10 tons per square foot (0.958 MPa), we must insert between the column and the soil a block that is

$$\frac{500 \text{ tons}/\text{ft}^2}{10 \text{ tons}/\text{ft}^2}$$

or fifty times as large in the horizontal plane as the cross-section of the column.

In SI units, $\dfrac{47.88 \text{ MPa}}{0.958 \text{ MPa}} = 50$

If the column is one-quarter square foot (0.023 m²) in cross-sectional area, the block must be 50 × ¼, or 12.5 square feet in area (50 × 0.023 m² = 1.15 m²). A block of concrete just over 3.5 feet square (1.07 m × 1.07 m) will do the job (17.73). This block is called a *spread footing*. Interestingly, this example requires a second sort of spread footing as well, because the concrete, although it is much stronger than the soil, is also incapable of directly sustaining the intense pressure of the steel column. A heavy steel *base plate* must be inserted between the column and the concrete footing to spread the load. The size of the base plate is computed in the same general manner as is the size of the footing itself.

A spread footing can be either an *isolated footing*, as in the preceding example, or a continuous *strip footing*, in which it is used under a concrete or masonry wall (17.74). A wall can be supported on isolated footings, however, if a *grade beam* is provided to spread the wall load among them. In soils of intermediate to low bearing capacity, isolated spread footings may be so large that it is easier and more economical to pour a single continuous reinforced-concrete *mat foundation* under the entire building than to construct the individual footings with only small spaces between them.

Sometimes a suitably firm stratum of soil or rock is buried beneath a considerable depth of soft soil that is incapable of supporting a building on spread footings. In this case, it often is possible to bore a hole down through the soft soil to reach the firm soil, to flare out the hole just above the firm stratum to give a larger bearing area, and to fill the entire hole with concrete. A column or grade beam may then be rested on top of this concrete *caisson* (17.75). An alternative possibility is to use a pile driver to pound a length of steel or precast concrete vertically through the soft soil until its lower end rests solidly on the hard stratum. This foundation device is known as an *end-bearing pile*.

If firm soil or rock is not within reach, as, for example, in filled swampland or waterfront areas, *friction piles* are commonly employed, made of wood, steel, or precast concrete. Each pile is pounded endwise into the soft soil until the friction of the soil against the sides of the pile reaches the point that the pile can sustain a load. Piles are usually driven in clusters, with a concrete cap over the top of the cluster to distribute the column load among the individual piles. If a column brings a load of 250 tons (227,000 kg) to earth and each pile can safely support 10 tons (9070 kg), a cluster of 25 piles will be needed. Five rows of 5 piles each would be appropriate.

A building in soft soil may sometimes be supported on a *floating foundation*, in which the weight of the building is balanced by the weight of soil removed during excavation. One story of excavated soil weighs about the same as five to eight stories of building, so, for example, a ten- to sixteen-story building can "float" on a two-story basement. The stress on the soil beneath the building is about the same after the building is built as it was before (17.76).

Sometimes a foundation must be designed to resist an upward force rather than a downward one, especially for the anchoring of air-supported or suspension structures. If suitable rock is available, one or more holes can be drilled, and cables or rods can be cemented into the holes with suitable adhesives. In softer soils, a piece of concrete must be buried so that the weight of the concrete plus the weight of the soil above it total more than the expected uplift. For temporary structures, heavy containers of sand or water may be placed on the surface of the ground as anchors, or small metal screw-anchors or stakes can be driven into the soil.

Further Reading

Rowland Mainstone. *Developments in Structural Form*. Cambridge, Mass., M.I.T. Press, 1975.

Mario Salvadori. *Why Buildings Stand Up*. New York, Norton, 1980.

Mario Salvadori, with Robert Heller. *Structure in Architecture*. Englewood Cliffs, N.J., Prentice-Hall, 1963.

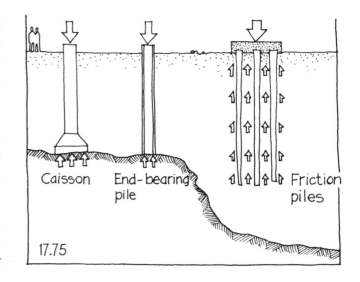

Caisson   End-bearing pile   Friction piles

17.75

wt. of excavated soil = wt. of building

Floating foundation

17.76

18
Providing for Building Movement

A building, even a seemingly solid, massive one, is never at rest. Its motions are usually very small ones, undetectable by the unaided eye, but most of them are of virtually irresistible force and would tear the building to pieces if not provided for in some way. The surfaces of the building would crack, twist, and tear; components would pull apart or be crushed together. At best, the building would become merely unsightly. At worst, it would become leaky and structurally unsound.

Building movement begins with the placement of the very first materials in the early stages of construction. The soil settles progressively under the foundations as the weight of the building grows. Most materials that are put in place wet—concrete, mortar, terrazzo, stucco—shrink slightly and tend to crack as they harden, whereas gypsum plaster expands slightly and pushes against adjoining materials. Lumber that is not sufficiently dry shrinks after installation. Beams, columns, and other structural elements, regardless of the material of which they are made, deflect gradually as their superimposed loads accumulate during construction. Further deflections, variable in magnitude, occur during the life of the building under shifting live loadings, including wind and seismic forces, and in some structural materials, most notably wood and concrete, a long-term sagging process known as *creep* takes place over a period of years.

Back-and-forth movements caused by thermal and moisture effects occur constantly. A building grows measurably larger in warm weather and smaller in cold weather. A roof, heated by the sun, grows larger in the middle of the day while the cooler walls below stay the same size. At night, the roof cools and shrinks. In subfreezing temperatures, the formation of ice from water within or beneath a building can crack materials or lift foundations by its expansion. Under humid conditions, wood and wood products expand, often quite noticeably, and when the air dries out, as in a heated building in winter, they contract and sometimes crack. Wood furniture that is inadequately glued often pulls apart at the joints during the peak of the heating season. Wooden doors and windows sometimes stick immovably in their frames in humid weather but fit too loosely under dry conditions. Where building components of different materials are juxtaposed, they are likely to move quite differently from one another. An aluminum window frame grows significantly smaller in cold weather, but the wood building frame in which it is mounted is little affected by temperature differences. A prolonged damp spell, however, expands the wood frame while leaving the aluminum window unchanged.

Certain unwanted chemical reactions can also cause buildings to move. As a metal corrodes, it also expands. Lime mortar or plaster that has not been fully hydrated before application will later expand as it incorporates moisture from the air into its crystalline structure. Portland cement reacts chemically with some minerals that may be inadvertently mixed with it when making concrete, causing destructive expansion. Chemically caused cracking, heaving, and spalling of masonry and concrete are occasionally seen in buildings, and the jamming together of metal components by corrosion is quite common. These conditions can be remedied only by carefully controlling the quality of the materials used during construction and by completely protecting corrosion-prone metals with appropriate coatings.

Control Joints and Expansion Joints

To accomodate the inevitable movements of a building without destructive results, designers take precautionary steps during the design process and throughout construction. The basic principle they follow is to provide the building and its components with the space and means to move without causing damage. The regularly spaced transverse cracks in an ordinary concrete sidewalk are a good example (18.1). They form intentional lines of structural weakness, created at the time the concrete is laid, in the knowledge that the concrete will shrink as it hardens and that the sidewalk will further shrink and expand as temperatures change and be heaved up here and there by frost or tree roots. If the cracks were not provided, these forces would form their own cracks in the sidewalk in a thousand different directions. The intentionally provided cracks, called *control joints*, absorb these forces in an orderly pattern and allow a

18.1

185

certain amount of tilting and heaving to take place without breaking the individual rectangles of concrete. Control joints are also provided at about 20-foot (6-m) intervals in concrete floor slabs that lie on the ground and in all concrete walls within buildings. They may be made with a special grooving trowel while the concrete is still wet, or, for a neater appearance, cut with an abrasive-bladed power saw after the concrete has begun to harden. Half the steel reinforcing bars are interrupted at each control joint to create a line of weakness that encourages cracks to form there rather than elsewhere (18.2).

Concrete block walls have a tendency to shrink and crack, and so they need control joints at intervals of 20 to 40 feet (6 to 12 meters), depending on the moisture content of the blocks at the time they are put in place (18.3). Exterior stucco walls also are prone to shrinkage, and control joints are recommended at spacings of about 10 feet (3m) to control cracking.

Interior wall and ceiling surfaces usually do not need control joints because they are made of gypsum plaster, which expands slightly as it hardens, rather than shrinking. But the expansion of plaster can cause compression cracking, and large plaster surfaces

Sealant

Discontinue half of steel at joint

Control joints in concrete wall and slab on ground

18.2

sealant

Control joint in concrete block wall

18.3

can also crack because of movement in the underlying structure. Thus long plaster walls and large ceilings should be subdivided every 30 feet (9 m) or so with *expansion joints.* In a typical expansion joint detail for plaster, the metal lath is discontinued at the line of the expansion joint, thereby creating a line of weakness that encourages movement in the wall along that line and not elsewhere. The flexible metal "bellows" strip gives a neat appearance to the joint and keeps the adjoining plaster surfaces aligned despite whatever movement may occur (18.4).

Another material that tends to expand slightly in a building is brickwork. Bricks are completely dry when they leave the kiln in which they are manufactured. In subsequent months and years they absorb small amounts of moisture and expand slightly. Expansion joints are recommended at maximum intervals of 200 feet (60 m) in brick walls (18.5). Exterior aluminum walls of buildings also need to have expansion joints to allow the metal components to expand as they are heated by the sun.

Wherever two materials with different movement characteristics come together in a building or wherever old and new construction come together in a remodeled project, it is wise to provide an *abutment joint.* A wood partition expands and contracts by relatively large amounts with changes in humidity, whereas a brick wall moves very little. Where they adjoin, therefore, a broad abutment joint filled with synthetic rubber sealant allows the two to move independently (18.6). Other typical locations for abutment joints are where a plaster wall abuts a stone foreplace, a wooden window abuts a concrete column, or the brick wall of a new addition meets the brick wall of the original building.

Detail of expansion joint in plaster
18.4

Expansion joint
in brick wall
18.5

An example of an abutment joint
18.6

Steel channel track is fastened only to ceiling

Elastic sealant

Vertical steel framing members slide freely in track

Wall surfaces are fastened only to vertical framing members

18.8

Structure-enclosure joint at top of nonloadbearing partition

Flexible rod anchors at top allow frame to deflect without applying load to panels

Rigid anchors at bottom support weight of panels

Structure-enclosure joint: Curtain wall panels

18.7

Structure-Enclosure Joints

Most large buildings today are not supported by their walls; quite the opposite is the case. That is, the interior and exterior walls of a building are supported by its structural frame. A typical large building is enclosed with *curtain wall* panels, and its interior is subdivided with *nonloadbearing partitions*. Neither the curtain wall panels nor the partitions are strong enough to support the load of the building's floors and roof, so it is important to provide *structure-enclosure joints* that ensure that the frame of the building and its walls can move completely independently of one another. A typical curtain wall panel is rigidly attached to the frame of the building at the bottom but is flexibly attached at the top by means of a flexing or sliding connection (18.7). This allows the floor beams of the building to deflect without applying any force to the panel. Inside the building, the tops of partitions are constructed with a slip joint in the wall framing and flexible sealant joints at the top edges of the wall surfaces (18.8). These allow the floor above to sag under load without applying any force to the top of the partition.

188

Shaded planes indicate locations of building separation joints

200' max. (60m)

18.9

Building Separation Joints

A building that is large in horizontal extent is not able to respond as a unit to foundation settlement, seismic distress, and thermal expansion and contraction because the accumulation of such forces becomes too great over the long dimensions of the building, resulting in destructive cracking and tearing. Thus a large building needs to be divided into smaller buildings, each of which can act as a compact, rigid unit in response to such movements. These divisions are best made at junctions between low and high portions of a building, junctions between wings, and other locations that constitute planes of geometric weakness (18.9). At each such plane, the structural frame of the building is interrupted completely so as to create a structurally independent building, with its own columns and foundations, on each side of the plane. The two buildings are separated by a gap of several inches to allow plenty of room for movement. The gap is closed by joint covers that are designed to allow the roof, walls, and floors to function normally despite any movement that may occur (18.10). At the roof, a rubber bellows keeps water out. At the walls and floors, metal plates and rubber gaskets are combined to create smooth, attractive surfaces that can adjust to movement without damage. These joints are commonly but imprecisely referred to as expansion joints. The term *building separation joint* is more descriptive, indicating that the building has been separated into independent parts along the plane of the joint. One part can

Building separation joint
18.10

189

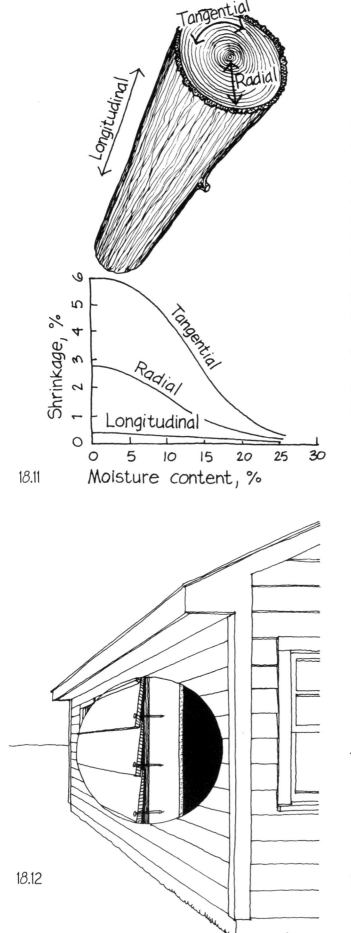

18.11

settle without affecting the other, and roof and wall surfaces are free to expand and contract without harm in response to changing weather conditions.

Providing for Movement in Wood

Of those materials, that are susceptible to moisture-induced movement, wood is the extreme example. The situation is aggravated by the large difference between movement parallel to the grain of the wood, which is slight, and movement perpendicular to the grain, which is quite considerable (18.11). The problem can be reduced by using lumber whose moisture content, through careful seasoning, has been brought to equilibrium with air of average humidity and by protecting the finished construction from extremes of moisture or dry heat. Care must then be taken to minimize the remaining effects of cross-grain movement.

Each horizontal wood siding board is nailed onto a house with a single row of nails located near its lower edge. Its upper edge is held loosely by the lower edge of the board above. This leaves each board free to expand and contract across its width as it gains and loses moisture (18.12).

Very old wooden doors were often made of vertical boards fas-

18.12

18.13

Panel   Stile

tened together side by side. These doors changed so much in width with changes in moisture content that they often jammed in their frames in the humid summer months but rattled loosely in the dry winter. The traditional wood-panel door is a good example of a form that evolved directly in response to this problem with the panels slip-jointed into the stiles and rails to allow for internal movement. Moisture-induced changes in the width of the door are limited to the changes in the widths of the two outside stiles, which total only about a third as much as the width change in a door made up entirely of vertical boards (18.13).

The floor structure of an ordinary wood-frame house, in which the wood grain runs horizontally, shrinks by a half-inch or so (about 13 mm) in height as the wood framing dries out during the first heating season. The walls of the house change height very little between one floor and the next because most of the height of a wall is made up of lumber whose grain runs vertically. Thus it is important when framing a house, especially one that has unusual spaces and forms, to put walls and floors together in a way that maintains the same amount of horizontal-grain wood from one side of the house to the other at each story (18.14). If this is not done, floors will

Correct: Both sides of building will shrink by equal amounts

Incorrect: Left side of building will shrink much more than right side

18.14

slope and plaster will crack because of the different amounts of vertical shrinkage between one area of the house and another. Where plywood exterior wall sheathing passes over the edge of a floor structure, it is wise to leave a horizontal gap of about half an inch (13 mm) in the plywood to allow the floor to shrink. On the interior of the a house, plaster does not usually pass vertically over the edge of a floor structure, but if it does, it should be interrupted with a horizontal control joint.

Further Reading

Edward Allen. *Architectural Detailing: Function, Constructibility, Aesthetics.* New York, Wiley, 1993, pp. 75–94.

19
Controlling Fire

Uncontrolled fire is a uniquely deadly and destructive occurence in human civilization. A forest fire or prairie fire is dangerous enough, but when a fire breaks out in a building, the danger is compounded simultaneously in a number of ways:

- A building supplies a concentration of fuel for an accidental fire. A wooden building is itself a source of fuel, but even a concrete or steel building is usually loaded with furniture, paper, carpets, and combustible building materials such as wood paneling and plastic insulating materials. Oil, gas, gasoline, paints, rubber, chemicals, and other highly flammable materials are often present in buildings.
- A building supplies many potential sources of ignition for accidental fires. Defective furnaces, spark-throwing fireplaces, leaky chimneys, unattended stoves, loose electrical connections, overloaded electrical wiring, and carelessly handled matches and cigarettes are but a few of the means by which a building or its contents may be set on fire.
- A building, stovelike, contains a fire and encourages its growth by concentrating its heat and flammable combustion gases. Where vertical passages through the building are open to the fire, strong convective drafts fan the flames, and new sources of fuel are made available to the fire in the upper reaches of the structure.
- A building holds dense concentrations of people, subjects them to the heat and gases generated by a fire, and restricts their escape (19.1). If a campfire gets out of control in a wilderness, few people are likely to be present, and there are a multitude of directions in which to escape. But if a fire of similar magnitude starts in a

19.1

school, a theater, a department store, or an office building, thousands of people may be within reach of the fire, and only a few escape routes are available.

- A building also serves as a barrier to firefighters. Whereas a wilderness fire can be fought from all sides. and even from the air, a fire in a tall building may be forty stories above the street, accessible only by stairway. Low, broad buildings can put an interior fire beyond the reach of fire hoses. Building fires expose firefighters to excessive heat, poisonous gases, explosions, dangerous heights, toppling walls, and collapsing floors and roofs.

These diverse effects of buildings on fire combine to produce a gruesome statistic. Twelve thousand American lives are lost in building fires each year, and 300,000 people are injured, often very seriously and painfully. Property losses due to building fires in the United States are measured in billions of dollars.

Fire begins when a supply of fuel and a supply of oxygen are brought together at a sufficiently high temperature to initiate combustion. As the fire burns, it consumes the fuel and oxygen, giving off various gases, particulate emissions, and large quantities of heat. Depending on the available fuel, the combustion gases may include carbon dioxide, carbon monoxide, hydrogen cyanide, hydrogen sulfide, and sulfur dioxide. Any of these is toxic if inhaled in sufficient concentrations.

People may be injured by fire in several ways. They may be burned, particularly in the lungs and respiratory passages by exposure to hot air, or on the skin by severe thermal radiation. They may be suffocated by oxygen-depleted air or poisoned by toxic combustion gases. Panic often contributes to loss of life in building fires; people may make irrational decisions with regard to personal safety (such as running back into a burning building to save personal effects), and they may injure one another by pushing, crowding, or trampling as they rush to escape. The most prevalent cause of death in building fires is suffocation or carbon monoxide poisoning that overtakes the victim after he or she has failed to find a means of escape because of dense accumulations of smoke.

In designing against fire in buildings, our first aim is to reduce the risk of human injury or death to as low a level as possible. Simultaneously, we wish to minimize fire damage to the building and its contents and to prevent the fire from spreading to neighboring buildings. We would like, of course, to eliminate *all* risk of fire, but contrary to popular myth, there can never be such a thing as a "fireproof" building. Steel obviously does not burn, but it does lose most of its structural strength and sag or collapse at a temperature that is well below its own melting point and the sustained temperatures frequently reached by ordinary building fires (19.2). Concrete is more resistant to fire than steel is, but its fundamental crystalline structure progressively disintegrates when exposed to fire, and if the fire lasts long enough, serious structural damage will result. Brick and tile, which are products of intense heat in the kiln, are not themselves weakened by fire, but their mortar joints are subject to disintegration, thereby weakening the entire masonry construction. Therefore our buildings cannot be made perfectly resistant to fire, but nevertheless we have developed a rather effective and rapidly improving arsenal of weapons to protect life and property against building fires.

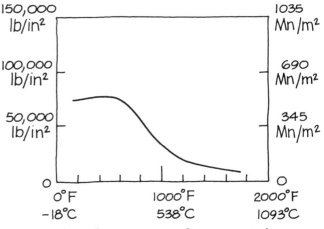

Average tensile strength of structural steel at various temperatures

19.2

Keeping Fire from Starting

A natural first step in building fire protection is to prevent fires from starting. Building codes and zoning ordinances regulate the combustibility of the materials with which buildings may be built in different areas of a city, as well as the conditions under which flammable and explosive substances may be stored in or near buildings. Proper building maintenance ensures that rubbish does not pile up anywhere, and firefighters and fire underwriters (the insurers of the building) inspect buildings periodically to see whether any unsafe concentrations of combustible matter have accumulated in them. Through these same means—codes, zoning ordinances, maintenance, and inspection—potential sources of accidental ignition are kept in safe working order. Heating devices, chimneys, electrical systems, electrical devices, and hazardous industrial processes are especially stringently controlled. Smoking is prohibited by law in many kinds of places, such as gasoline stations, certain types of industrial plants, and auditoriums.

Lightning can damage and set fire to tall buildings or buildings in exposed locations. A lightning bolt is the instantaneous release of a very high electrical potential between a rain cloud and the earth. Pointed metal rods connected directly to the earth through heavy electrical conductors furnish lightning protection for buildings (19.3). By leaking a charge off the points, the rods are often able to neutralize the electrical charges of clouds before lightning bolts form. But if lightning strikes the building, the rods and conductors offer a path to the ground of considerably less resistance than the building itself and thus provide a high degree of protection.

19.3

Keeping Fire from Spreading

Compartmentation of a building is designed to prevent the spread of fire, smoke, and heat beyond a restricted area of the building should

19.5

19.4

Fire walls

Unenclosed shaft: hot gases spread fire to higher floors

Enclosed shaft: fire is contained

19.6

a fire break out. Even on the scale of a house, a fire-resistant plaster wall and a solid wood door are required between an attached garage (where gasoline leaks pose a potential fire hazard) and the dwelling. In rowhouses, fire-resistant walls must be provided between dwellings. (19.4).

In larger buildings, compartmentation becomes increasingly important, both to protect the larger numbers of people inside and to prevent the unchecked spread of fire by hot combustion gases. Stairways and corridors used as escape routes must be isolated from the rest of the building by fire-resistant walls (usually of masonry, plaster, or concrete) and self-closing fire-resistant doors (usually of steel facings with an incombustible mineral core) (19.5). Fire-resistant walls and doors also are required as separations between different types of functions taking place in the same building. A boiler room, for example, must be separated in this manner from the rest of a building so as to contain any fire that might start there and prevent it from spreading. A woodworking shop or dry cleaning establishment must be separated from the remainder of a building that it shares with other functions.

Open vertical shafts of any kind, whether for stairs, elevators, ductwork, electrical wiring, or piping, must be enclosed with fire-resistant walls and self-closing fire-resistant doors at each floor, to prevent the convection of fire and combustion products through the building (19.6). The only exceptions to this rule are vertical *atriums*. Building codes define an atrium as a roofed, inhabited, multistory open space contained in a building. Atriums are commonly used in shopping arcades, hotels, and office buildings. To avoid the spread of fire through these vertical spaces, designers must comply with a number of building-code provisions: Minimum atrium widths of 20 to 48 feet (6 to 15 m) are required. The balconies around an atrium may be open to it, but surrounding rooms must be isolated from the

196

Vents normally closed

Curtain boards

Automatic sprinklers extinguish fire

19.7

Self-opening vent

Fly loft

Fire-resistant curtain

Stage

19.8

balconies and atrium by fire-resistant walls. An exception is made to this enclosure requirement for any three floors of the building that the designer may choose, allowing lobby spaces on several floors to be continuous with the atrium. The entire building that contains the atrium must be protected by sprinklers. And the atrium must be provided with a system of fans that will operate automatically in case of fire to bring fresh air into the space at ground level and exhaust smoke at the ceiling level.

Buildings with a large horizontal spread must be subdivided into smaller areas by means of fire-resistant walls and doors. In large single-story factories or warehouses where this is not practical, incombustible *curtain boards* must be hung from the roof to catch and contain the rising hot gases from a fire and a self-opening roof vent must be provided in each compartment thus formed to allow the hot gases to escape before they can spread the fire (19.7). The roof vent doors are held closed against springs by a *fusible link* of low-melting-point metal that releases them to open in case of a buildup of heat.

In theaters, where the backstage area is often filled with combustible scenery and temporary electrical wiring, the audience must be protected by a fire-resistant curtain held rolled up above the proscenium. If a fire breaks out, the curtain will drop, sealing off the stage from the audience. A large self-opening vent in the roof of the fly loft relieves the heat and smoke in the backstage area (19.8).

197

Fire-resistant roof

Parapet

Fire-resistant wall

Wired glass

19.9

Flame barrier

No spandrel

Spandrel resists upward fire spread

Spread of Fire Up the Face of a Building

19.10

UL

SODA-ACID FIRE EXTINGUISHER

19.11

Fusible link

Cap

Deflector

Orifice

19.12

Fire-resistant walls also are necessary on the exteriors of many buildings. The type of materials allowed in these walls and the permissible extent and treatment of windows and doors are governed by the proximity of each wall to the walls of neighboring buildings. If two buildings are within a certain minimum distance, each must have a *parapet*, a fire-resistant wall that projects a distance above the roof in order to prevent fire from leaping from one roof to the next (19.9). The fire-resistive qualities of roof materials are also regulated by law in urban areas, to prevent easy ignition of a roof by burning fragments thrown by a fire in an adjacent building. Wired glass, which holds together against flame for a considerable period of time, is usually required in windows that face a nearby structure. In multistory buildings, where fire on a lower floor can spread to upper floors by crawling up the face of the building floor by floor, two alternatives are open to the designer. A fire-resistant *spandrel* at least 3 feet (914 mm) high may be provided, or else a horizontally projecting *flame barrier*, also made of fire-resistant materials, at least 30 inches (762 mm) wide (19.10).

Extinguishing Incipient Fires

Rapidly quenching a small fire before it can grow large also is an effective way of preventing its spread. Such "first-aid" devices as portable extinguishers and fixed hose reels that can be used by building occupants help put out many small building fires before they can spread. The provision and clear identification of these devices are

198

Second floor sprinklers

Branch shutoff valve

Reserve tank

First floor sprinklers

Siamese connection

One-way flow valves prevent water loss if pressure fails in main or pumper truck

Water flow triggers alarm

Main shutoff valve

City water main

One or two pumper trucks can supply system via siamese connection

FIRE DEPARTMENT

Each sprinkler head protects 90 to 200 square feet of floor area (8 to 19 m²)

Typical Sprinkler Installation

19.13

required by law (19.11). More reliable and effective are *automatic sprinkler systems*, in which each sprinkler head is controlled by a plug or link of fusible metal that melts at a temperature of about 150°F (65°C) (19.12, 19.13). So efficient is the resulting spray of water in extinguishing a fire that rarely do more than one or two sprinkler heads have to discharge before the fire is put out. Sprinkler systems are costly to install, but the initial expense is often balanced by cost savings that accrue to the building owner because of the presence of sprinklers. Building codes commonly allow a sprinklered building several important concessions:

- Greater distances between exits are permitted in sprinklered buildings, which may have the effect of eliminating one or more stairways from a large building.

- Larger floor areas are permitted between fire separations in sprinklered buildings, which may result in the elimination of some fire-resistant walls and doors.
- Larger overall building areas and greater overall heights are permitted for sprinklered buildings.
- A lesser degree of fire protection may be permitted on some structural elements of a sprinklered building.
- Larger amounts of combustible building materials may be incorporated into a sprinklered building.

In addition to these code concessions, fire insurance rates are much lower for sprinklered buildings. Most fire underwriters refuse to insure a high-hazard building that has no sprinkler system.

For the occasional building in which sprinkler water would cause irreparable damage to the building contents—a library, a museum, an art gallery—analogous but more expensive systems are available to discharge inert gases or powders onto the flames. Nonwater systems also are useful in areas such as commercial kitchens where grease fires or other types of fires that cannot be extinguished by water may break out.

Protecting Human Lives

The most important function that we ask of a building in case of fire is that it let people reach safety quickly. An alarm system must alert them immediately to the presence of fire. Manually operated alarm boxes must be provided and identified at frequent intervals in a building. Automatic alarm systems, which sense smoke, heat, flame, or the ionization products of combustion, are becoming in-

Large rooms require two or more doors

Enclosed stairway

Elevators do not count as required exits

Enclosed stairway

Dead-end corridors restricted to 20' max. length (6m)

Enclosed stairway

Stairways must exit directly to outdoors

19.14

creasingly common and are now required by law in dwellings to combat the high percentage of fire deaths that occur while people are asleep. In some cases, besides setting off warning devices in a building, alarm systems are connected directly to fire department switchboards to avoid delay in summoning help.

Rapid, well-protected escape on foot to the outdoors is the best life-safety strategy for able-bodied people. In any building, a person emerging from a room must have two escape routes available in two different directions, so if one route is involved in fire, the other may still be used (19.14). A maximum permissible distance from the door of any room to the farthest protected exit is specified; it is usually 150 to 200 feet (40 m to 60 m). Illuminated exit signs must identify these routes, and these signs, together with sufficient emergency lights to illuminate the corridors and stairs, must be connected to a battery system that will energize them automatically if the building's regular lighting system fails (19.15). The corridors and stairs of each escape route must be protected from fire and smoke by fire-resistant partitions and self-closing doors. (The old, familiar, outdoor iron fire escape is no longer legal in new buildings.) The doors along an escape route may not lock against persons exiting from the building, and they all must open in the direction of travel from indoors to outdoors, to prevent possible interference with the flow of escapees. Exit doors in buildings that hold large numbers of people, particularly schools, theaters, and athletic assembly buildings, must be provided with *panic hardware* that opens the door automatically upon pressure from within. Revolving doors are made to fold outward and provide two unrestricted exitways if people try to turn the door in opposite directions at the same time (19.16). Exit stairs must

Exit sign and emergency lighting must be on independent, secure power supply

Glass in fire-resistant doors must be wired glass, and limited in area

Panic bar

19.15

19.16

Doors swing in direction of exit path

Lighting

44" min. (1120 mm)

Comfortable, consistent tread and riser proportions

Rail ends turn in

Landing as wide as stair

Emergency lighting

19.17

Horizontal exit →

← Fire resistant wall and fire doors

19.18

be comfortably and consistently proportioned to prevent stumbling, and they may not have excessive numbers of risers between landings (19.17). Stair landings may not be narrower than the stairs that lead into them. Stair railings may not have projecting ends that might catch clothing. Nothing may be stored in exit corridors or stairs. The widths of exit corridors, doors, and stairs, furthermore, must be determined in accordance with building-code formulas ensuring that they are adequate to allow the unencumbered escape of the maximum expected population of the building within a short period of time.

Not all occupants of buildings are able to escape by the means just described. Small children often cannot read exit signs and make rational decisions about how to escape. Prisoners are not free to leave their prisons. Bedridden patients in health care facilities can-

2-way communications unit and instructions

Area of Rescue Assistance

Illuminated sign

Exit

Exit stairway

Vestibule area of refuge

19.19

not move on their own. Many disabled people cannot negotiate stairs. For these persons, *areas of refuge* must be provided within many types of buildings. An area of refuge must be adjacent to a protected exit stairway, protected from smoke, and provided with communications devices that permit those taking refuge to summon firefighters to rescue them. A *horizontal exit* is often used to provide an area of refuge; it is simply a fire-resistant wall and doors that subdivide a floor of a building into separate areas that are, in effect, separate buildings (19.18). Escape from a fire on one side of the wall requires only horizontal movement through self-closing fire doors to the other side of the wall. Horizontal exits can provide refuge for very large building populations in health care, detention, and educational buildings. Smaller areas of refuge for the small populations of disabled people that are normally present in buildings can be provided by smoke-protected vestibules adjacent to exit stairways (19.19) or by enlarged landings in the stairways themselves.

These design guidelines for exitways are comprehensive. But if they seem excessive, one need only remember that each was drawn up to prevent the recurrence of past tragedies.

Protecting the Structure of the Building

Protecting the structural integrity of a building from the effects of fire is crucial to maintaining the value of the building, and is even more crucial to protecting its occupants, firefighters, and neighboring buildings. The taller the building is, the more necessary it is that neither the building nor any piece of it be allowed to fall. Even though we do not possess any "fireproof" materials for this, we do have materials sufficiently resistant to fire to help protect the building structure. Among these are fired-clay products—brick and tile—that are chemically unaffected by fire; a variety of mineral fibers that also are unaffected by fire; and concrete and plaster, both of which are composed in large part of hydrated crystals that absorb very large quantities of heat in order to evaporate their water of crystallization during a fire and thus offer a considerable barrier to fire during their slow disintegration. A more recent development in structural fire protection is the *intumescent coating*, available as either a paint or a thick trowel-on compound. When exposed to heat, the coating softens, releasing bubbles of gas that expand the coating to form an insulating layer over the substrate material.

When using any of these materials, the idea is to prevent the structural collapse of a building within the time that a fire will normally run its course or at least to delay collapse in low buildings until all occupants have escaped and firefighters have had a reasonable chance to save the building. Plaster or plasterboard walls and ceilings give wooden residences roughly a half-hour of protection from collapse. Low industrial and commercial buildings may be built of unprotected steel, in which case they are classified as "incombustible." In a hot fire their collapse would be rapid but unlikely before the occupants could get out through the easy escape routes. "Slow-burning" construction of timbers at least eight inches (200 mm) in minimum dimension lasts considerably longer in a fire than does unprotected steel. Building codes therefore recognize heavy timber construction as a special category suitable for buildings a story or two taller than would be permitted for unprotected steel. The ends of wooden beams and joists must be *fire-cut* wherever they

Square-cut beam   Fire-cut beam
19.20

Concrete

Lath and plaster

Suspended plaster ceiling

Spray-on insulation above non-fire-resistant ceiling

Fire protection of steel beams

19.21

enter masonry walls, in order to prevent the wall's toppling should the beams eventually burn through (19.20).

Most large buildings are constructed of either reinforced concrete or protected steel. The steel reinforcing bars in concrete beams and columns are buried a specified distance within the mass of concrete so as to be protected by its thermal capacity and natural fire-resistive properties. Steel beams and columns were first protected by embedding them in solid brick masonry and later by encasing them entirely in poured concrete. These expedients, though effective, were relatively expensive and added substantially to the structural load and structural cost of a building. Present-day alternatives include encasing steel members in lath and plaster, surrounding them with multiple layers of gypsum board, spraying lightweight mineral insulations in cementitious binders on them, and attaching preformed slabs of mineral insulation to them (19.21, 19.22). Steel beams and columns on the exterior of a building are not usually exposed to such high temperatures during a fire as those inside the building. Designers can determine by mathematical analysis the maximum temperature to which a given exterior steel member will rise in a fire, and if the temperature is sufficiently low, no fire protection need be added.

Helping Firefighters

It is vital that a building assist and protect firefighters during a blaze. A building's designers must furnish local fire authorities with infor-

Preformed mineral slabs

Concrete

Lath and plaster

Spray-on insulation

Fire protection of steel columns

19.22

Design error: Firetrucks cannot reach a building isolated in the middle of a complex of buildings.

Design error: Fire ladders cannot extend to windows for access or rescue.

19.23

Sole access to stair is across balcony

Standpipe

Hydrant

Siamese Connection

Balcony wall must be at least 50% open to air

Hydrant

Smokeproof Stairway Enclosure

19.24

mation regarding the configuration and construction of a building, its expected contents and use, and its facilities for assisting firefighters. Complexes of buildings must be planned so that fire trucks can drive to any building in the complex (19.23). Outdoor hydrants must be located within easy hose reach of the various buildings. Fire-truck ladders should be able to reach lower-floor windows. One exit stairway in a taller building must be placed in a *smokeproof enclosure* (19.24). This stair either is connected to the main spaces of the building only by open-air balconies or is automatically pressurized by a fan in case of fire. Within each exit stairway in multistory buildings, a *standpipe* must be furnished to which firehoses may be connected at any floor. To ensure a continous supply of water through the standpipe, a Y-shaped *siamese connection* must be connected to the pipe at street level. One or two pumper trucks may then couple to this connection to maintain pressure and volume in the standpipe if the city water mains cannot keep up with demand during a fire.

Because of their inherent unreliability, especially during a building fire, elevators and escalators may not be used as escape devices in buildings. But specially equipped elevators are required to assist firefighters in gaining quick access to the upper reaches of tall buildings. Elevators for firefighters must comply with elaborate precautions that ensure reliable smoke control, a secure supply of electricity, and complete isolation from the effects of the fire.

Further Reading

James Patterson. *Simplified Design for Building Fire Safety.* New York, Wiley, 1993.

20
Getting a Building Built

A building begins as a vague concept of need in someone's mind. If the need is a simple one and the person dexterous and ambitious, the steps needed to realize the concept are simple and direct. In some primitive societies, one or more members of the family or tribe scratch a floor-plan circle or rectangle of suitable size on the bare ground and assemble locally gathered materials—mud, stone, reeds, snow, logs, or poles—into a building on the spot. The design and details of the building require little thought because they are traditional to the society. The suburban American do-it-yourselfer, whether needing a tool shed or an entire house, generally takes somewhat more elaborate steps. He or she spends time developing plans on paper or spends money purchasing ready-made plans, in order to resolve as many functional problems as possible before starting construction. The paper plans also allow accurate estimating of the necessary quantities of building materials and labor and facilitate negotiations with the local building inspector for a permit to build. Once everything is in order, materials are bought and delivered, tools are prepared, and construction can begin.

Organizing the Larger Project

For larger building projects, more complicated arrangements are necessary. A large number of people and organizations are needed: Not just the owner and local building inspector but also an architect; various engineers and specialist design consultants in such fields as structure, foundations, heating, plumbing, electrical work, acoustics; a general contractor; subcontractors and materials suppliers; and

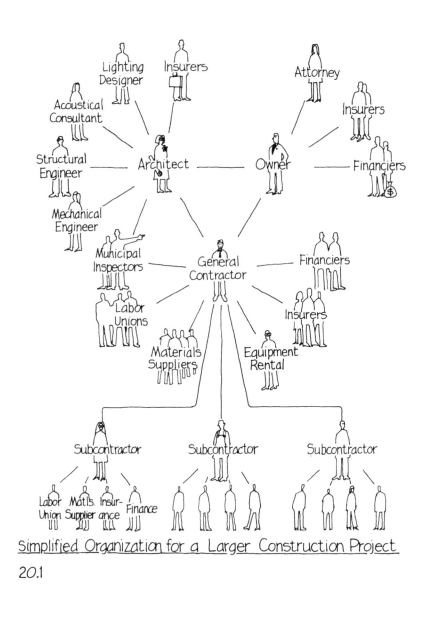

Simplified Organization for a Larger Construction Project

20.1

SPECIFICATION

Chez Rover
R. Dogg, Owner

Foundation:	Concrete, 2500 psi
Floor:	Concrete, steel trowel finish
Structure:	#2 Pine boards, ship-lapped on walls
Roofing:	#1 Red Cedar Perfections, laid 5" to weather
Painting:	One coat oil-base primer, two coats exterior latex paint· Furnish color samples to owner for selection

A simple specification

20.2

a small army of financiers, lawyers, and insurers (20.1). With so many persons involved, with so much money changing hands, and with the ever-present hazards of accident, fire, vandalism, inclement weather, labor disputes, inflation, and materials shortages and delays, firm, written understandings must be established among the various people regarding who is responsible for what, especially if something should go wrong. As a basis for these understandings, all must agree precisely on what is to be built and how. The "what" and "how" are the purposes of the architect's *specifications* and *working drawings*.

The specifications comprise a written document enumerating in detail the type and quality of all the materials to be used in a building, the standards of workmanship to be expected, and which trades will be responsible for which portions of the work (20.2). The working drawings (sometimes called the *blueprints*) show the size, location, and configuration of all parts of the building, presented in terms of what each tradesperson needs to know in order to get the building built in its intended form (20.3). The specifications and working drawings are, for practical purposes, the sole means of translating the design ideas of the owner and the architect into an actual building. They serve as the basis on which construction financing is granted, the basis for various insurances, the basis for estimating and bidding construction costs, the basis for the general construction contract and all subcontracts, the basis for material supply contracts, and the basis for a legal permit to build the building. As such, they must be complete, clear, unambiguous, and understandable (20.4, 20.5). They must be written and drawn in a language that can be understood by the people who will provide and place the materials. Beauty is of no importance in these drawings, but clarity and precision are.

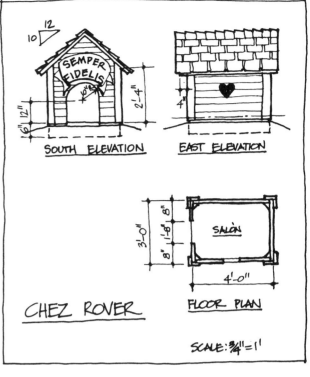

A simple working drawing   20.3

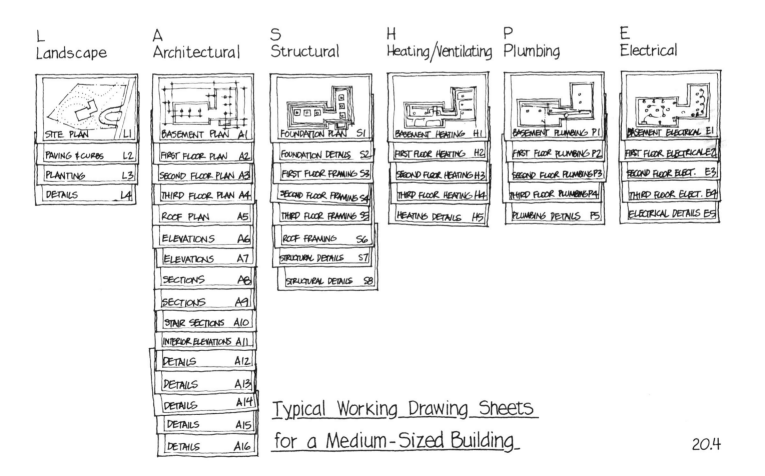

Typical Working Drawing Sheets
for a Medium-Sized Building   20.4

DIVISION 1	GENERAL REQUIREMENTS		DIVISION 9	FINISHES
01010	Summary of work		09110	Nonloadbearing wall framing
01021	Cash allowances		09200	Lath and plaster
			09500	Acoustical treatment
DIVISION 2	SITEWORK		09650	Resilient flooring
02150	Shoring and underpinning		DIVISION 10	SPECIALTIES
02200	Earthwork			
02350	Piles and caissons		10160	Metal toilet compartments
			10500	Lockers
DIVISION 3	CONCRETE			
			DIVISION 11	EQUIPMENT
03100	Concrete formwork			
03200	Concrete reinforcement		11050	Library equipment
03300	Cast-in-place concrete		11400	Food service equipment
DIVISION 4	MASONRY		DIVISION 12	FURNISHINGS
04210	Clay unit masonry		12300	Manufactured casework
04220	Concrete unit masonry			
			DIVISION 13	SPECIAL CONSTRUCTION
DIVISION 5	METALS		13034	Sound conditioned rooms
05100	Structural metal framing			
05300	Metal decking		DIVISION 14	CONVEYING SYSTEMS
05700	Ornamental metal		14210	Electric traction elevators
DIVISION 6	WOOD AND PLASTICS		DIVISION 15	MECHANICAL
06100	Rough carpentry		15400	Plumbing
06200	Finish carpentry		15500	Heating, ventilating, and air conditioning
DIVISION 7	THERMAL AND MOISTURE PROTECTION			
07190	Vapor retarders		DIVISION 16	ELECTRICAL
07200	Insulation		16120	Wires and cables
07250	Fireproofing		16140	Wiring devices
07500	Membrane roofing		16500	Lighting
			16700	Communications
DIVISION 8	DOORS AND WINDOWS			
08100	Metal doors and frames			
08500	Metal windows			
08700	Hardware			

Typical Specification Sections for a Medium-Sized Building

20.5

Problems of Construction

A building under construction creates many temporary disruptions and dislocations in its vicinity. The soil and vegetation are torn up. Roads and sidewalks are often obstructed, and natural surface drainage patterns interrupted. Heavy construction vehicles often accidentally break the pavement. Noise, dust, and fumes gather around construction work. Power tools and construction machinery present hazards to fingers and limbs. Tools and materials may fall or be blown by wind from higher levels of the building. Edges of floors and holes in floors for pipes, wires, ducts, stairs, and elevators create a risk of accidental falls. The chances of accidental fire increase during construction, with debris accumulating and various torches and heaters in use. The partly finished building is attractive to thieves, vandals, and adventure seekers, making it doubly vulnerable to fire and accident. Therefore the construction process itself needs careful design attention in order to minimize its danger and unpleasantness and to maximize its efficiency and economy.

Temporary utilities are needed during the construction process: water, electricity for power tools and temporary illumination, telephone lines, toilets, and waste removal services. Construction workers need parking or other transportation arrangements. The contractor must provide a system of temporary drainage to keep excavations free of water and to control surface drainage. Trucks bringing materials to the site need delivery routes. An area for unloading materials is required, adjacent to dry, safe areas where materials can be stored until needed. There must be lifting and carrying devices to unload trucks, stack and unstack materials, lift materials and workers to the various levels of the building, and transport materials across each level.

On many projects the contractor must erect temporary fences and barriers of various kinds to protect the public from the hazards of the work and to protect the work from intruders. Trees must be fenced and padded against accidental damage by construction machinery. If excavations are in unstable soil or too close to roads or adjacent buildings, they must be *shored* to prevent collapse of the surrounding soil. If the excavation is to go below the level of the foundations of adjacent buildings, those buildings may have to be supported temporarily against subsidence or sliding (20.6, 20.7).

As the building rises, workers need scaffolding and ladders for access to the various surfaces of the building. Many structural elements need temporary support: knee braces for walls, formwork for concrete, centering for masonry arches, and temporary diagonal braces of plank or cable throughout wood or steel frames. All these will later be removed as the structure becomes self-supporting. For safety and convenience, contractors may install temporary floors of wood planking in steel building frames until the permanent floors are in place and temporary railings have been installed at edges and openings of floors. Temporary protection against the weather is required in several areas of the building site: The contractor and subcontractors need one or more portable field offices. Sheds or trailers often store tools and valuable materials on the site or shelter specific areas of work such as those around large power saws for cutting wood or masonry. Waterproof tarpaulins shelter piles of materials. In severe weather, tarpaulins act as roofs or walls throughout a building

Shoring an Excavation
With Sheet Piling

1. Piledriver sinks continuous perimeter of steel sheet piling into ground

2. Excavation proceeds within sheet piling

As excavation deepens, sheet piling must be braced.

20.6

Alternative Methods of Bracing Sheet Piling

1. Cross-lot bracing

2. Rakers

3. Tiebacks (tension ties into firm soil)

20.7

211

20.8

site to shelter work and workers from wind, rain, snow, or cold air. In winter, temporary heating stoves protect concrete or masonry work against freezing before they have thoroughly hardened, or they help paint and plaster to dry. In very hot weather, sunshading may have to be provided (20.8).

Workers on a construction job are exposed to many dangers; building contracting has one of the highest rates of on-the-job injury of any industry in the United States. Many protective devices are therefore required for the various trades. The hard safety helmet is universal, to protect the head against dropped objects or from bumping against overhead hazards. Hard-toed safety shoes protect feet from dropped tools or materials. Nonslip soles serve an obvious safety function. Goggles keep flying chips and dust from power tools out of the eyes and protect eyes from the sparks and glare of welding. Leather gloves, aprons, dust-filtering respirator masks, and safety belts or safety lines are required for certain trades. Most power tools have built-in safety features such as self-returning blade guards, anti-kickback devices, and self-opening switches to shut off the tool if it is accidentally dropped. First-aid kits and fire extinguishers are kept close at hand, and instructions about medical and fire assistance are prominently posted. Medical and hospitalization insurance for workers is required by law. A safety officer is appointed by the contractor on each construction site to ensure that all aspects of the work are clean and safe.

The workers normally own their small construction tools— hammers, handsaws, and so forth. Other tools belong to the general contractor or subcontractors. But if a contractor does not like to keep a large inventory of construction equipment, he or she may rent or lease very large or highly specialized tools from an equipment-rental firm.

Every shipment of material that goes into a building must be checked on delivery to ensure that it meets the designer's specification. Each piece of lumber or plywood comes from the mill with a printed identification of its species and grade that makes on-site inspection easy. Structural steel is delivered with a certificate from the steel mill of its composition and quality. Most other building materials are similarly stamped or pedigreed with indications of their origins and quality.

Materials such as concrete and mortar, which are put in place wet, cannot be thoroughly checked for quality at the time of their placement, since there is no sure way of knowing what their strength will be after they have hardened. The standard procedure is to cast several small samples of material from each batch in special molds. These samples are carefully marked, recorded in a book along with the locations in the building where the corresponding batch of material was used, and kept on the site for a standard period of hardening. They are then transported to a laboratory where their strength is determined by crushing them in a calibrated hydraulic press. If the crushing strength is above the specified minimum value, all is well. If it is not, work done with the batches of material from which the samples were taken may have to be torn out and done over.

With the aid of modern measuring and leveling instruments, buildings are built with a surprising degree of precision, but they are not like watches or cameras. One must assume that even the best building components—because of their large size, shipping damage they may have suffered, water they may have absorbed in transit or on the job site, and variations in temperature—may not be square, flat, true, plumb, perfect, or accurate at the time they are installed in a building. One must also assume that a worker may not always measure or install a piece exactly as it should be, especially in the rougher sorts of work such as concrete work and wood framing. For a few building components, such as structural steel, there is an industry-wide standard specifying the maximum amounts of various sorts of distortions and inaccuracies that can be expected in the product when it arrives at the construction site. For most components, however, we must assume that plus or minus one-quarter inch (6 mm) accuracy is reasonable to expect in buildings but that discrepancies of an inch or several inches (25 mm or more) sometimes must be accepted. Under these conditions, joints in which one piece of material simply laps over another are the easiest and safest to make (20.9). Where materials must be butted at two or more sides, it is essential that intentional gaps be provided to allow for inaccurate positioning and fitting. The openings for window and door units in wood-frame walls are always larger than the units themselves. When the units are installed, they can then be leveled and located accurately by means of small wedges around the perimeter. The siding covers the resulting gap on the outside, and the interior wall finish conceals it on the inside. Concrete or metal exterior wall panels are installed with generous perimeter gaps, as much for thermal movement and structural deflection as for ease of installation. The metal mounting clips on such panels provide generous adjustments for accurate leveling and locating before a permanent attachment is made.

In planning a construction job, it is important that those materials that must present a good, finished appearance be installed as late in the process as possible and that they be protected from damage until the last worker is out of the building. In many buildings, for example, it would be easiest to install the finish flooring early in construction, during the framing operation. If this were done, however, the surface would be exposed to the abrasion, chipping, scratching,

Overlapping joints: Lots of margin for error

Butt joints: Less margin for error

Butt joints on four sides: Least margin for error

20.9

214

indentations, dripping, and spotting caused by the feet, tools, materials, spillage, and miscellaneous accidents of all the subsequent work in the building. Instead, even at the cost of some inconvenience, installing finish floors is one of the very last jobs to be done in a building.

Designers must also consider carefully what is to be left exposed in a building. It might be attractive to expose the wood framing in a wall—but what will the wall really look like, with the natural defects in the lumber, the grade-marking stamps, the dents left by the carpenter's hammer, the leftover pencil marks, and the electrical wiring and plumbing pipes drilled coarsely through? If a wall's framing is to be seen, it demands close attention to appropriate lumber grades and a careful routing of pipes and wires. It also demands a higher and more time-consuming quality of workmanship than a framing carpenter is normally asked to do. Usually it is cheaper to follow the standard procedure of bringing in gypsum wallboard workers and painters to cover the wall in several successively better-finished layers of work, letting the carpenter, electrician, and plumber work in their customarily rough and efficient ways. It is readily apparent when examining any of the traditional ways of putting buildings together in our society that a principle is generally followed of sequencing construction so that each of the final trades covers up and smooths over the work of the previous trades. The fourth-from-last trades in a typical building install large areas of flat material—siding, wall panels, lath, gypsum wallboard—that crudely cover the exposed innards of the building. The third-from-last crews are the smoothers-on of gooey substances—sealants, plaster, wallboard joint compound—that obscure the worst gaps in the flat materials. The next-to-last crews install flooring, cover plates, cover strips, and moldings of various sorts. The last crew, the painters, brighten and conceal all these layers with a thin cosmetic and preservative coating, ready for the final cleanup of construction debris, the final inspections of all parties concerned, and the handing of the keys to the owner. The building, after a long and often troubled period of gestation, is born at last.

The Cost of Building

Buildings are inherently very expensive objects. Expense can be measured ultimately in two quantities, the amount of physical resources consumed and the human time consumed. The physical resources can be assessed only in relative terms, but with human time we can be much more precise. The average house in America requires about one-fifteenth of a human's working lifetime to produce. An average Manhattan skyscraper uses, in total, the equivalent of the entire useful lives of fifty to one hundred workers in its construction and the equivalent of several lifetimes per year in its maintenance. Very large buildings often cost several times this amount.

As to *why* buildings are so expensive, this is best learned by working on the construction of a building. Even a small building uses copious tonnages, volumes, and areas of expensive materials, most or all of which must be lifted, positioned, and joined by human labor. The number of nails, bricks, or bolts consumed is often staggering, and each such component involves the expenditure of a finite and nontrivial amount of human time. The number of separate operations required to complete even the simplest building detail is quite surprising. Managing workers, ordering materials, thinking through problems, planning the next stages of construction, keeping records, and paying bills also take up large amounts of time. The totals rise alarmingly fast, and one soon realizes that we have become accustomed to constructing very large and very expensive shelters in our society.

Economy in building construction, once the design of the building has been established, is a matter of good management. Good management requires the best and most efficient use of workers, tools, materials, and money. As much work as possible should be done under shelter, preferably in a factory, where working conditions are ideal and there is a high level of mechanization. Workers need to be choreographed carefully so that they are neither standing idle nor getting in one another's way. Materials need to be obtained at the lowest possible price, but only from reputable suppliers. They should be delivered as needed. If they arrive on the site too late, they will hold up work. If they arrive too early, they will take up storage space on the site, are more likely to be damaged before installation by weather or accident, are more subject to pilferage, and have to be paid for earlier. A good building contractor treads a tightrope, bidding low enough to get work in competition with other contractors but high enough to realize a profit or at least break even, and then managing the project closely and knowledgeably, both to maintain the expected profit margin and to produce a well-built building. Construction management is a risky and highly skilled profession, and good contractors are not a readily available commodity.

21
Keeping a Building Alive and Growing

Even before a building is completed, Nature begins to destroy it systematically. Gravity, wind, and seismic movements constantly test the stability of the structure. The ultraviolet wavelengths of sunlight fade and decompose organic building materials through molecular breakdown. From the atmosphere, rainwater dissolves carbon dioxide and sulfur dioxide to form weak carbonic and sulfuric acids that eat away at stone and encourage the oxidation of metals. Where two adjacent metals of dissimilar electrolytic potentials are wetted by rainwater, a galvanic reaction occurs, causing rapid decomposition of the anodic metal. Water encourages the growth of molds, mildew, and fungi that attack many building materials, particularly wood and wood products. Water also encourages several types of wood-destroying insects, and weeds, vines, and trees whose roots burrow into tiny building cracks and wedge them inexorably larger. Falling water spatters soil onto the lower reaches of exterior walls, nourishing insects and fungi. As water freezes in soil, it heaves and cracks foundations and pavings. Freezing water spalls chips from the surfaces of concrete and masonry. Wind transports dust, spores, and seeds and deposits them on buildings. Mice and rats set up residence inside and gnaw passages through a building. Domestic animals rub, chew, and scratch building surfaces and deposit decay-breeding excrement in obscure corners. The human inhabitants of a building do their share to tear it down, too, tracking in moisture and dirt, spilling, spattering, staining, charring, banging, scuffing, scratching, breaking, discarding debris, wearing out doors and drawers, keeping destructive pets, rearing destructive children, and creating smoke, soot, and cooking fumes that stain building surfaces. Nature bears no special grudge against buildings; for the most part these are the same natural forces that level mountains, divert rivers from their beds, change lakes into meadows and meadows into forests, and turn old materials into new ones throughout the natural world. Change is the constant factor in Nature. Birth, growth, maturity, decline, death, decay, and rebirth are the stages in all natural cycles. So too with buildings, but humans like to keep the cycle under human control, to maintain each building in human use until its death suits human purposes.

The forces of deterioration in buildings can be grouped into three categories: Some forces pose such strong or immediate threats to the usefulness of the building that they must be neutralized at all reasonable cost. Other forces are inevitable, but we can cope with them satisfactorily on a day-to-day basis. And paradoxically, certain forces of deterioration can contribute to the beauty and utility of the building—if we will let them.

Safeguarding the Building

Among the first category of forces, the most dangerous are those threatening the stability of a building's foundations. We avoid frost heaving by founding the building below the deepest level at which the soil freezes in winter. We avoid excessive settlement by designing the foundations carefully with respect to the bearing capacity of the supporting soil. To prevent erosion of the soil from around and under foundations, roof-water drainage systems must be kept in good working order, and any major pipe leaks inside or near the building must be repaired promptly. In dry, windy locations, plantings or other protective devices must be employed against wind erosion. Areas immediately adjacent to basement walls must be kept clear of trees, to avoid root damage. Buildings resting on driven piles of untreated wood should be periodically inspected to ensure that nearby wells or pumps at nearby construction projects have not lowered the water table below the tops of the piles, for unless they are totally submerged, decay will set in.

If a building's foundations have settled but the building is not irreparably damaged, *underpinning* is usually an effective remedy. New foundations of larger capacity are constructed under or alongside the existing ones, and the building is jacked onto the new ones.

Structural weaknesses also fall into the "dangerous" category. Ordinarily a building's structure is strong enough to begin with, but if faulty design or increased loadings cause structural inadequacies when the building is being used, one can often add new beams, columns, or bracing.

Structures require certain types of maintenance. Steel structures must be kept from dampness and rust by either the surrounding layers of a building or the maintenance of paint or some other protective coating on all exposed surfaces. Any important bolted joints in wood frames need to be retightened to compensate for wood shrinkage after the building has been heated for an initial period after construction; access holes or access panels must be provided in any covering materials to allow this. Wood fungi and wood-destroying insects must be kept out of wooden structures. Some wood fungi, such as the blue-gray stain found on recently sawed, unseasoned lumber or the white flecks seen in some woods, are merely unsightly and cause no structural damage. Others, with colloquial names like *dry rot* and *wet rot*, are exceptionally destructive. Wood-boring insects, of which there are many species in various parts of the world, are uniformly dangerous.

All these wood-destroying organisms consume wood as food, need moisture, and need air. The chief means of controlling the organisms are, therefore, to poison the wood, to keep the wood completely dry to deprive the organisms of moisture, or to keep the wood completely submerged in water to deprive them of air. Various chemical substances called *preservatives* are used commercially to poison wood against both insects and fungi. They are not very effective if merely applied to the surface and should instead be dispersed throughout the cells of the wood by pressure treatment in a factory. Certain species of wood are naturally resistant to insects and decay, by virtue of chemical substances that grow naturally in them. Redwood, cypress, and cedar are the most common American woods with this property.

Keeping wood dry or wet may seem like contradictory aims, but wood in either condition is safe from attack. Wood that is moist but not submerged or wood that is alternately wetted and dried offers both moisture and air to destructive organisms and is therefore strongly attacked. Wood that is in or very near to the soil is especially vulnerable. Wood laid directly on a brick or stone foundation should be protected from capillary moisture with a damp-proof layer of impervious plastic or asphalt. Wood beams resting in pockets in foundation walls should have similar protection and should be given plenty of space to "breathe" on all sides.

Where one piece of wood is connected to another in an exterior location, rainwater is held between them by capillary action, and decay is rapid. The covered bridge illustrates one logical response to this problem: The hundreds of joints in the wood trusses supporting the bridge are kept dry by a waterproof roof and walls (21.1). If the bridge were not covered, it would become structurally unsound within several years because of the decaying of its connections. Where weather protection of wood connections is not possible, preservative treatment, or at least a heavy application of paint, stain, or

21.1

asphalt, can slow deterioration, but exposed wood connections should be avoided except in benches, railings, fences, and other secondary constructions. Even in these, periodic inspection and maintenance are required to replace rotting components before they become dangerous.

If wood is kept completely submerged, no air is available and the wood is safe from both insects and decay (unless the water is seawater, making the wood susceptible to marine borers). This effect is chiefly used in wood foundations placed below the water table. If the water table falls, however, decay will set in just above the water line, as it does in untreated wood posts used for supporting docks in freshwater.

Termites are especially liable to attack a building that has untreated wood parts extending into the ground or one with wood scraps or tree stumps buried near the building. They are capable of attacking dry wood, however, by carrying water from the ground to the wood. The most common (and most damaging) type of termite found in the United States is the subterranean termite, which nests in the soil but takes its food from the wood of a building above. In order to reach the building, the insects build hollow shelter tubes of mud, wood dust, and excreta over the intervening foundation construction and then tunnel into the wood itself. Where termite infestations are common, the soil in the immediate vicinity of the building should be poisoned, and sheet metal *termite shields* should be installed between the foundation and the wood structure (21.2). The shields do not prevent the entry of termites, but they do cause the insects to have to build their shelter tubes over the shield, where they can be seen, rather than through cracks in the foundation. If tubes are seen on the shields, an exterminator can further treat the soil.

Dry wood termites, which need very little moisture, do not require contact with the soil and are found in wooden buildings in the tropics and subtropics. Infested buildings must be covered with plastic sheets and fumigated with poison gas. Other types of termites and wood-destroying insects are found in various parts of the world, each requiring its own set of preventions and cures.

Closely associated with decay and termite prevention is the prevention of water leaks in buildings. Aside from fire or earthquake, nothing can bring down a building faster than the internal decay caused by a leaky roof. Roofs, rainwater drainage systems, walls, and windows must be maintained diligently. Plumbing leaks and conditions of excessive condensation must be attended to quickly. In the ordinary wood-frame house, water damage and decay from condensation are common in wooden window sashes across the bottom of each pane of glass and in wooden subfloors beneath toilet tanks. Leakage problems and their associated water damage and decay

Subfloor

Termite shield

Foundation

21.2

220

occur frequently next to chimneys and around roof gutters. Through decay of the roof boards around leaks, such problems are compounded rapidly unless taken care of as quickly as they occur.

Roof maintenance includes keeping drainage systems operational, leakproof, and free of clogging debris, removing soil and growing plants that may settle in crevices, and inspecting for leaks or signs of deterioration. Shingles of any sort are gradually eroded by water, ice, and wind; are decomposed by the destructive powers of the sun; and may be split or torn by ice, wind, or tree branches. Membrane roofs erode less rapidly but are susceptible to damage by expansion and contraction of the roof deck, vapor blistering and rupture, and abrasion from excessive foot traffic.

The mortar joints in masonry are susceptible to damage by the freezing and thawing of absorbed water. Masons can shape and compact mortar joints to make them shed water rather than trap it or absorb it (21.3). Even with such precautions, however, the mortar deteriorates progressively, usually over decades, and from time to time it is necessary to rake out the damaged mortar near the surface and repoint the masonry with new mortar. Many building maintenance people think climbing vines accelerate the deterioration of masonry because their roots penetrate the surface and their leaves keep it moist between storms. Building owners must weigh this factor against the undeniable charm of climbing vines, their contribution to summertime cooling through shade and leaf-surface evaporation, and their insulating role in winter.

Continuous inspection is required to maintain a building's fire hazards at an acceptable level. Rubbish must be cleared promptly. Chimneys, appliances, and the loads on electrical circuits must be checked periodically to ensure safe operating conditions. Exits must be kept clear, and fire doors must be kept closed but operable. Misplaced or missing extinguishers must be replaced, and alarm and emergency lighting systems must be checked regularly. In certain types of buildings, especially schools, occasional fire exit drills are advisable for the safety of the occupants.

Intolerable health hazards in plumbing systems include blocked or leaking pipes, pipes that are susceptible to freezing and therefore to bursting, and cracked or defective plumbing fixtures. Inadequate heating or a lack of natural light or ventilation are hazards sufficient to warrant vacating a building until they are corrected, as are accumulations of garbage or infestations of vermin. Window screens to keep out flies and biting insects are a necessity for health in most areas of the world.

Last in our discussion of critical maintenance problems in buildings are the human enemies of buildings, vandals and arsonists. When no ulterior motive is apparent, vandalism and arson seem to

Mortar Joint Profiles   21.3

Weather-Resistant

Concave

Vee

Non-Weather-Resistant

Weathered

Flush

Beaded

Extruded

Raked

occur mainly in buildings that are either in poor repair or abandoned. Inhabited buildings in good repair are likely to suffer damage only if they seem psychologically threatening to the vandals. Schools and low-income housing are frequent victims, especially if they appear authoritarian and depressing. Buildings in which each inhabitant feels a certain personal involvement would seem to be the answer, but we have as yet no sure guidelines for designing and building such structures.

Routine Building Maintenance

Routine building maintenance includes many sorts of repair, renewal, and cleaning operations. On the exterior of a building, impervious wall surfaces such as glazed tile, porcelain enamel on steel, glass, aluminum, and stainless steel have extremely long lifetimes under normal circumstances and need no maintenance other than periodic washing and occasional replacement of the mortar or sealant between units. Exterior paints, stains, and varnishes deteriorate quickly in sunlight and rain and must be renewed every few years. With white paint this rapid degradation has some advantage; the progressive chalking and washing away of the surface of the paint film keep the coating clean and bright in appearance.

The droppings of pigeons, starlings, sparrows, gulls, and other birds contribute to exterior maintenance problems in some buildings. Eliminating snug crannies from the exteriors of buildings deals with much of the problem. Devices that produce unpleasant sounds or electric shocks, or that have rows of spikes to prevent roosting, may be needed in extreme cases.

Window glass quickly accumulates layers of dirt on both sides. In time these will obscure vision and block daylight. Periodic washing is made easier by using window types that allow both sides of the glass to be reached from inside the building. Otherwise, ladders are necessary to reach the windows of low buildings, and movable suspended staging is needed for taller buildings. Windows must be designed to make occasional replacement of broken panes easy, preferably working from inside the building. Most glazing compounds harden with age and eventually crack and fall away, needing replacement. Window frames need periodic inspection for corrosion, decay, leakage of air or water, excessive tightness or looseness of operation, and wear or breakage of hardware.

Interior surfaces of buildings are generally safe from the destructive effects of sun, rain, and wind, but they are exposed instead to the wear, tear, and soil of human occupancy. Walls and ceilings collect dust and dirt from the air and from the hands, heads, feet, and furniture placed against them. In areas such as kitchens and bathrooms where walls are especially exposed to soiling, gloss or semi-gloss enamel paints make them easier to wash. Smooth *wainscots* of glazed ceramic tile or plastic laminate are preferable in heavily used facilities (21.4). Doors, windows, and their wooden casings are usually coated with gloss or semigloss finishes to make finger marks easy to remove. When interiors are repainted, the first step is to repair any plaster cracking. Serious plaster cracking is often indicative of structural problems or water leakage, however, and should not be smoothed over before a diagnosis can be made. When choosing colors of paint, wallpaper, or wood paneling, we should consider what effect the new color will have on lighting levels in the room. Only white and the very lightest tints are highly reflective of light; other finishes may achieve an effect that is both excessively somber and intolerably dark.

Floors, which undergo the abrasions of grit trodden underfoot, are the most subject to wear of any interior building surfaces, and they also are a source of dust that is kicked up by passing feet and deposited on walls and furnishings. Floor maintenance is therefore the largest single component of day-to-day building care. We can keep out much foot-borne dirt by using a doormat or grille just inside the entrance door. Vacuuming, dusting, sweeping, and scrubbing remove dirt before it piles up too deeply. Waxing some types of floor surfaces offers some protection against wear, and makes washing the floor considerably easier. Floors of hard stone or hard tile are highly resistant to abrasion and are easily washed. Soft stone, soft tile, and wood floors are abraded much more quickly. In most cases, wood floors can be sanded and revarnished after severe abrasion. Soft tiles and stones occasionally need replacement. On public stairways, where wear is exceptionally severe and eroded stairs present a particular safety problem, hard materials should be used. Stair treads are available with nonslip surfaces of extremely hard abrasives.

The maintenance of floors, countertops, and wainscots is made easier, and their appearance generally improved, if their surface has a mottled or streaked color pattern. Such patterns camouflage small splotches and streaks of dirt, making them much less noticeable than they would be on a plain-colored surface. Plain-colored materials frequently cost more than otherwise identical mottled ones, because even the tiniest manufacturing defect will be cause for rejecting a plain-colored product, whereas it might not be noticed in a mottled one.

Graffiti can be a large problem in public places. The would-be artist usually is discouraged if faced with a surface so rough, irregular, or richly patterned that any superimposed message is likely to be illegible, if it is possible to apply it in the first place. An exceptionally

Tile wainscot

21.4

smooth, easily cleaned or easily repapered surface, on the other hand, encourages the addition of *ad hoc* names, notes, and pictures. As long as the accumulating pattern is pleasing, it can be retained. Obscenity or excessive messiness can be obliterated, and the process can begin anew.

Except for its mechanical systems, a building has few moving parts that need care. Drawers, doors, and windows require occasional adjustment and lubrication. Hinges, latches, and locks are especially prone to wear and breakage. Doors that accommodate large numbers of people, in markets, schools, and other public buildings, require more frequent maintenance and occasional replacement of worn working parts.

Systematic programs of maintenance are required for all the mechanical systems in a building. The air filters of heating, ventilating, and cooling equipment must be cleaned or replaced at regular intervals. Burners need occasional cleaning and adjustment for maximum efficiency of combustion. Motors, fans, pumps, and compressors require lubrication and replacement of rubber belts. Less frequently, ductwork may need to be vacuumed clean.

Plumbing fixtures must be cleaned regularly and their drains kept free of obstructions. Faucets and toilet valves need constant repair. Water supply piping may in time fill with mineral scale and have to be replaced. Waste piping is prone to clog now and then with hair, paper, cooking fats, or invading tree roots. Devices ranging from a length of stiff wire to elaborate rotary knives can be introduced at cleanout ports in the piping to clear the obstacles. Water heaters are especially susceptible to scaling from mineral-laden water, and their electrical or fuel-burning components need periodic attention.

Incandescent bulbs, fluorescent tubes, and fluorescent ballasts are the items in a building's electrical system requiring the most frequent replacement. Regular cleaning of fixtures and occasional cleaning and painting of ceilings and walls also are required for maximum performance of the electrical lighting system. Light switches and electrical appliances wear out relatively quickly. The other components of the electrical system do not usually wear out, but electrical systems as a whole become obsolete fairly rapidly. Older systems are universally too small in capacity, do not furnish enough outlets, and do not meet modern standards of grounding protection. Future developments are certain to eclipse today's most up-to-date installations in a few years. Fortunately, new wiring is fairly easily installed in existing structures, especially where plenty of conduit capacity is available.

Elevators and escalators are generally serviced at close intervals by specialists associated with the manufacturers of the devices, and they are inspected regularly for safety by representatives of the local municipality. Elevators in particular are extremely complex and diverse in their mechanism and controls and are subjected to heavy wear. Because elevators also present a unique potential for human disaster, their mechanisms are designed with very large factors of safety; numerous safety devices are incorporated into their design; and maintenance must be frequent and thorough.

Designing for Growth and Change

Among the more subtle arts of an experienced designer is using the natural forces of deterioration to improve the building. There are few things more satisfying than seeing a building grow more attractive with age, rather than shabbier. To construct such a building, one must first recognize the basic problem that the surfaces of the building are both the visible face of the building and the surfaces that must withstand the abuse of sun, rain, wind, soot, dirt, and human wear. Any material that grows steadily worse in appearance when exposed to these forces should be avoided. A new car furnishes numerous examples of such materials: When it emerges from the showroom, it gleams seductively with bright, flawless enamel, polished chromium, and sparkling curves of glass, and it cradles the human body on plump, shining tufts of upholstery amid deep-pile carpeting. With each passing day, however, the car becomes less attractive: The paintwork chalks and fades. Any scratch or dent is immediately visible as a prominent blemish. Rust spots mar the chromium. The glass and paintwork tend to look even dirtier than they really are. The upholstery sags and the carpets accumulate dirt that refuses to be coaxed out. A motorist who buys a car for its visual appeal is doomed to a life of hard maintenance and ultimate disappointment, because the car will never again look as good as it did on the day it was purchased.

Consider, by contrast, a roof of cedar shingles. The shingles are somewhat garishly colorful when installed but rather quickly begin to turn gray in the sunlight and rain. For some months they are not very attractive but look a bit dirty and streaky. Then the color begins to blend and deepen, and the roof takes on a comfortable, silvery gray tone that becomes richer with the passing years. Rain erodes the softer bands of spring growth from the grain of the wood and adds texture to the roof. Lichens or mosses may add color. With no maintenance at all, the roof will not only last for several decades but will actually grow more attractive each year. Whereas the automobile starts life with a perfection of finish that can only grow less perfect with age, the cedar roof sidesteps the question of perfection entirely and acquires an ever-richer patina whose beauty has no limit.

There are many building materials that have this same quality. Redwood and cypress are similar to cedar in their weathering properties. Unfinished interior wood in tabletops, doors, and railings that is constantly handled and rubbed looks spotty for a time but then begins to glow with the natural polish given it by human hands. Brass door handles are etched chemically over time by the sweat of hands, to expose the fascinating crystalline pattern of the metal. Copper in the outdoor environment changes slowly from a bright, reflective orange metal to a rich tapestry of blue-green oxide. The oxide clings tightly to the metal to protect it from further deterioration. Lead roofs oxidize to a pleasant white. Aluminum is a metal with similarly self-protective oxides, but the oxides look dirty and streaky and are not especially attractive. Most exterior aluminum is therefore chemically oxidized in the factory, often with the addition of a permanent black or brown color, and becomes a material that grows neither better nor worse with age. Most ferrous metals rust destructively, but a steel alloy has been developed that has a tenacious, self-protecting oxide and assumes a pleasing color and texture after an initial period of splotchiness.

Masonry generally looks progressively better as it accumulates grime and as the mortor weathers to a more subtle color. Climbing vines further enhance its beauty year by year. Unglazed ceramic tile floors or floors of natural stone slabs often wear into pleasing contours underfoot. Glazed ceramic surfaces on masonry change little in appearance over the years and present a bright counterpoint to the softening, deepening colors of the materials about them. Because age so often darkens colors, surfaces that begin life dark in color tend to age more gracefully than light surfaces do. If a surface of white paint or whitewash, however, is frequently renewed, it will in time become pleasantly smooth in texture and will show off to good advantage adjoining areas of darker colors.

Surfaces made up of many small units generally age more attractively and are easier to repair than large, smooth planes. A crack or flaw in a floor-to-ceiling sheet of glass is visually annoying, potentially dangerous, and requires a skilled crew and expensive equipment to replace. But cracks in a small pane or two of a large multipane window are not particularly disturbing to the eye and do not require replacement of the panes unless they leak water or air. If replacement is necessary, a single semiskilled person can do it with a couple of dollars' worth of materials. The large sheet of plate glass must be washed to perfection every few weeks if it is to appear clean, whereas the multipane window can get quite dirty before it becomes disturbingly so. Similarly, a courtyard paved with bricks or small stones has maintenance advantages over one paved in concrete or asphalt. A wall paneled in narrow wood boards is apt to age more gracefully than one made of large sheets of beautifully veneered plywood. A floor of irregular stones or primitive clay tiles shows less evidence of the ravages of time than does one of polished marble slabs.

Secondhand building materials offer many advantages with respect to their visual characteristics: They are already worn, weathered, and hardened by time. In many cases they have already acquired a pleasant patina. They are often richer in design and detail than contemporary materials. They are sometimes cheaper than new materials. And they generally bring a welcome sense of history and continuity with the past into a new building. They blend more and more naturally with the building as it acquires marks of the injuries, repairs, and changes of its own lifetime, to produce a structure that records its own history on its exposed surfaces.

Buildings should be able to absorb life's hard knocks without looking the worse for them. Normal weathering and wear should not diminish the beauty of the finishes. Reasonable amounts of dirt and grime should look quite acceptable on the various surfaces of the building. And the normal, pleasant clutter of the various objects of people's daily lives should not look out of place because the building seems to have been constructed for superfastidious visitors from another planet. Building maintenance is not an end in itself but is intended to make life more livable for the building's inhabitants through the slow, dignified aging process of the building itself.

Addition and remodeling are eventually important to the usefulness of most buildings. Through these processes, a building can grow and adapt to changing human requirements, and the useful life of a building can be extended indefinitely. Remodeling usually involves removing at least some of the interior finishes, partitions, and mechanical equipment of a building, reconfiguring the interior and perhaps the facades, and applying new finishes. Remodeling is more difficult if the interior has many load-bearing partitions or if the floor structure is difficult to cut and change, as it is in many concrete buildings. It is easier if partitions, floors, stairs, and mechanical services are relatively simple to demount and relocate. Adding onto a building is possible in the horizontal direction, the vertical direction, or both. For vertical additions, much expense and disruption can be avoided if the original structure is made to accept additional floors without overstressing the columns and if elevators, stairs, and mechanical systems are planned from the outset to serve the extension. Horizontal additions are bound to look awkward if the original building is a complete, closed form like a dome, a cylinder, or a hyperbolic paraboloid shell. They are easiest to fit when the original

21.5

building rambles a bit already and when one or more natural points of connection are provided along the periphery of the existing pedestrian circulation system.

With periodic remodeling and constant maintenance, a building can live for a very long time. A number of buildings from Roman times are still in use. Even a wooden building, if kept safe from water and fire, can last for centuries. But buildings are abandoned or torn down every day. Sometimes health or safety problems are the reason. Sometimes a building simply cannot be brought up to modern standards of convenience because it is too small or its original configuration is too unyielding to alteration. More commonly, a building becomes uneconomic, through changing needs of its occupants, excessive costs of maintenance and repair, or because it occupies a piece of land so valuable that the owner wishes to build a much larger building in order to maximize the return on investment. In most such circumstances, the building is dismantled and trucked away in pieces by a building demolition contractor. Some of its components may be saved and sold, but usually the entire building ends as broken chunks in a dump.

In rural areas it is not difficult to find a barn or shed dying a natural death after many years of service (21.5). It is sad to know that the optimism, human energy, and skill that originally went into the making of the building are now to be lost forever, but it is a joyous experience to see how Nature takes back the building materials it once yielded, to convert them to other uses. There is dignity in the sagging of decaying wood and reassurance in the slow absorption of the wood by the earth. There is beauty in the gentle, supremely patient attack of Nature on masonry and concrete, as weather softens the surfaces, and tendrils of plants reach into tiny pores and cracks to begin the long process of prying and wedging that will someday, probably lifetimes hence, reduce even these materials to earth. The plants gradually cover the dying building with a shroud of green leaves and bright blossoms, and it becomes a new object in the landscape, a picturesque promise of the new and better order with which Nature will replace it.

The Building Blocks
of Architecture

Active
Mechanisms

Enclosure

Site

22
Building Components and Building Function

So far we have examined the characteristics of the outdoor environment, compared them with the environmental requirements of people and society, and noted the range of functions that we expect a building to perform in reconciling the differences between the two. We have discussed at considerable length the various physical mechanisms employed in buildings to perform these functions. It now remains to look briefly at the common components from which we assemble buildings, to see what functions we expect each to perform and by what combination of mechanisms each works. Simple words such as *wall* or *roof* denote very complicated components that perform a surprising range of functions in a building.

Let us begin with the component we call *the site*. The site is a building's all-important outer perimeter of devices for modifying the outdoor environment. Trees on the site can block the sun's rays, cool the air, divert the winter wind, and provide visual privacy. The site can keep water away from the foundations. It can protect a building from noise or fire by keeping it sufficiently distant from neighboring buildings. By careful placement and orientation of the building on the site, useful outdoor areas can be created; pockets of warmer or cooler microclimate can be set up; and the penetration of the sun into the building can be controlled for optimum comfort in all the seasons of the year. For many buildings, the site also provides water and disposes of sewage—and may even provide food.

A second perimeter of devices to modify the environment are contained in the enclosure of the building. Here the major work of the building is done: Sunlight is blocked, selectively admitted, and reflected. The passage of air, heat, moisture, sound, and living creatures is closely controlled. Level surfaces are created and stacked

231

for human occupancy, supported on walls or columns. The enclosed volume is divided into a convenient arrangement of rooms, linked by passages both vertical and horizontal.

Within these two perimeters are the active mechanisms that generate or pump heat, circulate air, provide light, energize tools, distribute water, and collect liquid wastes. It is best to restrict the role of active devices as far as possible to that of fine-tuning the internal environment to optimum conditions, once the heavy work of environmental modification has been performed by the passive devices of the site and the building enclosure. Such a design approach has the advantage, of course, of cutting down on energy consumption in the building. Even more important, it offers maximum comfort and convenience by leveling out temperature flows, reducing noise from mechanical equipment, reducing air pollution, and providing more favorable levels of natural illumination. This approach also helps place people in a more natural relationship with the outdoor environment, one in which they can understand and appreciate more fully the majestic cycles of Nature and the relationship of these cycles to human life. Machines, no matter how powerful, can never substitute fully for the good design judgment of the designer who sites and configures the building, for it is the enclosure of the building, not the mechanical equipment, that must create the basic conditons for human satisfaction, both spiritual and physical.

We are able to make satisfactory buildings, it would seem, from almost anything. Some materials need little processing: mud, broken stone, fieldstone, snow, grasses, reeds, leaves, bamboo, natural asphalt, tree trunks and branches. With a modest expenditure of time and energy, we can make hard-fired bricks, squared lumber, paper, stone blocks, and plaster. With still more processing, cement, glass, metals, rubber, and plastics become available. One builds with what one can obtain in a given locale, within a given set of economic restrictions. Through the military, the Peace Corps, or foreign architectural commissions, American architects and engineers have often found themselves building with mud, straw, or bamboo, seeking to cope with unfamiliar climates and patterns of life. Even our own life patterns continue to change, and new materials of construction reach the market every month, each promising certain advantages over the materials it hopes to replace.

Designers in such situations learn to evaluate new or strange materials as to what each can do best and what its disadvantages and weaknesses are. How strong is a material in tension, compression, and shear? How will it be affected by water? Will it allow water vapor to pass? What are its thermal properties? How much will it expand and contract with changes in moisture or temperature? Can its surface be left exposed in a floor or wall? How will the material be affected by fire? What are its acoustical properties? How can the material best be put in place? How will it cope with normal wear and weathering? If laboratory test figures are unavailable, experienced designers can still judge these qualities rather well by hefting, pulling, poking, bending, scratching, wetting, and holding a match to the sample or by seeing how the material is used and has weathered in existing buildings. Having learned what the material can and cannot do, designers must then determine where it can be of use in a building and with what other materials it should be teamed to make building components that perform all the functions required of them.

The accompanying table (22.1) shows the major functions performed by various building components. An exterior wall probably

	Site	Foundation	Structure	Floors	Walls	Windows	Doors	Roofs	Ceilings	Partitions	Finishes	Furnishings	Fireplaces	Heat/vent/A.C.	Plumbing	Electrical
Provides clean air	●					●	O							●	O	O
Provides clean water	·							·							●	·
Removes and recycles wastes	·											·		·	●	·
Controls thermal radiation	●		·	·	●	●		●	●		●			●	●	·
Controls air temperature	●		·	·	●	●	O	●	●				O	●		·
Controls thermal qualities of surfaces			·	●	O	O				·	·	●		O		·
Controls humidity	●	·	·	O	●	●	O	●	●		·			●	·	·
Controls flow of air	●		·	O	●	●	O	●	O	O				●		·
Optimum seeing and visual privacy	●		·	O	●	●	●	●	●	●	●	·		·		●
Optimum hearing and acoustic privacy	●	·	O	●	●	●	●	●	O	●	●	●	●	O	·	·
Controls entry of living creatures	●	O	·	O	●	●	●	●	O		●					·
Provides concentrated energy	·							·								●
Provides channels of communication					·	·	·			·	·					●
Provides useful surfaces	●	·	·	●	O	·	·	·			●	●	●			
Provides structural support	●	●	●	●	●				●	·	O					
Keeps out water	●	●	·	·	●	●	O	●			·				·	·
Adjusts to movement		●	●	O	O	O	O	O	O	O	O			O	O	O
Controls fire	●		●	●	●	●	●	●	●	●	●	●	●	●	●	●

Key: ● Major function O Minor function · Sometimes plays a role

22.1

233

serves more important functions than does any other part of a building. No single material can do all these jobs well. As a result, even the wall of an ordinary wood-frame residence is extraordinarily sophisticated in its combination of materials. Reading from exterior to interior, such a wall commonly includes several coats of exterior paint, wood siding, a spun-bonded polyethylene air barrier paper, plywood sheathing, wood two-by-six framing, mineral-fiber insulation, electrical wiring, heating ducts, a plastic sheet vapor retarder, gypsum wallboard, and several coats of interior paint. About fifteen separate construction operations, carried out by six different construction trades, are required to make this wall. But its efficiency in performing its appointed functions is unsurpassed.

Windows and doors are special cases of "wall"; they are specially designed to allow controlled penetration of the wall's environmental defenses. A door primarily controls the passage of people but often acts as a valve or filter for the selective passage of air, heat, animals, insects, and light. A window is one of the most fascinating of the building's components. A standard residential window of the most common type allows for the simultaneous and independent control of

Natural illumination
Natural ventilation
View out
View in
Passage of insects
Passage of water
Passage of heat—radiant, conducted, convected

Considering this multiplicity of functions, a window is a surprisingly simple mechanism. To designers, the possibilities of a window are limitless. Consider some of the following choices in designing a single window for a building:

Orientation of window
Location of window in the wall
Size of window
Proportions of window
External shading devices
Mode of window operation (fixed, sliding, etc.)
Material and color of frame
Type of glass
Type of shade or shutter
Type of curtain, material, color
Type of insect screen

Windows are important to designers not only as functional elements of the building enclosure but also as major elements of the visual patterns of both interior and exterior, as revealers of particular views, as illuminators of interior space, as gatherers of solar heat, and sometimes as the means of passage between interior and exterior. To achieve one's design goals in these many respects, one must learn to manipulate the technical choices at one's disposal. The results can approach the sublime: A sunny, plant-filled bay window. A cathedral rose window of richly colored stained glass. A large pane of glass that hovers invisibly before a panoramic view of a wooded valley below. A snug window seat for reading on a rainy Saturday afternoon. A skylight that illuminates a bright tapestry. But the results can also be mundane, even depressing: A "picture window" that pictures only a street full of parked cars and simultaneously destroys interior privacy. A tenement window that faces on a bleak air shaft. A too-small window that leaves an interior space too dark.

The story is much the same for each of the other components of a building: Each must serve a multiplicity of functions. Each must be made of a combination of materials of complementary capabilities. Each offers to a designer its unique set of aesthetic possibilities to be exploited or, at the designer's peril, to be ignored. These components are the building blocks of architecture, the only stuff with which a designer can work the unique magic that results in a satisfying building. The only solid basis for architectural creativity is an ordered and accessible knowledge of how buildings work. There is a natural order to architecture, and true design freedom springs from an everyday, easy familiarity with this order.

This book has outlined the natural order of physical function in buildings. Architecture has other important functions, too—each building serves an economic function, justifying its existence in dollars and cents, and a symbolic function, evoking emotions in those who experience it. But these are the province of other books. Here the message is simply that the scientific fundamentals of building are always the same. A house of snow in the Arctic obeys the same physical laws as does one of bamboo in the tropics, and a steel-framed skyscraper is not so far removed from a tree house as we would sometimes believe. A designer who understands from first principles how to moderate the forces of Nature for human occupancy is prepared to build well under any circumstances.

Glossary

Where a term is adequately defined in the text, the page on which the definition occurs is cited.

Absorptance, 48

Absorption cycle, 82, 83

AC. *See* Alternating current

ACTIVATED CHARCOAL FILTRATION   The cleansing of air or water by passing it through a volume of charcoal that is specially produced to have a very large ratio of surface area to volume. This activated charcoal is highly effective in absorbing many types of contaminants.

ACTIVE   Adjective used to describe any building system that requires the application of energy from an external source for its function, as contrasted with a passive system, which uses only ambient flows of energy.

ADIABATIC   Adjective describing a change in the volume of a gas without the loss or gain of heat.

AEROBIC   Adjective describing a biological process that occurs only in the presence of oxygen.

Air barrier, 108

Air chamber, 34

ALTERNATING CURRENT   An electric current that reverses direction at rapid, regular intervals, usually 60 times per second in the United States.

ANAEROBIC   Adjective describing a biological process that occurs only in the absence of oxygen.

Anticlastic, 163

Area of refuge, 203

Artesian well, 33

Atmospheric inversion, 7

Atrium, 196

Autumnal equinox, 5

AWNING   A sloping rooflike cover projecting outward over a window or door.

AWNING WINDOW   A window that opens by being pushed outward along its lower edge and is hinged along its top edge.

BALLAST, FLUORESCENT   An electrical assembly in a fluorescent light fixture that serves both to provide the high voltage necessary to start the lamp and to limit the current to the lamp once it is started.

Base plate, 182

BEAM   A solid structural member that resists bending forces by means of a latticelike pattern of internal forces of tension and compression.

Bearing wall, 156

Buckling, 157

Bus bar, 137

BUTTRESS   A structural device in which the dead weight of stone or brick combines with the angular thrusts of arches or vaults to produce a resultant force that falls safely within the foundations of the building.

Caisson, 182, 183

Camber, 175

Cant strip, 104, 105

CANTILEVER   The portion of a beam or truss that projects beyond its last point of support.

CAPILLARY ACTION   The drawing of water through a fine hole or crack by the combined forces of cohesion in the water and adhesion between the water and the material through which it is drawn.

Capillary break, 110

CASEMENT WINDOW   A window that swings open at one side and is hinged at the other.

Catenary, 161

CAV. *See* Constant air volume system

Cavity wall, 106

Centering, 166

Cesspool, 40

CHASE   A hollow space especially provided in a building to house a run of pipes, wires, or ducts.

Chimney, 93

CHORD   The top or bottom linear element of a truss.

CIRCUIT   A single loop of electrical wiring, capable of serving a limited number of fixtures or outlets.

CIRCUIT BREAKER   A device that shuts off electrical flow automatically if the capacity of an electrical circuit is exceeded, thus preventing damage to the circuit.

CLERESTORY   A vertical window placed at the junction of two roof planes.

COLUMN   A linear vertical element of structure that supports primarily vertical loads.

COMPARTMENTATION   The subdivision of a building by fire-resistant walls and/or floors in order to restrict the spread of a building fire.

COMPRESSION   A squeezing together.

Compression cycle, 82

COMPRESSIVE STRESS   The magnitude of compression in a material, measured in units of applied force per unit area.

CONCRETE   A rocklike material produced by mixing together Portland cement, sand, gravel, and water and allowing this mixture to harden.

CONDENSATE   A liquid created by condensation.

CONDENSATION   The changing of a material from a gaseous state to a liquid state.

Conduction, 47

Conduit, 136

Constant air volume system, 84, 85

CONTINUITY   In a structure, the property of having structural elements joined together rigidly so they may act as a single structural unit.

Control joint, 185, 186

Convection, 47

CONVECTIVE   Adjective describing a process that uses convection as its mode of heat transfer.

CONVECTOR   A device for heating air by means of steam or hot water that circulates through metal tubing that is exposed to the air. A convector usually has metallic fins attached to the tubing to increase its surface area for better heat transfer, and the entire assembly is commonly housed in a sheet metal cabinet with openings for the circulation of air.

Corbel, 179, 180

CRAWL SPACE   A continuous access area, not tall enough to stand in, beneath the ground floor of a building.

Creep, 184

CROSS CONNECTION   A faulty plumbing installation that allows sewage to be drawn into water supply pipes in case supply pressure is lost.

CROWN   A slight curvature.

Curtain board, 197

DAMPER   A moveable metal flap that acts as a valve for airflow in a duct, a fuel-burning appliance, or a fireplace.

DC. See Direct current

Dead load, 153

Decibel, 125

DECIDUOUS   A tree that drops its leaves in winter.

DEFLECTION   The amount by which a given point on a structural member moves when the member is placed under a given load.

DEW POINT   For any mass of air containing water vapor, the temperature at which the water vapor begins to condense. The dew point varies depending on the water content of the air: The higher the water content is, the higher the dew point will be.

DIFFRACTION   The bending of light waves or sound waves by their being passed across sharp edges, especially a series of edges whose spacing is similar to the wavelength of the light or sound.

DIRECT CURRENT   An electric current that is constant in direction.

DOME   A structural form consisting of an arch rotated about its vertical centerline. A dome is often a hemisphere or some other segment of a sphere.

DOUBLE-HUNG WINDOW   A window with two sashes, both of which slide on vertical tracks.

Downspout, 103

DRIP   Any building feature that forces water to fall clear of the building at that point rather than run along the surface.

DUCT   A round or rectangular tube through which air is circulated.

EAVE   The lowest edge of a sloping roof.

Echo, 129

EFFLUENT   The supernatant of decomposed sewage.

Elastic modulus, 155

Emittance, 48

Equinox, 5

Evaporative cooler, 86, 87

EXPANSION JOINT   A linear device that allows a material to expand without damaging itself.

FACADE   The principal exterior face of a building.

Factor of safety, 155

Fire-cut, 204

FLASHING   A continuous strip of sheet metal or plastic that acts as a barrier to the passage of water.

Flat arch, 164, 165

Flat-plate collector, 79, 80

Floating foundation, 183

Fluid-filled structure, 180

Fluorescent, 114

FLUX   A flow of energy.

FLYING BUTTRESS   A buttress in which the lateral thrusts are transmitted from the vault or arch to the vertical mass of the buttress by means of sloping arches.

FORMWORK   A structure of wood or metal that temporarily provides shape and support to a concrete or masonry building element that is not yet self-supporting.

Frost heaving, 111

FUNICULAR   Having the form that would be taken by a hanging rope that supports a given set of weights, or having the inversion of that form.

FUSIBLE LINK   A connector made of a special alloy with a very low melting point, used for the automatic control of fire safety devices in buildings.

GABLE   A roof consisting of two sloping surfaces that meet at a level ridge.

GASKET An elastic strip used to seal a joint between two adjacent components.

GLARE Excessive contrast in brightness between a visual task and its surroundings.

GLAZED Having a glassy surface.

GLAZING The installation of glass in a building. Also the application of a glassy finish to a ceramic material.

GLAZING COMPOUND An elastic material used for sealing around panes of glass.

Grade beam, 182

Ground fault interrupter, 137

Gutter, 103

GYPSUM A naturally occurring mineral, hydrated calcium sulfate, used to make plaster, wallboard, structural fireproofing, and other building materials.

Hard water, 33

HEAT EXCHANGER A device for transferring heat from one medium to another, such as from water to air or air to air. An automobile "radiator" is a water-to-air heat exchanger.

Heat pump, 82

HEAT SINK A mass or substance with a very large thermal capacity compared with the amounts of heat flowing through a given thermal system.

H.I.D, High-intensity discharge lamp, 121

HOPPER WINDOW A window whose sash is hinged along the bottom edge and swings inward.

Horizontal exit, 202, 203

HOT WIRE A current-carrying electrical wire that is not grounded.

Hydronic, 81

Hypothermia, 17

Ice dam, 103, 104

INCANDESCENT Adjective describing a substance that is heated to such a temperature that light is emitted.

INFILTRATION The gain or loss of air in a building through cracks and defects in the enclosure of the building.

INFRARED Literally "below red"; the electromagnetic wavelengths longer than those of red light.

Intumescent coating, 204

Inverse square law, 64

Inversion, 7

Inverted roof, 62

Isolated footing, 182

JOIST A slender beam used repetitively at narrow spacings to support a floor, ceiling, or flat roof.

KNEE BRACE A temporary diagonal brace used to support walls or columns during construction. A permanent diagonal brace that joins a column above its midpoint.

Labyrinth joint, 107

LAMP A lightbulb or light-emitting tube.

LANDING A broad platform on a stair.

LATENT HEAT The heat required to change the phase of a material without altering its temperature.

LATH Any mesh or sheet material used as a base to which to apply plaster.

Leaching field, 40

LIME Calcium hydroxide, produced from limestone or seashells and used as an ingredient of mortar or plaster.

LINTEL A beam that supports a wall above a window or door opening.

Live load, 153

LOUVERS Closely spaced parallel strips of material used to obstruct the passage of light or rain while allowing the passage or air.

Lumen, 120

Luminance, 122

Masking noise, 131, 132

MASONRY Stonework, brickwork, or concrete blockwork.

Mat foundation, 182

Mean radiant temperature, 65, 66

MEMBRANE ROOF A roof that is waterproofed by means of a single impervious sheet of material.

MONITOR A rectangular box that projects above a flat roof to facilitate natural illumination and/or ventilation.

MORTAR The substance used for cementing together masonry units.

MRT. See Mean radiant temperature

Neutral wire, 135

NIGHT SOIL Human excrement.

NOCTURNAL RADIATION The radiation of heat from terrestrial objects to the night sky.

Nosing, 146, 147

One-way, 177

PANEL OF A TRUSS A portion of a truss bounded by a lower chord, an upper chord, and two vertical members.

Panic hardware, 201

PARAPET A wall that projects above the surrounding roof surfaces.

PASSIVE Adjective used to describe any building system that uses only ambient flows of energy, without the application of energy from an external source.

Pattern staining, 51

PEDIMENT The ornamented triangular end of a gable roof in classical architecture.

Pile, end-bearing, 183

Pile, friction, 183

Plate girder, 178

PORTLAND CEMENT A gray powder used with water to cement together sand and gravel to make concrete; also used in mortar and stucco.

POST-TENSIONING The application of compressive force to a concrete structural member by means of steel strands that are tensioned after the concrete has hardened.

PRECAST CONCRETE Concrete that is cast and hardened away from the building site and then put in place in the building as a rigid component.

Preservative, 219

Pressure equalization chamber, 108–110

PYROLYSIS The heating of materials to reduce them to their constituent components.

QUOINS Ornamental rectangular blocks of masonry built into the exterior corners of a building.

Radiation, 47

RADIATIONAL COOLING   The cooling of terrestrial objects by radiation of heat from the objects to the night sky.

RAFTER   A slender, sloping beam used repetitively at narrow spacings to support a sloping roof.

Rainscreen, 108–110

Reflectance, 48

Regenerative wheel, 96, 97

REGLET   A slot provided for tucking in the edge of a flashing or a roof membrane.

REGULATOR, GAS   A device for reducing and controlling the pressure of gas at the point of use.

REINFORCED CONCRETE   A common type of construction in which concrete is used to carry compressive stresses and steel bars are embedded in the concrete to carry tensile stresses.

Reinforcement, sound, 129

Relative humidity, 59

RELAY   An electrical switch that is controlled by another electric current.

RESONATOR   A hollow chamber that vibrates sympathetically and therefore absorbs sound energy at a given frequency.

Reverberation time, 130

Ribbed slab, 177

RIDGE, ROOF   The highest edge of a sloping roof, the line along which the two planes of a gable roof intersect.

Rigid frame, 178

RISE OF STAIR   The total vertical dimension of a stair.

RISERS   The vertical planar elements of a stair.

Roof Monitor. See Monitor

ROOF VENTILATOR   A device, usually of metal, that encourages the passage of air through a roof.

RUN OF STAIR   The total horizontal dimension of a stair.

Safe working stress, 155

SASH   The portion of a window frame, often movable, that holds the glass.

SCAFFOLDING   Temporary platforms for the convenience of building workers, usually supported on frames of metal or wood.

SCUPPER   A hole through a parapet wall for draining water from the roof.

Sealant, 107

Self-opening roof vent, 197

SENSIBLE HEAT   Heat that raises or lowers the temperature of a material without changing its phase.

SEPTIC TANK   A watertight underground tank designed to foster the anaerobic decomposition of sewage and to separate the decomposed sewage into effluent and sludge.

SERVICE PANEL   A metal box containing the circuit breakers for a number of electrical circuits and from which the wiring for these circuits radiates.

SHEAR   A slipping tendency along a plane in a material caused by parallel but opposite forces applied to the two sides of the plane, much as a pair of scissors apply parallel but opposite forces to the two sides of a plane perpendicular to the plane of a sheet of paper.

SHEAR PANEL   A planar element of structure that resists lateral loads by means of forces within its plane.

SHEAR STRESS   The magnitude of shear in a structural member, measured in units of applied force per unit area.

SHELTER BELT   A swath of trees planted to obstruct the wind.

SHINGLE   A small flat piece of material overlapped with similar pieces on a vertical or sloping surface in such a way that water cannot penetrate.

SHORING   A temporary structure erected to support an earthwork or a freshly poured concrete structure against collapse.

SHORT CIRCUIT   An accidental or inadvertent interconnection of a hot wire with a neutral wire.

SI UNITS   Système International d'Unités, a rationalized system of measurement based on the meter.

SIAMESE CONNECTION   A Y-shaped fitting at the base of a building that allows one or two pumper trucks to connect to a building's standpipe or sprinkler system.

SILL   The horizontal lower edge of a window or door.

SIMPLE SPAN   A beam or other structural device that is supported at its two ends.

Single phase, 134, 135

SKYLIGHT   A window in a roof.

SLAB   A horizontal planar element of concrete, used most commonly as a floor, roof, or roadway.

SLAB-ON-GRADE   A concrete slab that rests directly on the ground.

SLUDGE   The precipitate of decomposed sewage.

Smokeproof enclosure, 206

SNOW FENCING   A slatted fencing used to induce drifting of snow so as to keep the snow away from roads or paths.

SOLAR FLUX   The flow of energy from the sun.

Solstice, summer, 4

Solstice, winter, 5

SPACE FRAME   A three-dimensional truss that spans with two-way action.

Spalling, 106

SPANDREL   The zone between the tops of the windows of one story of a building and the bottoms of the windows of the next story.

SPECIFIC HEAT   The ratio of the unit heat storage capacity of a material to that of water.

Specifications, 208–210

SPLAY   A divergence in the surfaces of a window frame.

Spread footing, 182

Sprinkler system, 199, 200

STANDING WAVES   Single-frequency modes of vibration, causing reinforcement of the sound at the given frequency.

Standpipe, fire, 206

Step ramp, 145

STIFFENER   A ridge of material added to a structural element to increase its resistance to buckling or shearing.

STIRRUPS   U-shaped pieces of stell bar used to reinforce concrete beams against shear failure.

Strain, 155

Stress, 154–156

STRING COURSE   A projecting horizontal molding running across the facade of a building.

Strip footing, 182

STRUT   A short structural element acting in compression.

SUPPLY PIPING   The system of pipes that furnish fresh water, both hot and cold, to the plumbing fixtures in a building.

Surface film, 51

SYNCLASTIC   Adjective describing a surface that has the same sense of curvature, either concave or convex, along both its principal axes.

TENSILE   Having to do with tension.

TENSILE STRESS   The magnitude of tension in a material, measured in units of applied force per unit area.

TENSION   A stretching or pulling apart.

Termite shield, 220

TERRAZZO   A decorative concrete flooring produced by grinding and polishing a slab made of colored marble chips and a selected color of cement.

TERRESTRIAL RADIATION   Thermal radiation from or among objects on earth.

THATCH   A roofing made of bundles of reeds, grasses, or leaves.

THERMAL BREAK   A layer of low-conductivity material interposed between parts of a metal frame to reduce its conduction of heat.

THERMAL BRIDGE   A high-conductivity path for the transmission of heat through an otherwise well-insulated building assembly.

Thermal capacity, 51

Tholos, 180

Three-phase, 135

TIE   A simple tensile structural member or a simple tensile connecting device.

Total energy system, 84

TRANSFORMER   A device for reducing or increasing the voltage of alternating current by means of two coils of a differing number of turns of wire wrapped around a single magnetic core.

Trap, plumbing, 39

TREADS   The horizontal planar elements of a stair.

TRUSS   A structural spanning device in which the loads are translated into axial forces in a triangulated system of slender members.

Tungsten halogen lamp, 121

Two-way, 177

UNDERPINNING   Strengthening the foundations of a building by supporting the building temporarily on jacks while adding new foundation components.

UNIT AIR CONDITIONER   A small, self-contained electric cooling and dehumidifying machine, usually mounted in a window or a specially made hole in an exterior wall of a building.

Unit ventilator, 86

Vacuum breaker, 36

Vapor pressure, 60

Vapor retarder, 61

Variable air volume system, 84–86

Vasomotor regulation, 16

VAULT   A structural form consisting of an arch translated along an axis not in its plane, or of a combination of such translations.

VAV. *See* Variable air volume system

Vent, plumbing, 39, 40

Vernal equinox, 5

VISUAL TASK   The focus of attention in an illuminated environment; the object one is trying to see.

Voussoir, 164

Waffle slab, 177

WAINSCOT   An interior wall facing that starts from the floor but does not extend to the ceiling.

Wash, 110

Water hammer, 35

Water softener, 33

WEEP HOLE   An opening in a wall whose function is to drain to the exterior any water that may accumulate in the wall, whether from leakage or condensation.

Working drawings, 209

WYTHE   A vertical layer of a masonry wall that is one brick, one block, or one stone thick.

Yield point, 155

Index